M

J O U ...

i...

M O H ...

COUNTRY ...

As written by

H.M. van den Bogaert

with artwork by

George O'Connor

and color by

Hilary Sycamore

First Second

NEW YORK & LONDON

First Second

New York & London

To my Dad, who loves the Mohawk.
And to MommaRose, who loves my Dad.

English language translation copyright © 1988 by Syracuse University Press
Illustrations copyright © 2006 by George O'Connor

Published by First Second
First Second is an imprint of Roaring Brook Press, a division of Holtzbrinck Publishing Holdings Limited Partnership
175 Fifth Avenue, New York, NY 10010

Distributed in Canada by H. B. Fenn and Company Ltd.
Distributed in the United Kingdom by Macmillan Children's Books, a division of Pan Macmillan.

Designed by Danica Novgorodoff

Library of Congress Cataloging-in-Publication Data

Bogaert, Harmen Meyndertsz van den.
Journey into Mohawk Country / as written by H.M. van den Bogaert, with artwork by George O'Connor and color by Hilary Sycamore. –1st ed.
p. cm.
Children's illustrated version of: A journey into Mohawk and Oneida country, 1634-1635. 1988.
ISBN-13: 978-1-59643-106-5
ISBN-10:1-59643-106-7
1. New York (State)–Description and travel–Early works to 1800–Comic books, strips, etc. 2.Bogaert, Harmen Meyndertsz van den–Travel–New York (State)–Comic books, strips, etc. 3.Dutch–New York (State)–History–17th century–Comic books, strips, etc. 4. Mohawk River Region (N.Y.)–Description and travel–Early works to 1800–Comic books, strips, etc. 5. New York (State)–Description and travel–Early works to 1800–Juvenile literature. 6. Bogaert, Harmen Meyndertsz van den–Travel–New York (State)–Juvenile literature. 7. Dutch–New York (State)–History–17th century–Juvenile literature. 8. Mohawk River Region (N.Y.)–Description and travel–Early works to 1800–Juvenile literature. I. Bogaert, Harmen Meynderstsz van den. Journey into Mohawk and Oneida country, 1634-1635. II. O'Connor, George, III. Sycamore, Hilary. IV. Title.

F122.1 .B62 2006
917.47_10444–dc22
2006040232

First Second books are available for special promotions and premiums.
For details, contact: Director of Special Markets, Holtzbrinck Publishers.

First Edition September 2006

Printed in China

10 9 8 7 6 5 4 3 2 1

A Few Words by way of Introduction:

"Even old *New York* was once *New Amsterdam*."
  —*Jimmy Kennedy* and *Nat Simon*, "Istanbul (not Constantinople)"

New York did not exist in 1634.

There were hundreds and hundreds of miles of wilderness that white men had yet to claim, let alone see. The land was far from uninhabited, though. Dozens of *Native American* tribes, each with its own language, customs, and way of life, had lived in this territory for thousands of years. By the 1630s, however, some new players began to appear on the scene.

An outfit called the *Dutch West India Company* established a few shaky footholds in what they dubbed *New Netherland.* The main colony, *New Amsterdam*, was a rough-and-tumble town of no more than a few hundred people located on the southernmost tip of what the *Algonquin* natives called *Manhatas (Manhattan) Island.* Some 100 miles up the *North River* (now known as the *Hudson*), the *Dutch* established *Fort Orange*, a tiny military outpost, on the site where the city of *Albany* stands today.

The whole reason the *Dutch* and other *European* explorers came to *North America* in the first place was to procure. . . wait for it. . . beaver pelts. These wildly popular skins were treated with mercury to remove the fur and then transformed into hats by the haberdashers of *Europe*. The craze for beaver hats was in full swing across the *Atlantic*, and the pelts couldn't arrive fast enough.

In order to obtain the necessary beaver skins, *Dutch* traders relied on their friends in the *Mohawk* nation. Allied with the *Dutch* for many years, the *Mohawk* were the easternmost tribe of the powerful *League of the Iroquois*. *The League* (from west to east, the *Seneca*, the *Cayuga*, the *Onondaga*, the *Oneida* and the *Mohawk*) comprised the most powerful military force of the region. Renowned as fearless and fearsome warriors, the *Mohawk* outnumbered the *Dutch* by the thousands.

A twenty-three-year-old barber/surgeon with the unwieldy handle of *Harmen Meyndertsz van den Bogaert* set out into this world with little else aside from his two companions. Together, they traveled some 100 miles into the interior of the continent to hash out a new trade agreement with the *Iroquois*. Shortly before our story begins, trade on the *Mohawk River* had dried up. Fewer and fewer *Mohawk* were making the trip to *Fort Orange*, fewer and fewer beaver pelts were being traded, and the *Dutch* operation was becoming dangerously unprofitable. The *French* had started up some colonies of their own further north, along the same rivers as the *Dutch* settlements, and the traders in *New Amsterdam* suspected that the *French* intended to use their advantageous positioning to cut the *Dutch* out of the action and corner the beaver market themselves.

Van den Bogaert's mission was simple: to rescue the fortunes of the *Dutch* colony. He kept a journal of his travels, and that journal (translated from the *Dutch* by *William Starna and Charles Gehring*) makes up the text of this comic. None of his entries have been altered or abridged; all is as *Van den Bogaert* recorded it. His words provide a glimpse into a much different time and place, and above all into his state of mind. So please, sit back and enjoy your journey into *Mohawk Country*....

—*George O'Connor, Jan. 9, 2006, New York City*

The Journal
of
Harmen
Meyndertsz
van den
BOGAERT

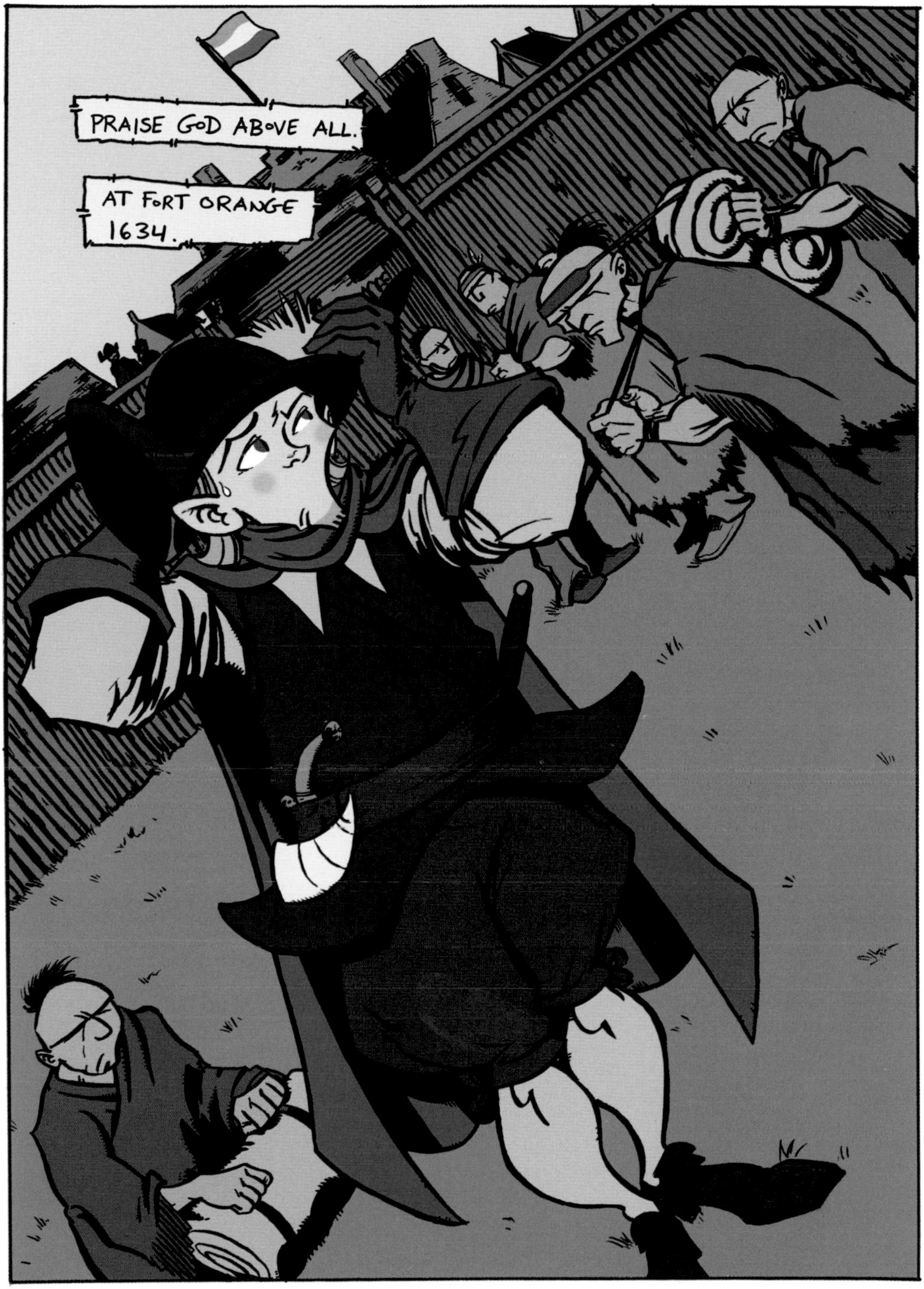
PRAISE GOD ABOVE ALL.
AT FORT ORANGE 1634.

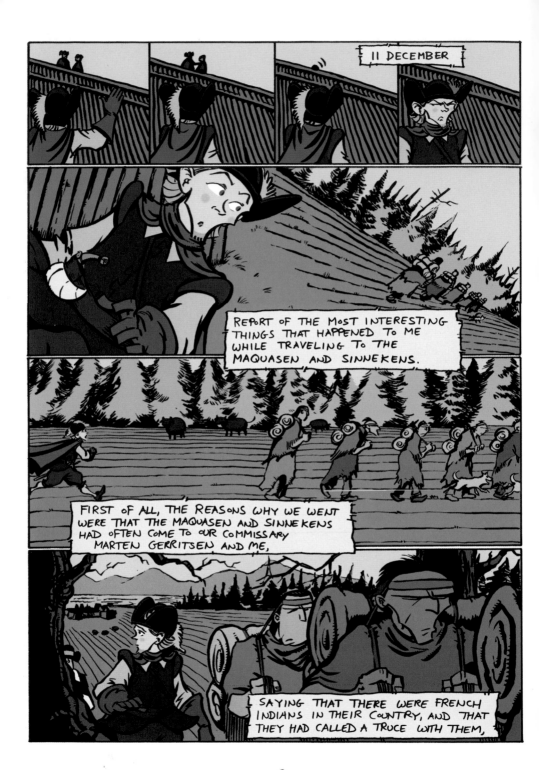

11 DECEMBER

REPORT OF THE MOST INTERESTING THINGS THAT HAPPENED TO ME WHILE TRAVELING TO THE MAQUASEN AND SINNEKENS.

FIRST OF ALL, THE REASONS WHY WE WENT WERE THAT THE MAQUASEN AND SINNEKENS HAD OFTEN COME TO OUR COMMISSARY MARTEN GERRITSEN AND ME,

SAYING THAT THERE WERE FRENCH INDIANS IN THEIR COUNTRY, AND THAT THEY HAD CALLED A TRUCE WITH THEM,

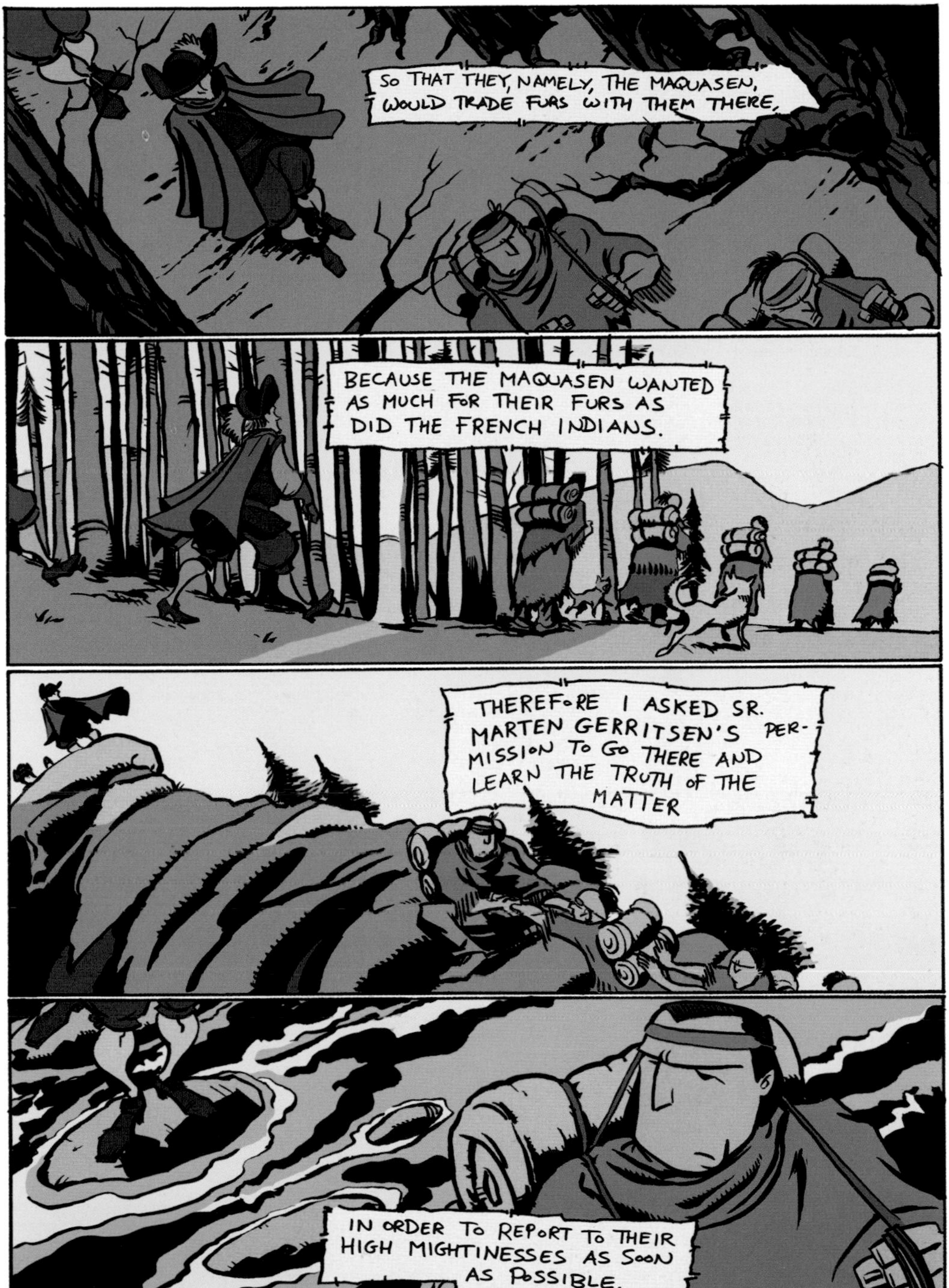
SO THAT THEY, NAMELY, THE MAQUASEN, WOULD TRADE FURS WITH THEM THERE,
BECAUSE THE MAQUASEN WANTED AS MUCH FOR THEIR FURS AS DID THE FRENCH INDIANS.
THEREFORE I ASKED SR. MARTEN GERRITSEN'S PERMISSION TO GO THERE AND LEARN THE TRUTH OF THE MATTER
IN ORDER TO REPORT TO THEIR HIGH MIGHTINESSES AS SOON AS POSSIBLE,

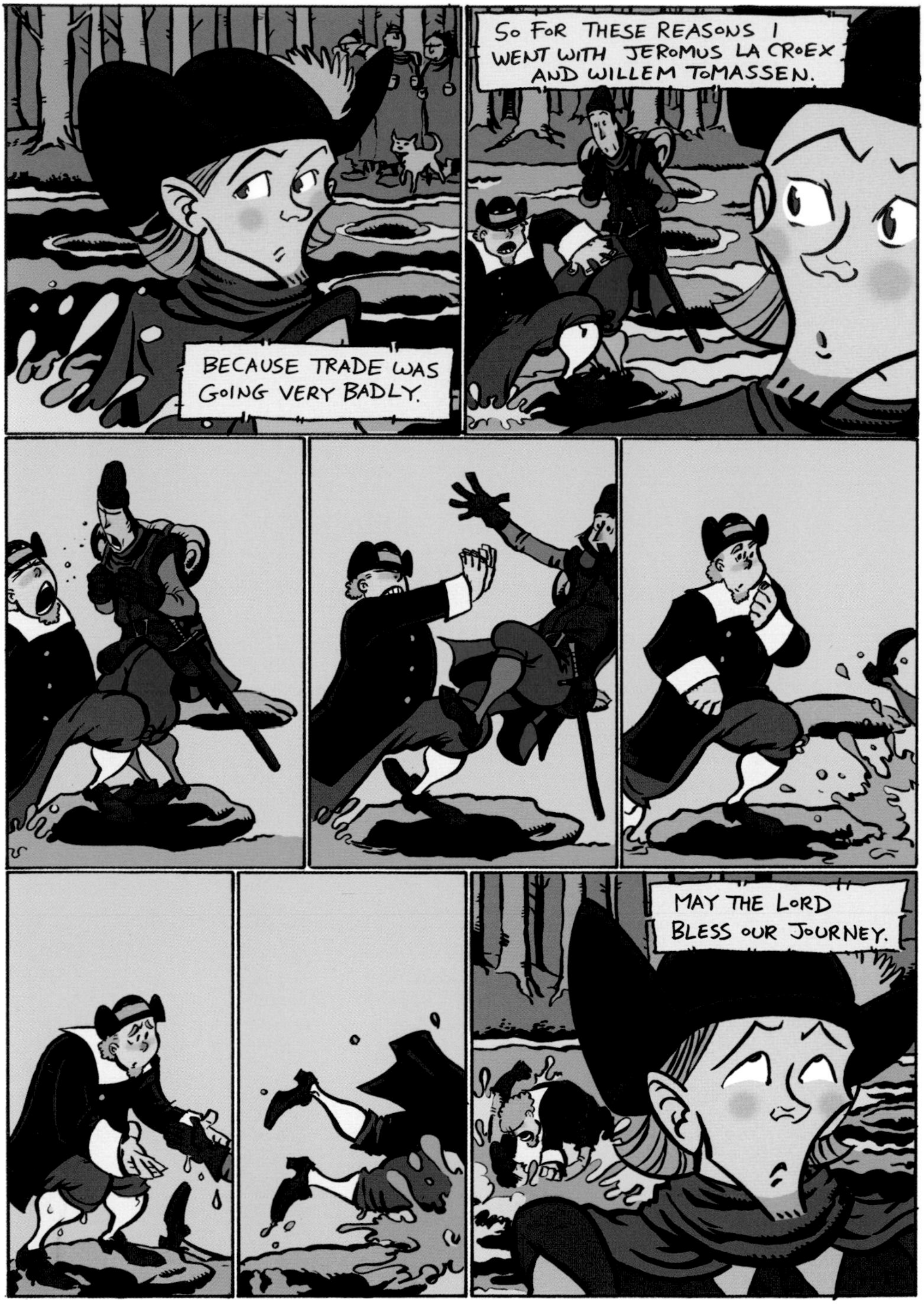
BECAUSE TRADE WAS GOING VERY BADLY.
SO FOR THESE REASONS I WENT WITH JEROMUS LA CROEX AND WILLEM TOMASSEN.
MAY THE LORD BLESS OUR JOURNEY.

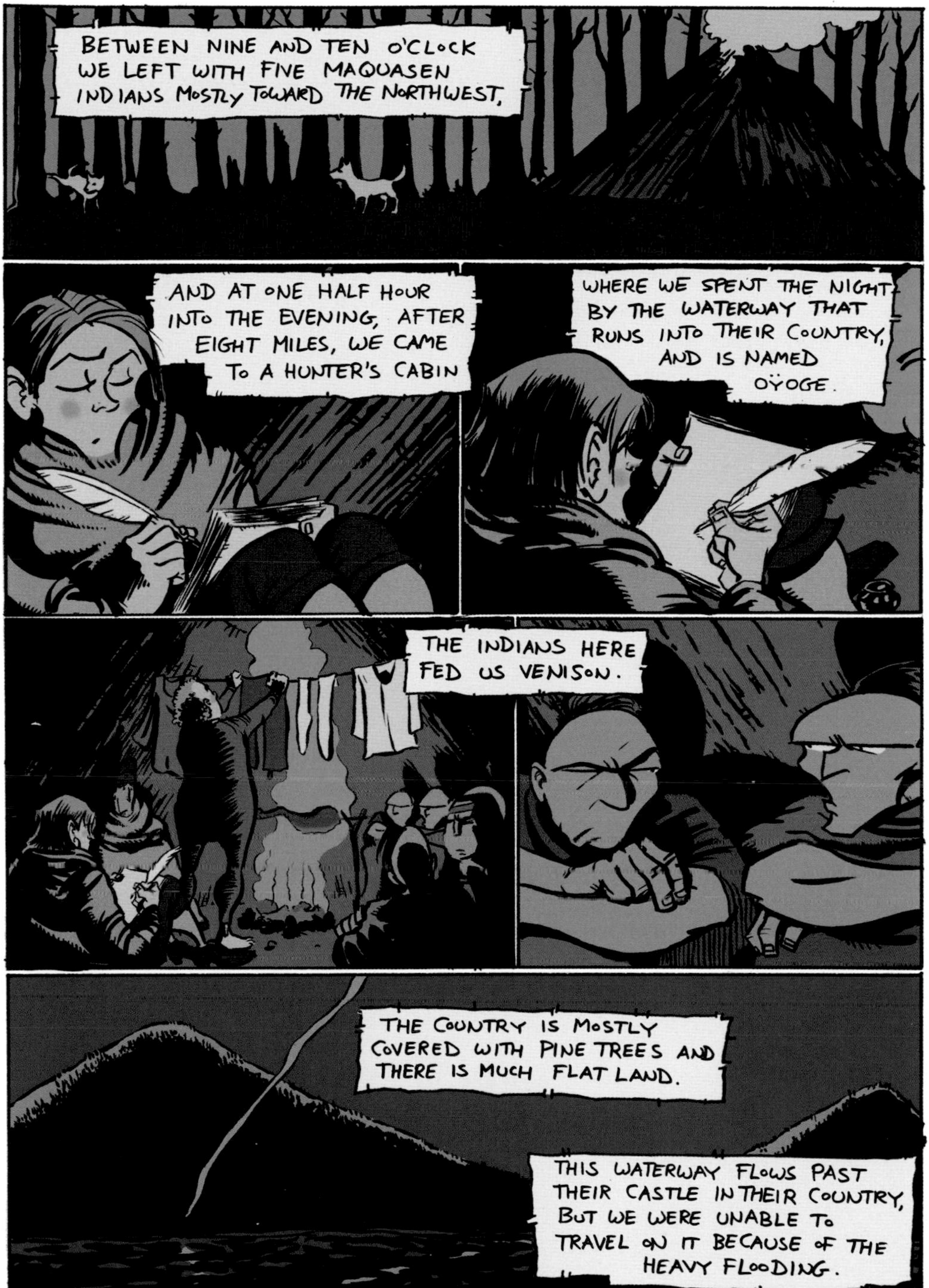

BETWEEN NINE AND TEN O'CLOCK WE LEFT WITH FIVE MAQUASEN INDIANS MOSTLY TOWARD THE NORTHWEST,
AND AT ONE HALF HOUR INTO THE EVENING, AFTER EIGHT MILES, WE CAME TO A HUNTER'S CABIN
WHERE WE SPENT THE NIGHT BY THE WATERWAY THAT RUNS INTO THEIR COUNTRY, AND IS NAMED OŸOGE.
THE INDIANS HERE FED US VENISON.
THE COUNTRY IS MOSTLY COVERED WITH PINE TREES AND THERE IS MUCH FLAT LAND.
THIS WATERWAY FLOWS PAST THEIR CASTLE IN THEIR COUNTRY, BUT WE WERE UNABLE TO TRAVEL ON IT BECAUSE OF THE HEAVY FLOODING.

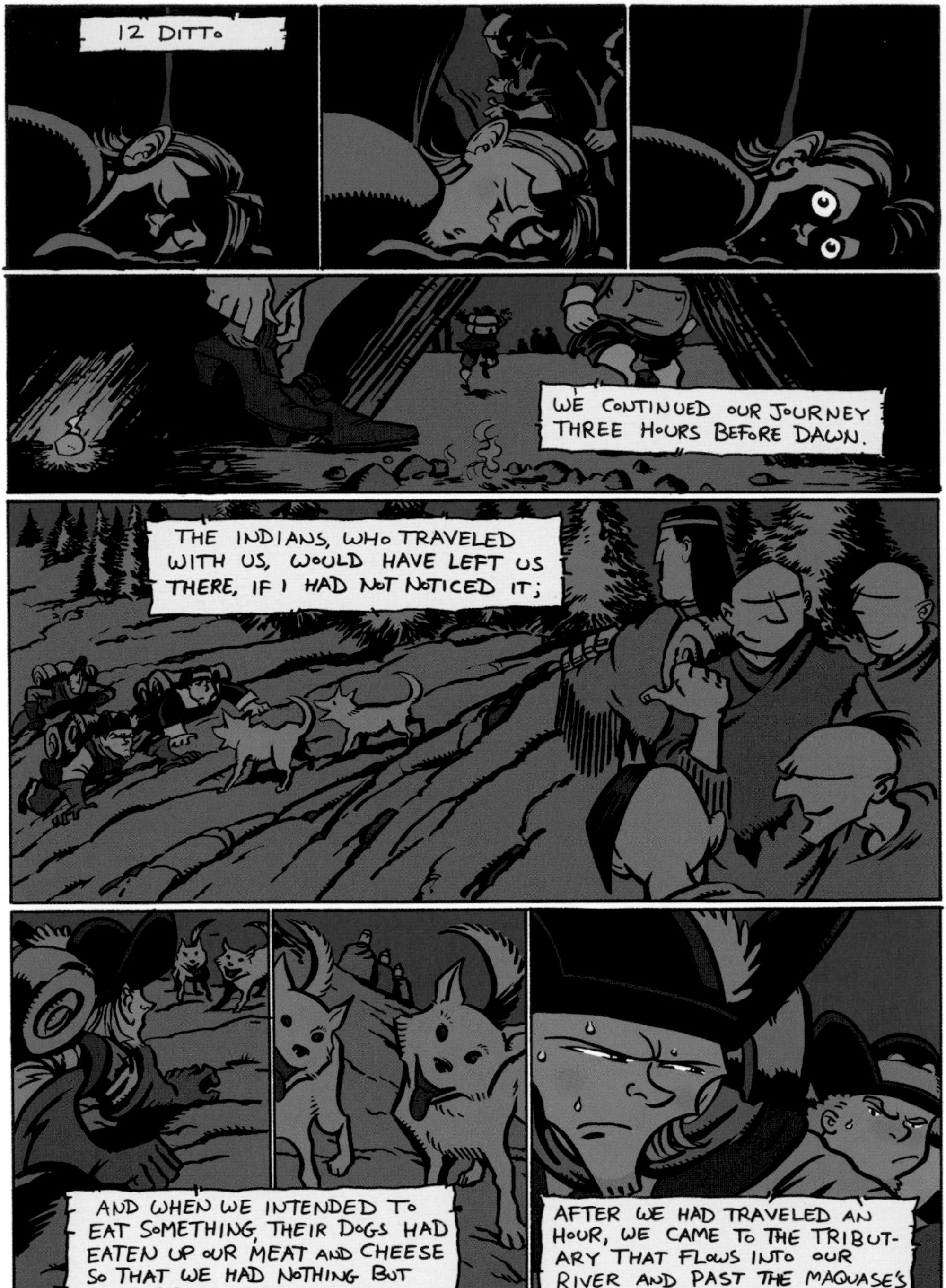
12 DITTO
WE CONTINUED OUR JOURNEY THREE HOURS BEFORE DAWN.
THE INDIANS, WHO TRAVELED WITH US, WOULD HAVE LEFT US THERE, IF I HAD NOT NOTICED IT;
AND WHEN WE INTENDED TO EAT SOMETHING, THEIR DOGS HAD EATEN UP OUR MEAT AND CHEESE SO THAT WE HAD NOTHING BUT DRY BREAD TO TRAVEL ON.
AFTER WE HAD TRAVELED AN HOUR, WE CAME TO THE TRIBUTARY THAT FLOWS INTO OUR RIVER AND PAST THE MAQUASE'S VILLAGES.

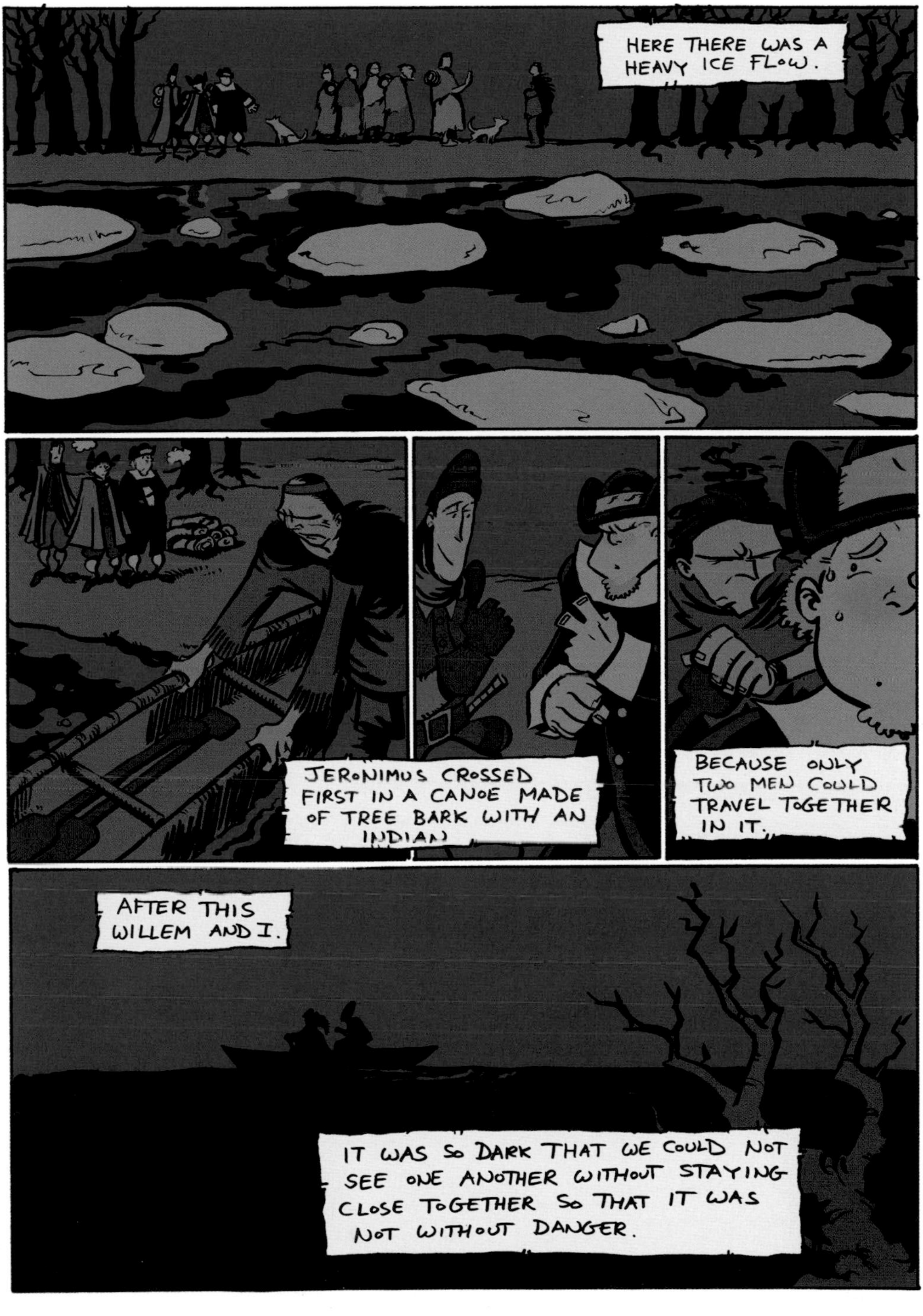
HERE THERE WAS A HEAVY ICE FLOW.
JERONIMUS CROSSED FIRST IN A CANOE MADE OF TREE BARK WITH AN INDIAN
BECAUSE ONLY TWO MEN COULD TRAVEL TOGETHER IN IT.
AFTER THIS WILLEM AND I.
IT WAS SO DARK THAT WE COULD NOT SEE ONE ANOTHER WITHOUT STAYING CLOSE TOGETHER SO THAT IT WAS NOT WITHOUT DANGER.

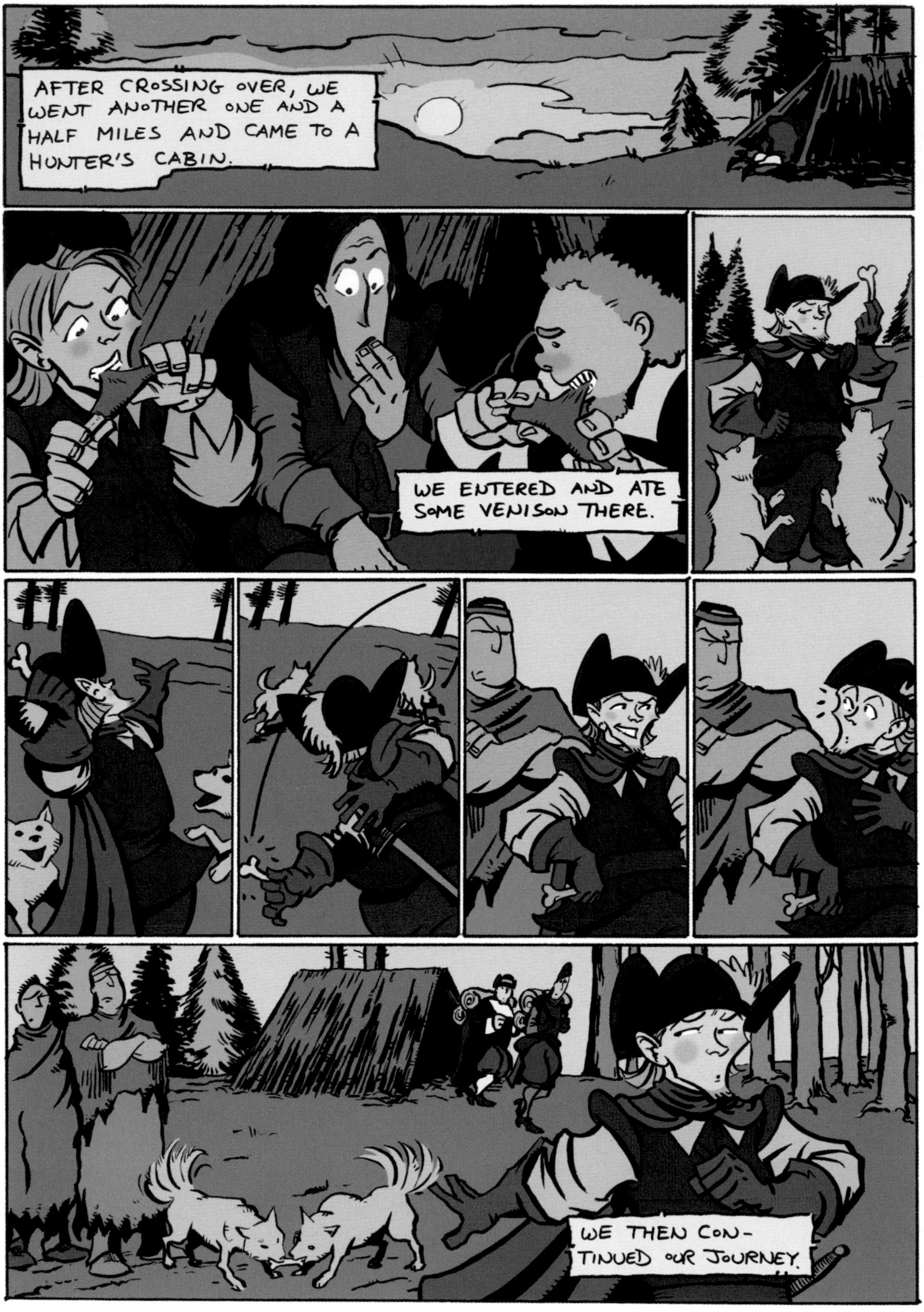
AFTER CROSSING OVER, WE WENT ANOTHER ONE AND A HALF MILES AND CAME TO A HUNTER'S CABIN.
WE ENTERED AND ATE SOME VENISON THERE.
WE THEN CONTINUED OUR JOURNEY.

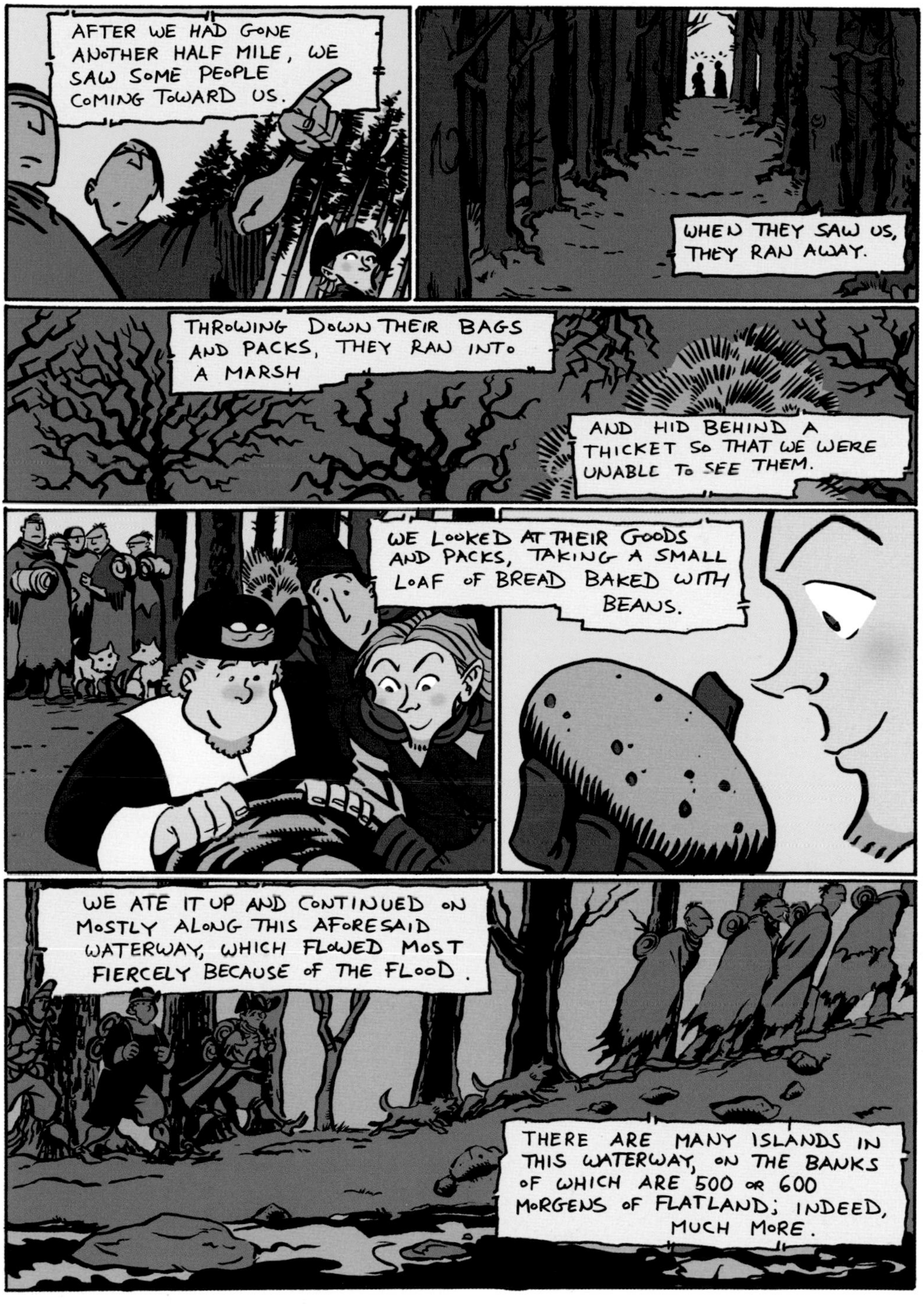
AFTER WE HAD GONE ANOTHER HALF MILE, WE SAW SOME PEOPLE COMING TOWARD US.
WHEN THEY SAW US, THEY RAN AWAY.
THROWING DOWN THEIR BAGS AND PACKS, THEY RAN INTO A MARSH
AND HID BEHIND A THICKET SO THAT WE WERE UNABLE TO SEE THEM.
WE LOOKED AT THEIR GOODS AND PACKS, TAKING A SMALL LOAF OF BREAD BAKED WITH BEANS.
WE ATE IT UP AND CONTINUED ON MOSTLY ALONG THIS AFORESAID WATERWAY, WHICH FLOWED MOST FIERCELY BECAUSE OF THE FLOOD.
THERE ARE MANY ISLANDS IN THIS WATERWAY, ON THE BANKS OF WHICH ARE 500 OR 600 MORGENS OF FLATLAND; INDEED, MUCH MORE.

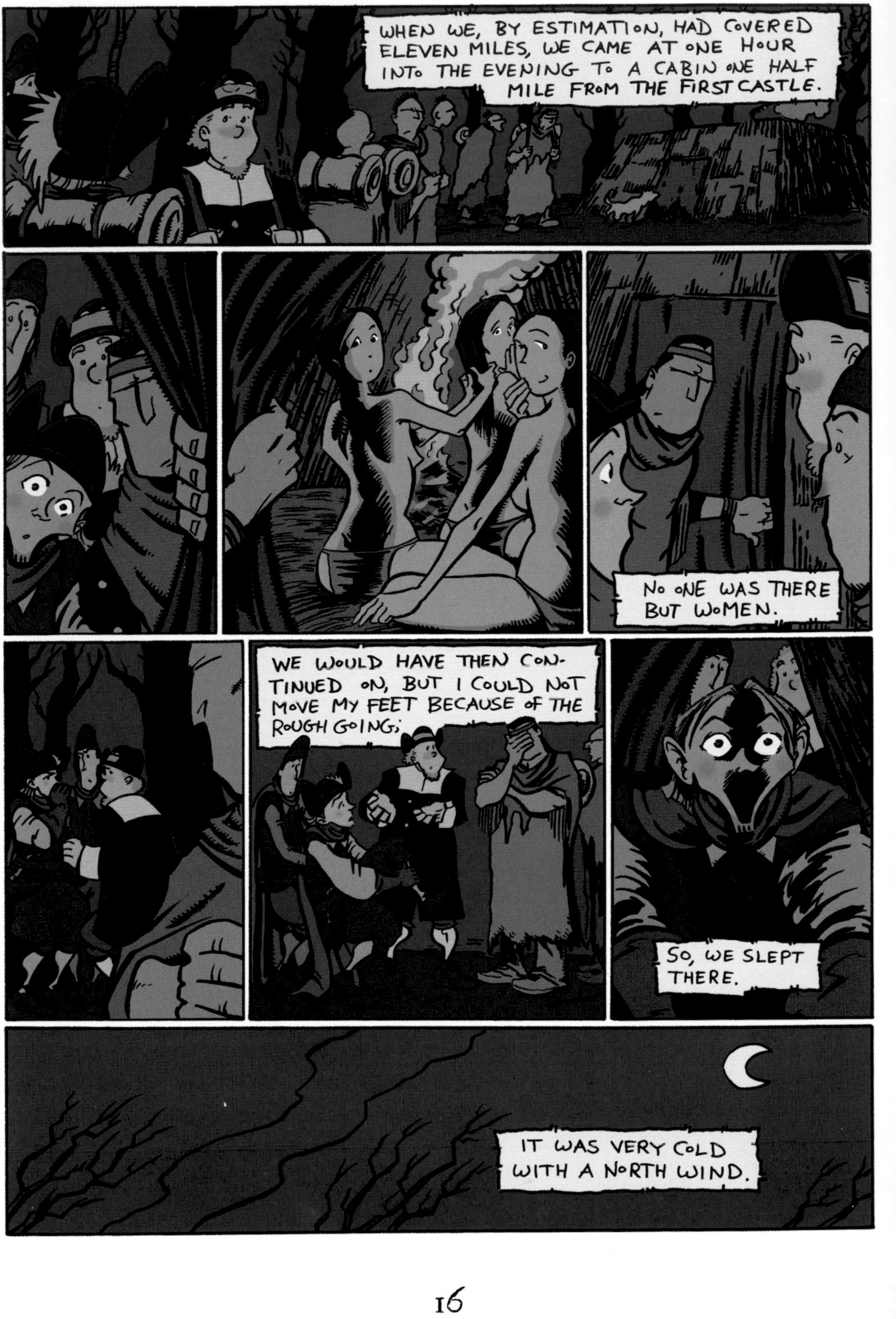
WHEN WE, BY ESTIMATION, HAD COVERED ELEVEN MILES, WE CAME AT ONE HOUR INTO THE EVENING TO A CABIN ONE HALF MILE FROM THE FIRST CASTLE.
NO ONE WAS THERE BUT WOMEN.
WE WOULD HAVE THEN CONTINUED ON, BUT I COULD NOT MOVE MY FEET BECAUSE OF THE ROUGH GOING;
SO, WE SLEPT THERE.
IT WAS VERY COLD WITH A NORTH WIND.

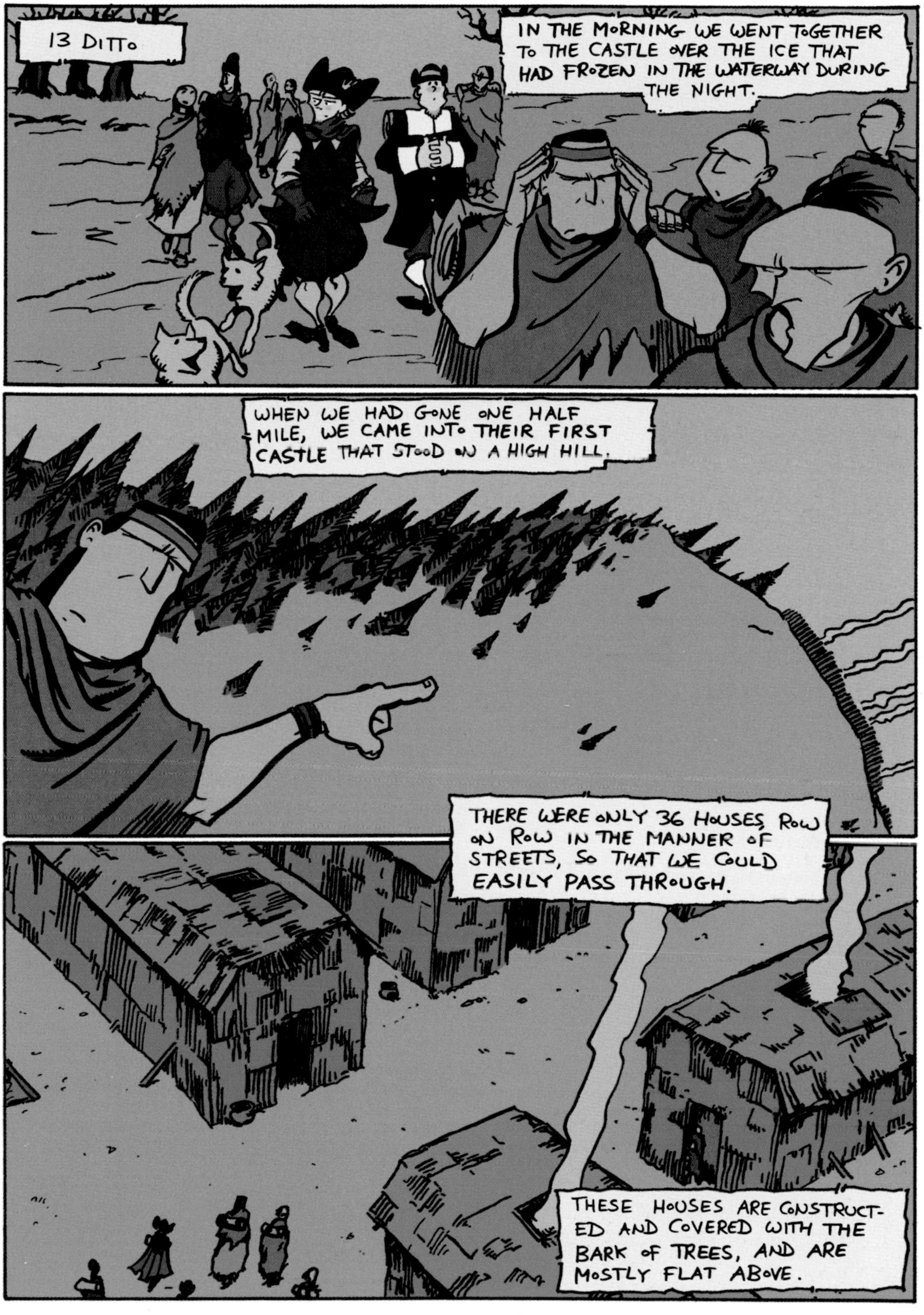
13 DITTO
IN THE MORNING WE WENT TOGETHER TO THE CASTLE OVER THE ICE THAT HAD FROZEN IN THE WATERWAY DURING THE NIGHT.
WHEN WE HAD GONE ONE HALF MILE, WE CAME INTO THEIR FIRST CASTLE THAT STOOD ON A HIGH HILL.
THERE WERE ONLY 36 HOUSES, ROW ON ROW IN THE MANNER OF STREETS, SO THAT WE COULD EASILY PASS THROUGH.
THESE HOUSES ARE CONSTRUCTED AND COVERED WITH THE BARK OF TREES, AND ARE MOSTLY FLAT ABOVE.

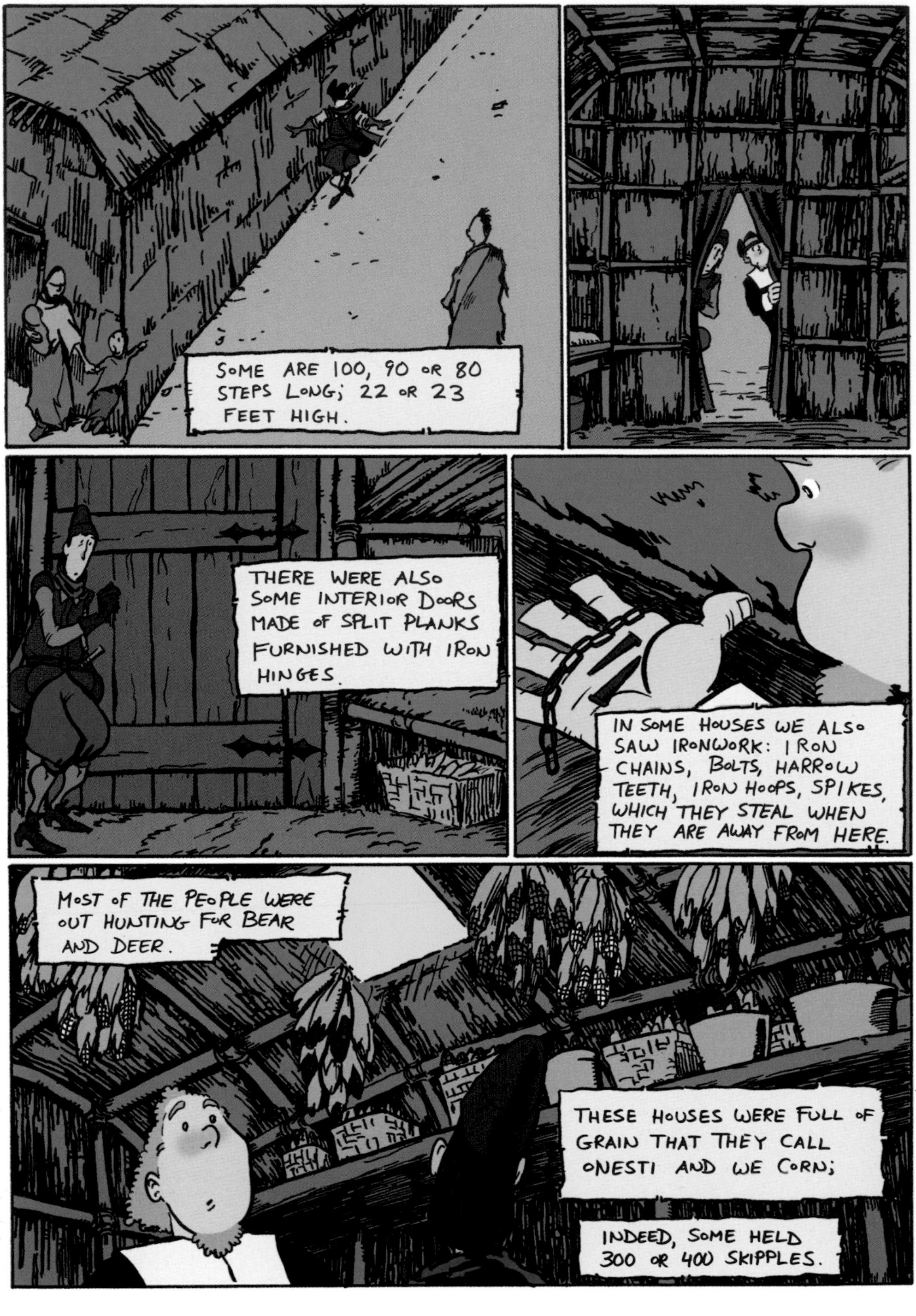
SOME ARE 100, 90 OR 80 STEPS LONG; 22 OR 23 FEET HIGH.
THERE WERE ALSO SOME INTERIOR DOORS MADE OF SPLIT PLANKS FURNISHED WITH IRON HINGES.
IN SOME HOUSES WE ALSO SAW IRONWORK: IRON CHAINS, BOLTS, HARROW TEETH, IRON HOOPS, SPIKES, WHICH THEY STEAL WHEN THEY ARE AWAY FROM HERE.
MOST OF THE PEOPLE WERE OUT HUNTING FOR BEAR AND DEER.
THESE HOUSES WERE FULL OF GRAIN THAT THEY CALL ONESTI AND WE CORN;
INDEED, SOME HELD 300 OR 400 SKIPPLES.

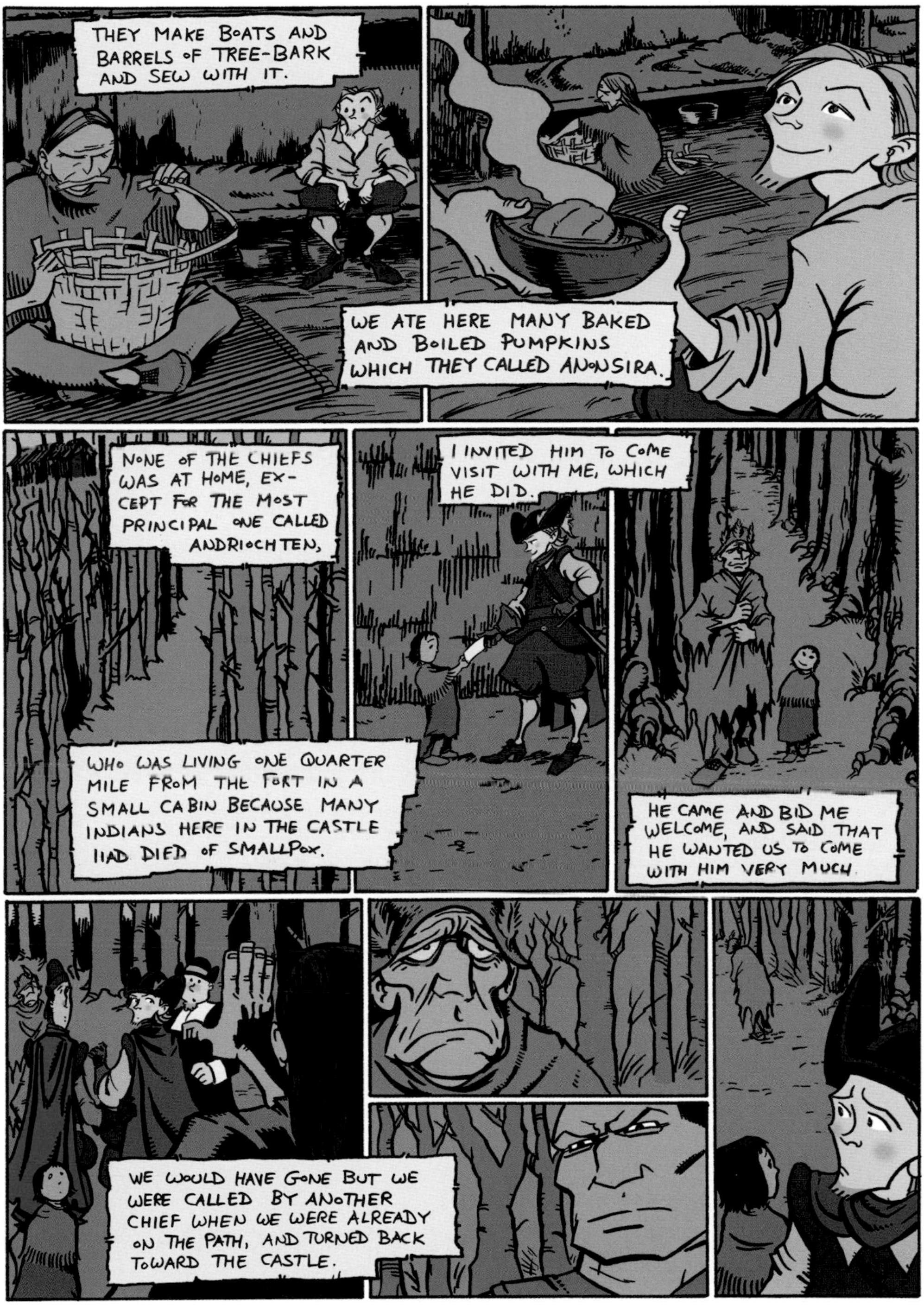
THEY MAKE BOATS AND BARRELS OF TREE-BARK AND SEW WITH IT.
WE ATE HERE MANY BAKED AND BOILED PUMPKINS WHICH THEY CALLED ANONSIRA.
NONE OF THE CHIEFS WAS AT HOME, EX-CEPT FOR THE MOST PRINCIPAL ONE CALLED ANDRIOCHTEN,
WHO WAS LIVING ONE QUARTER MILE FROM THE FORT IN A SMALL CABIN BECAUSE MANY INDIANS HERE IN THE CASTLE HAD DIED OF SMALLPOX.
I INVITED HIM TO COME VISIT WITH ME, WHICH HE DID.
HE CAME AND BID ME WELCOME, AND SAID THAT HE WANTED US TO COME WITH HIM VERY MUCH.
WE WOULD HAVE GONE BUT WE WERE CALLED BY ANOTHER CHIEF WHEN WE WERE ALREADY ON THE PATH, AND TURNED BACK TOWARD THE CASTLE.

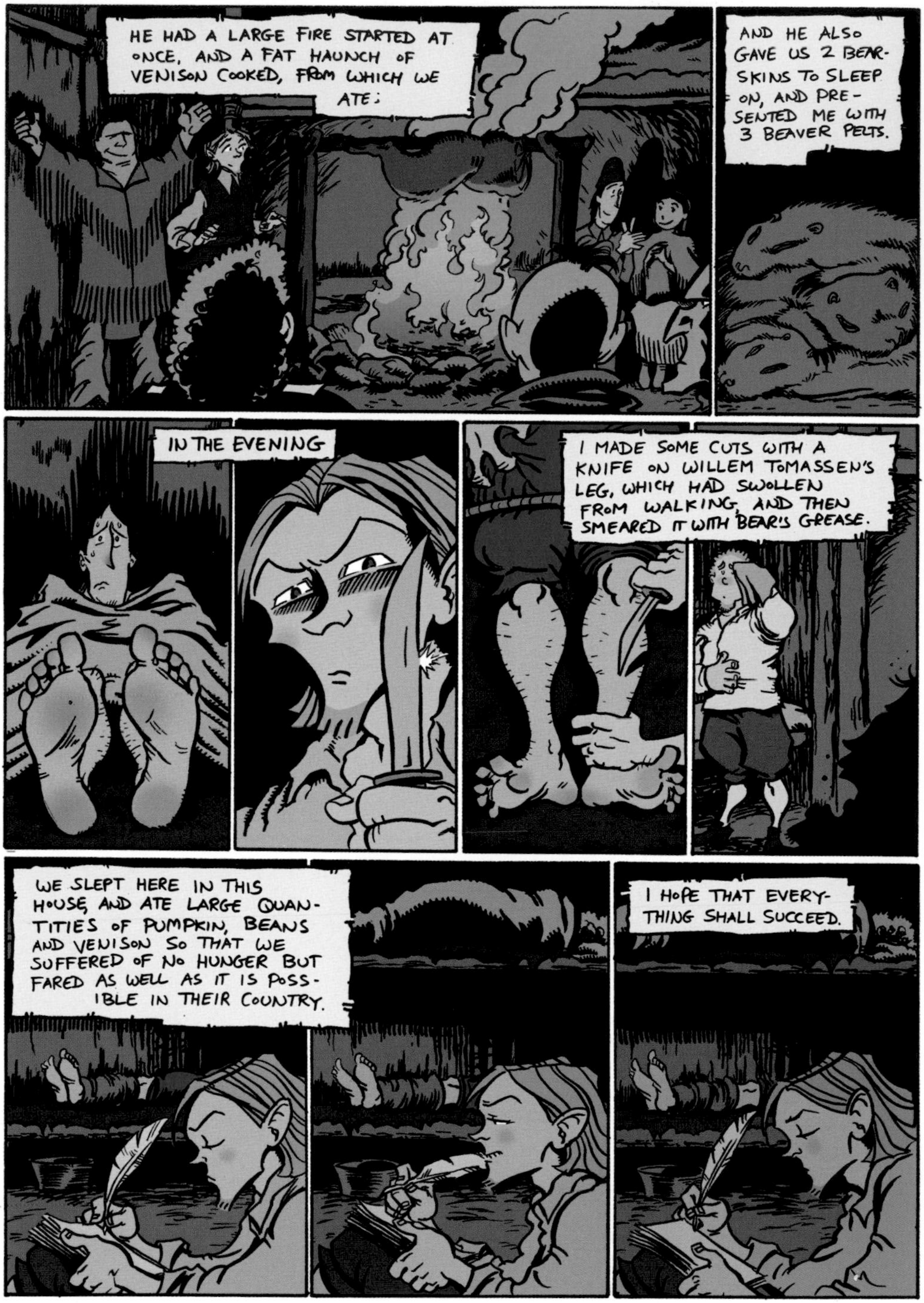
HE HAD A LARGE FIRE STARTED AT ONCE, AND A FAT HAUNCH OF VENISON COOKED, FROM WHICH WE ATE;
AND HE ALSO GAVE US 2 BEAR-SKINS TO SLEEP ON, AND PRE-SENTED ME WITH 3 BEAVER PELTS.
IN THE EVENING
I MADE SOME CUTS WITH A KNIFE ON WILLEM TOMASSEN'S LEG, WHICH HAD SWOLLEN FROM WALKING, AND THEN SMEARED IT WITH BEAR'S GREASE.
WE SLEPT HERE IN THIS HOUSE, AND ATE LARGE QUAN-TITIES OF PUMPKIN, BEANS AND VENISON SO THAT WE SUFFERED OF NO HUNGER BUT FARED AS WELL AS IT IS POSS-IBLE IN THEIR COUNTRY.
I HOPE THAT EVERY-THING SHALL SUCCEED.

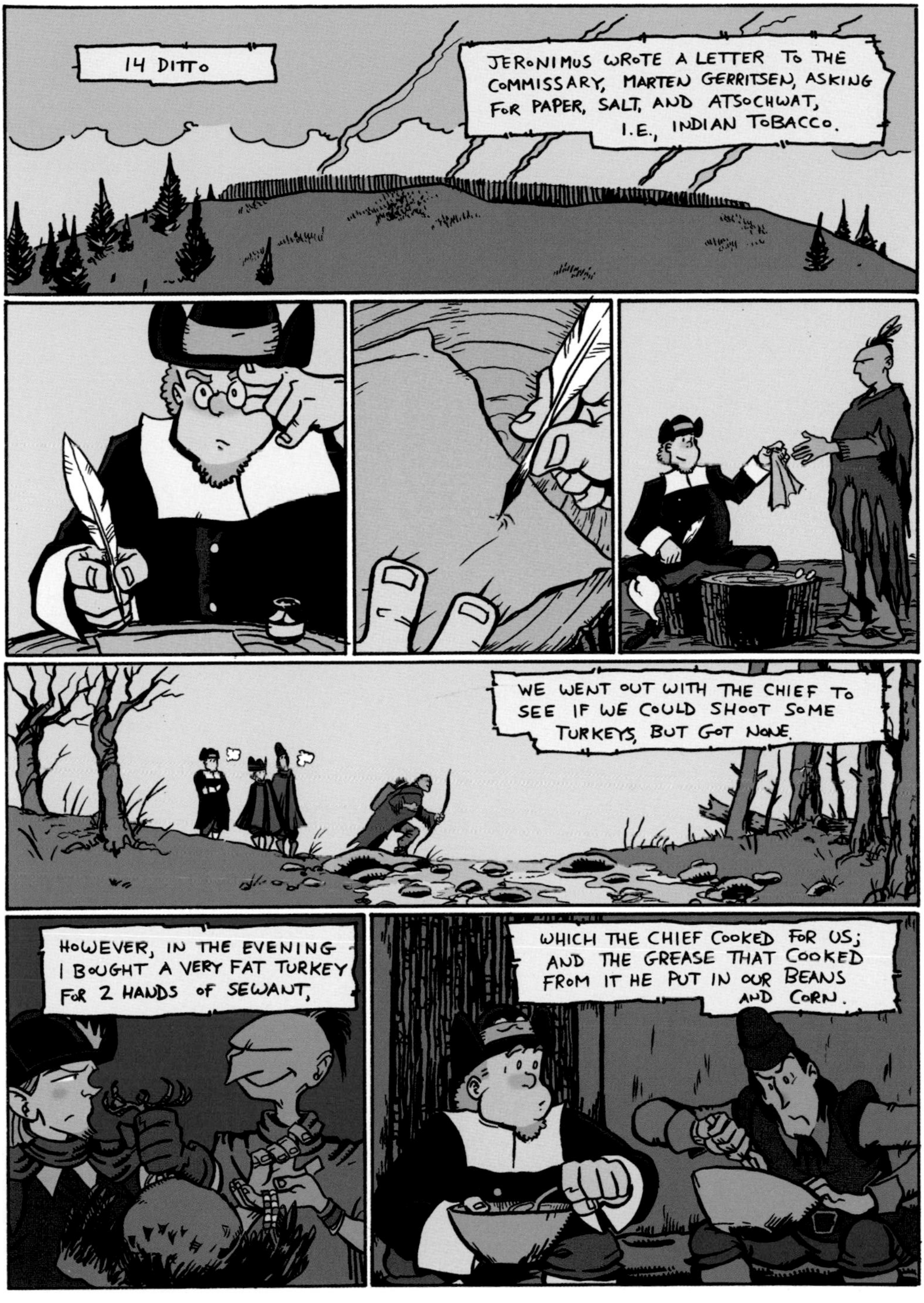
14 DITTO
JERONIMUS WROTE A LETTER TO THE COMMISSARY, MARTEN GERRITSEN, ASKING FOR PAPER, SALT, AND ATSOCHWAT, I.E., INDIAN TOBACCO.
WE WENT OUT WITH THE CHIEF TO SEE IF WE COULD SHOOT SOME TURKEYS, BUT GOT NONE.
HOWEVER, IN THE EVENING I BOUGHT A VERY FAT TURKEY FOR 2 HANDS OF SEWANT,
WHICH THE CHIEF COOKED FOR US; AND THE GREASE THAT COOKED FROM IT HE PUT IN OUR BEANS AND CORN.

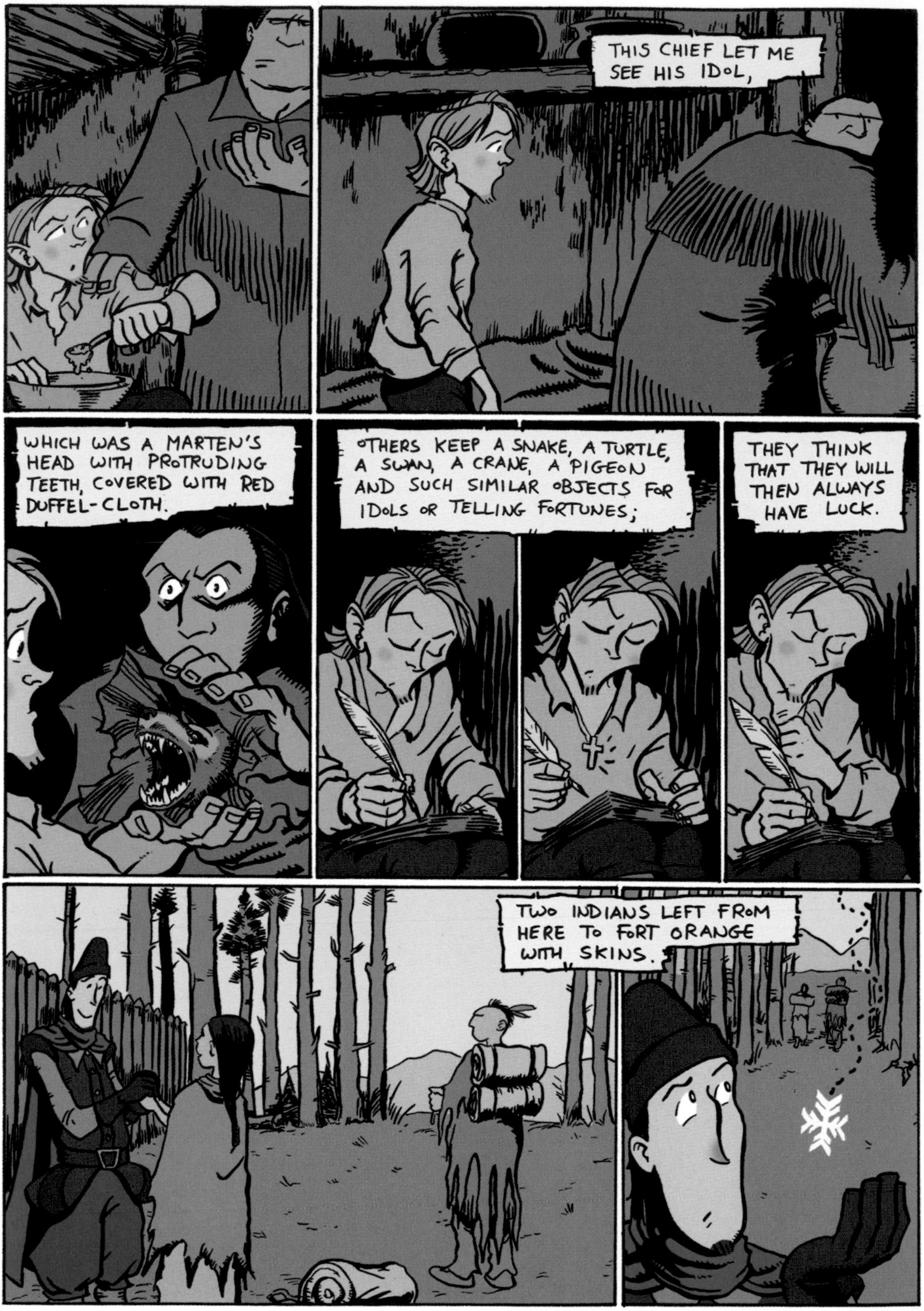
THIS CHIEF LET ME SEE HIS IDOL,
WHICH WAS A MARTEN'S HEAD WITH PROTRUDING TEETH, COVERED WITH RED DUFFEL-CLOTH.
OTHERS KEEP A SNAKE, A TURTLE, A SWAN, A CRANE, A PIGEON AND SUCH SIMILAR OBJECTS FOR IDOLS OR TELLING FORTUNES;
THEY THINK THAT THEY WILL THEN ALWAYS HAVE LUCK.
TWO INDIANS LEFT FROM HERE TO FORT ORANGE WITH SKINS.

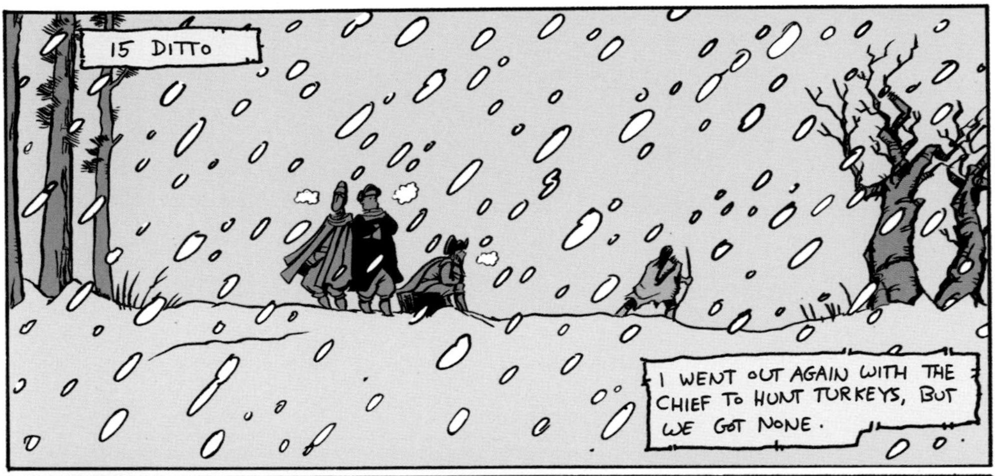
15 DITTO
I WENT OUT AGAIN WITH THE CHIEF TO HUNT TURKEYS, BUT WE GOT NONE.

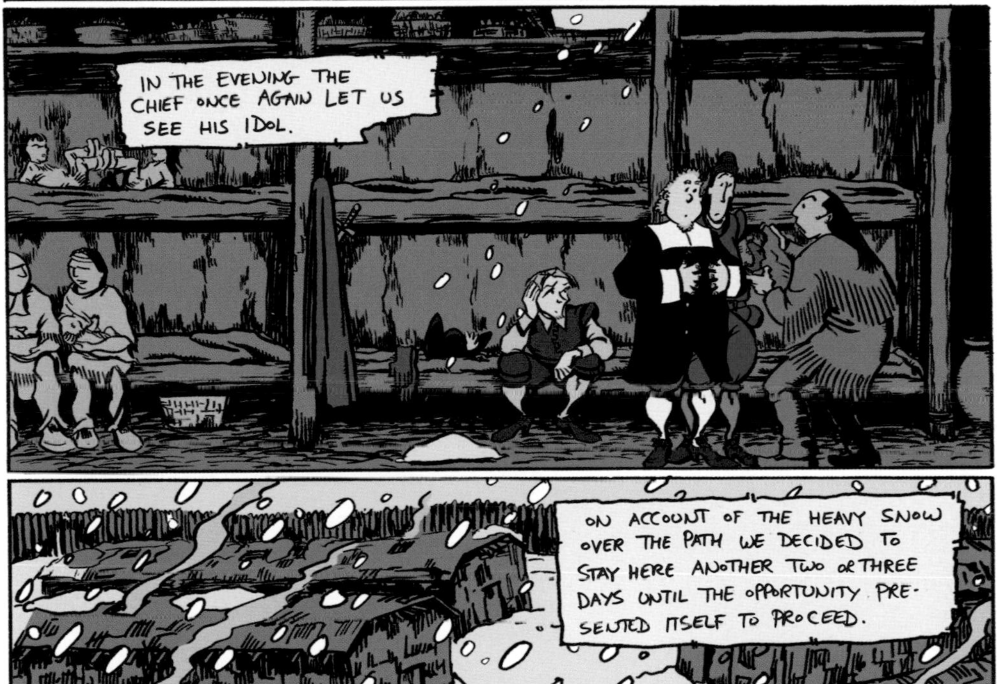
IN THE EVENING THE CHIEF ONCE AGAIN LET US SEE HIS IDOL.

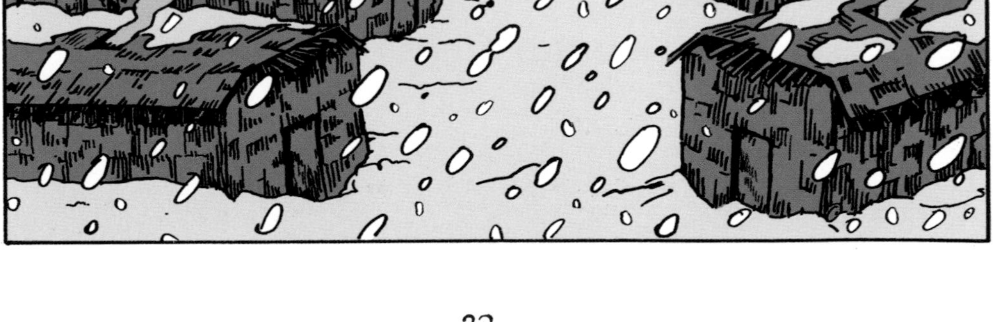
ON ACCOUNT OF THE HEAVY SNOW OVER THE PATH WE DECIDED TO STAY HERE ANOTHER TWO OR THREE DAYS UNTIL THE OPPORTUNITY PRESENTED ITSELF TO PROCEED.

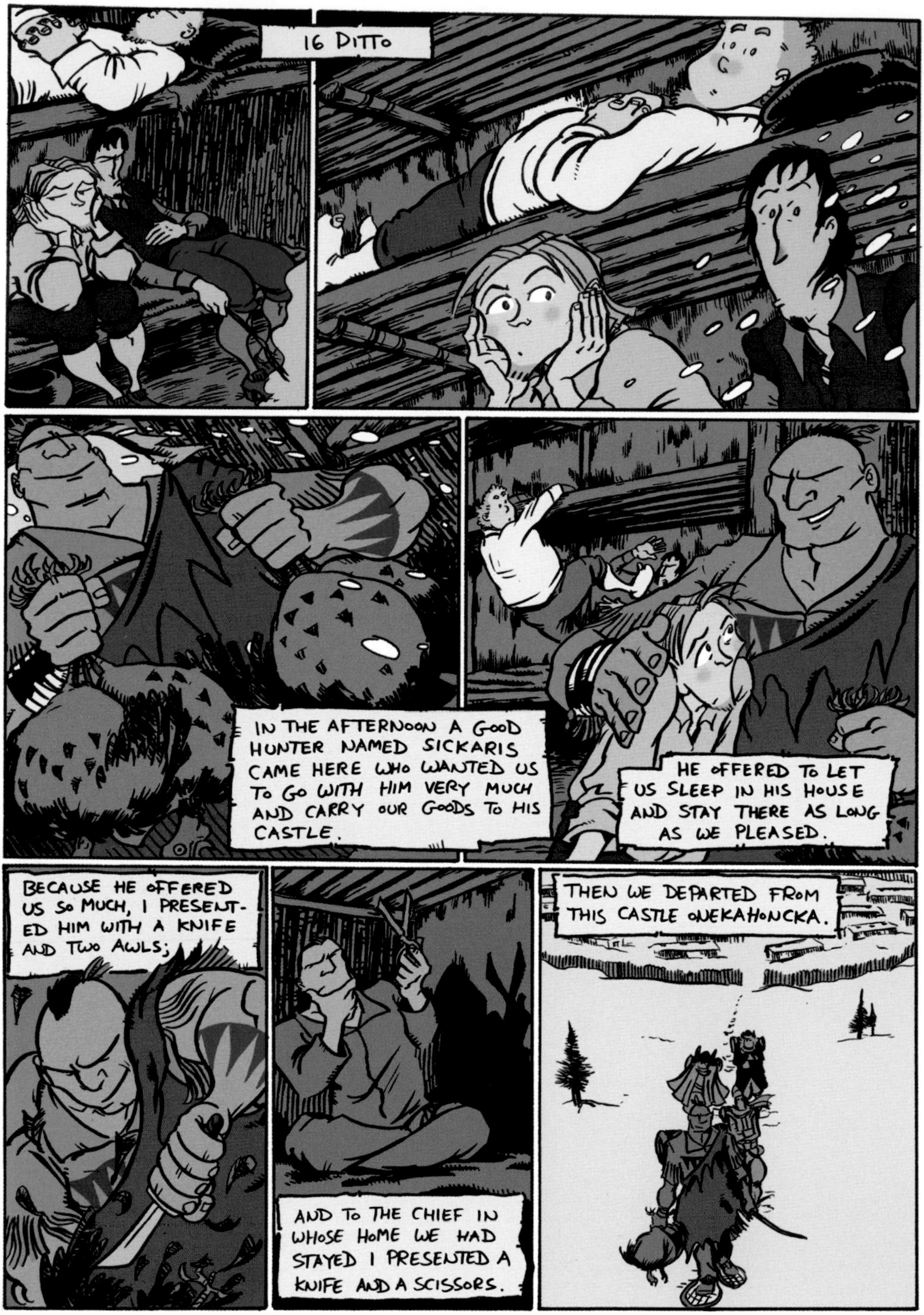
16 DITTO
IN THE AFTERNOON A GOOD HUNTER NAMED SICKARIS CAME HERE WHO WANTED US TO GO WITH HIM VERY MUCH AND CARRY OUR GOODS TO HIS CASTLE.
HE OFFERED TO LET US SLEEP IN HIS HOUSE AND STAY THERE AS LONG AS WE PLEASED.
BECAUSE HE OFFERED US SO MUCH, I PRESENTED HIM WITH A KNIFE AND TWO AWLS;
AND TO THE CHIEF IN WHOSE HOME WE HAD STAYED I PRESENTED A KNIFE AND A SCISSORS.
THEN WE DEPARTED FROM THIS CASTLE ONEKAHONCKA.

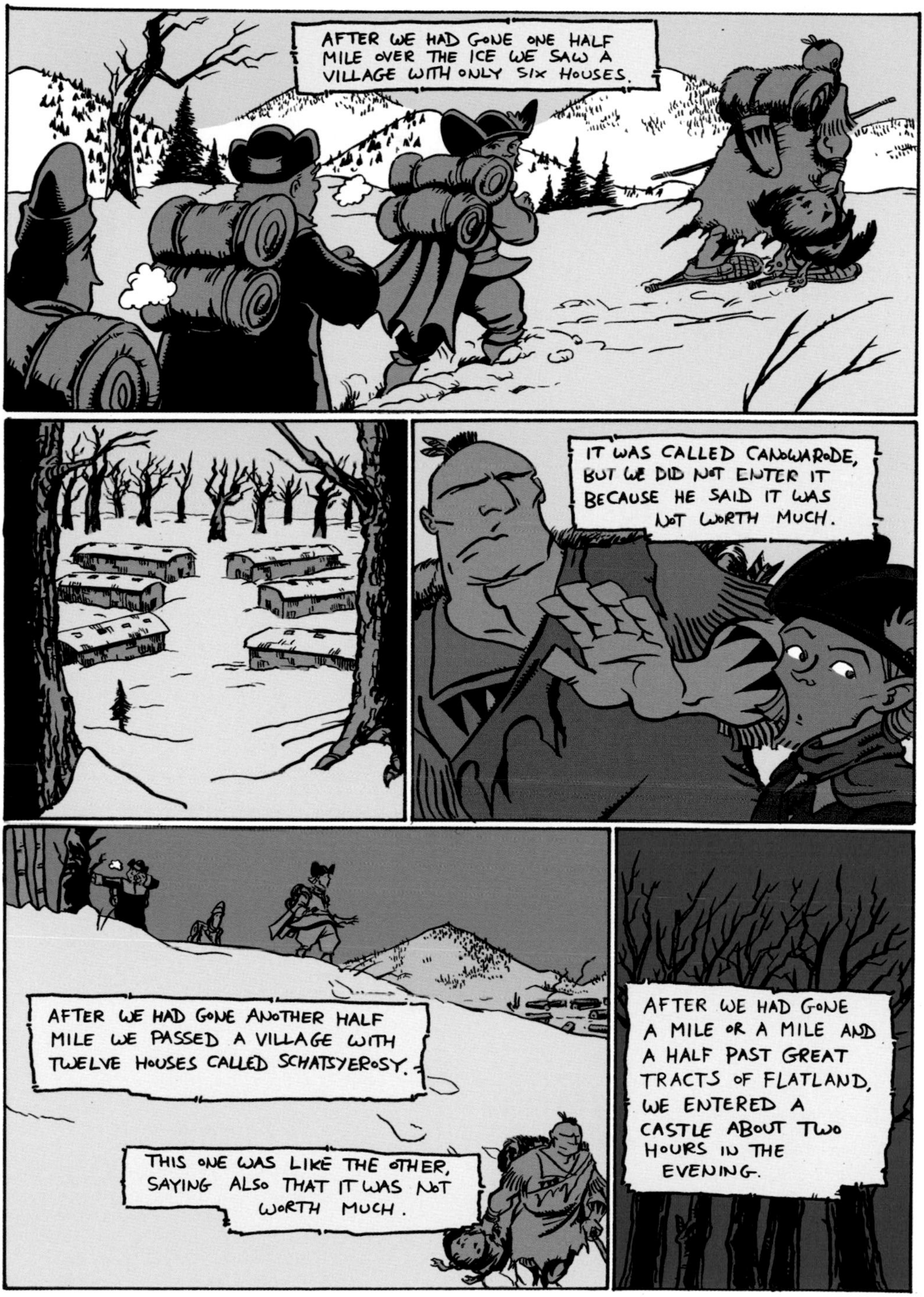
AFTER WE HAD GONE ONE HALF MILE OVER THE ICE WE SAW A VILLAGE WITH ONLY SIX HOUSES.
IT WAS CALLED CANOWARODE, BUT WE DID NOT ENTER IT BECAUSE HE SAID IT WAS NOT WORTH MUCH.
AFTER WE HAD GONE ANOTHER HALF MILE WE PASSED A VILLAGE WITH TWELVE HOUSES CALLED SCHATSYEROSY.
THIS ONE WAS LIKE THE OTHER, SAYING ALSO THAT IT WAS NOT WORTH MUCH.
AFTER WE HAD GONE A MILE OR A MILE AND A HALF PAST GREAT TRACTS OF FLATLAND, WE ENTERED A CASTLE ABOUT TWO HOURS IN THE EVENING.

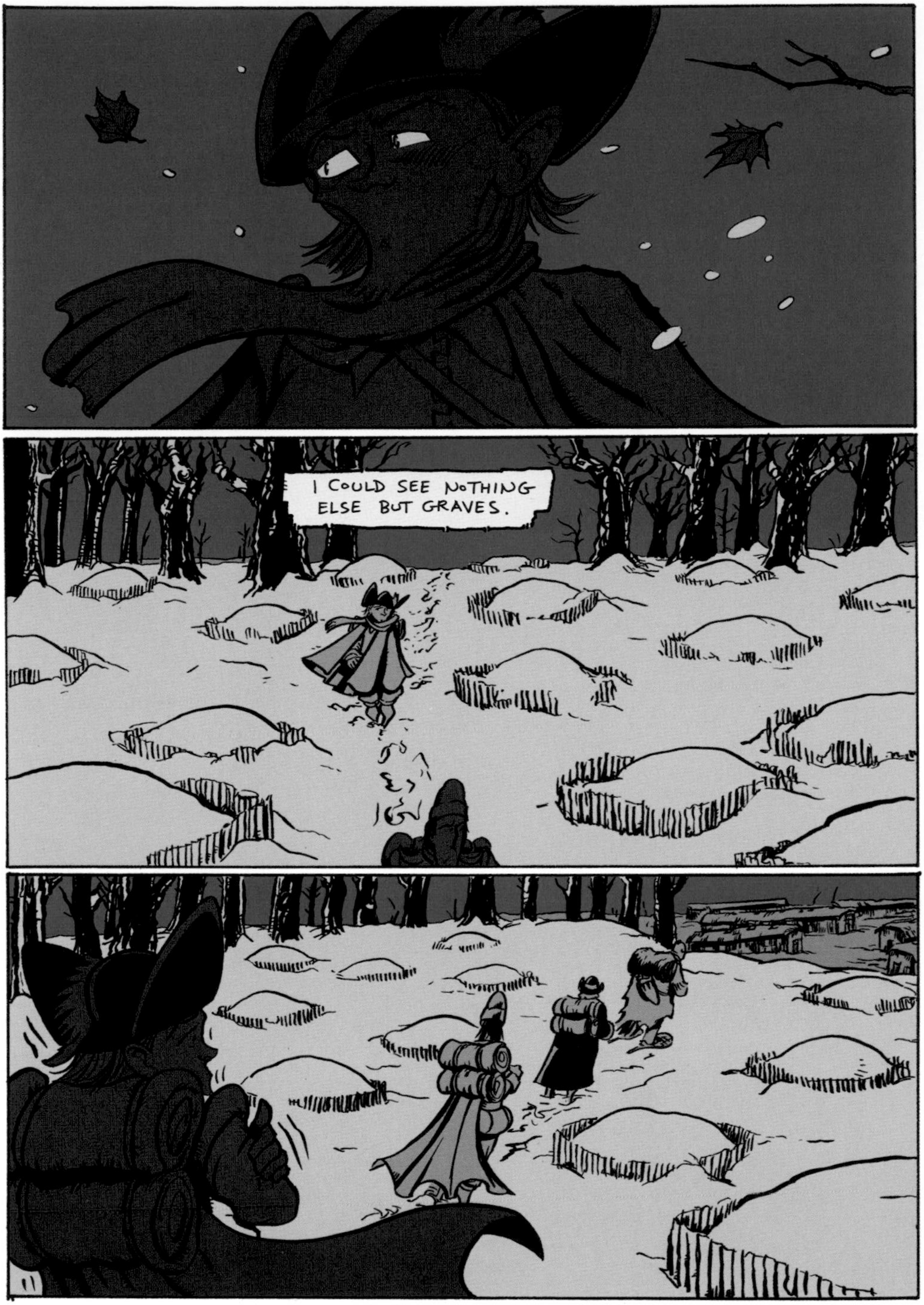
I COULD SEE NOTHING ELSE BUT GRAVES.

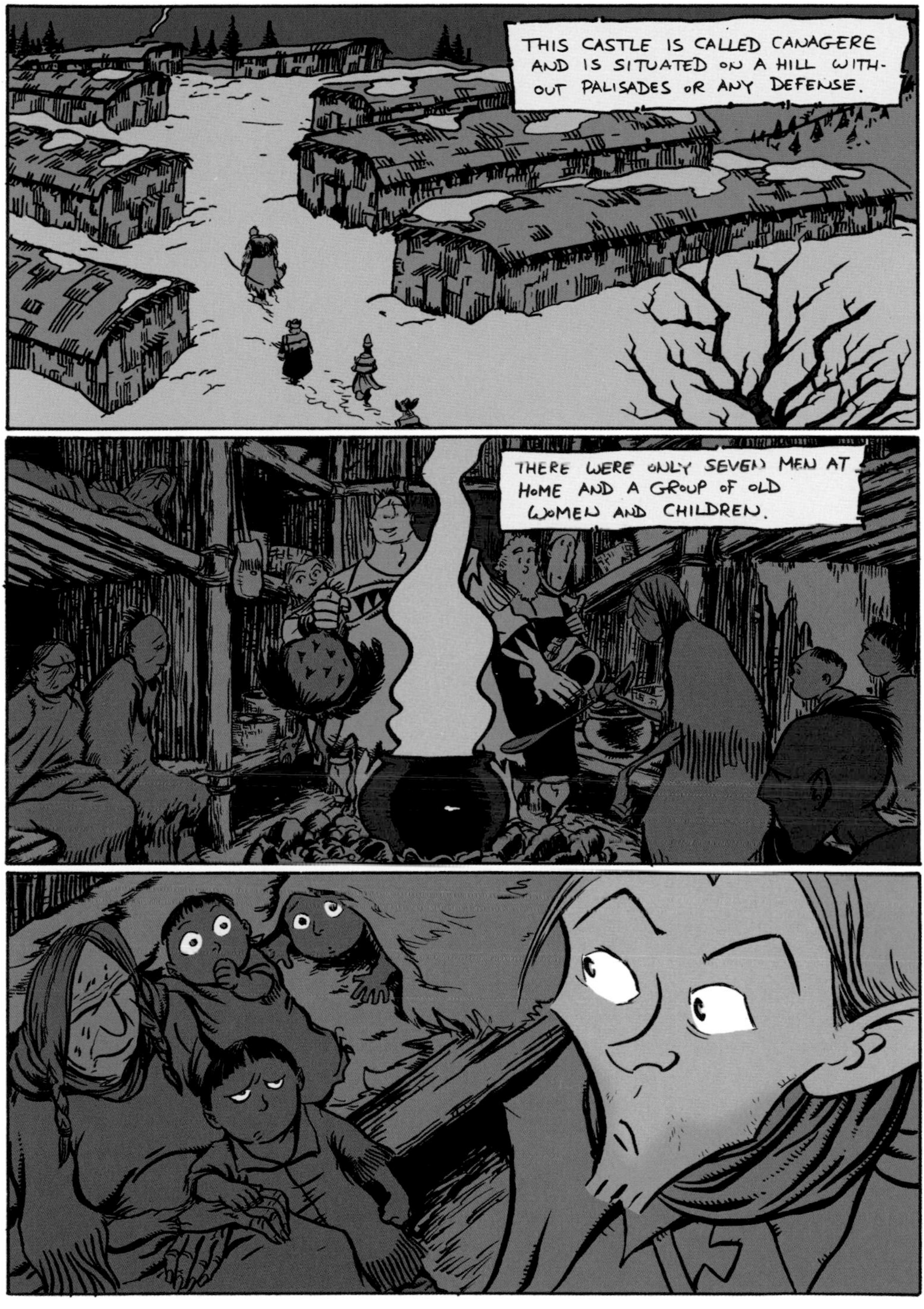
THIS CASTLE IS CALLED CANAGERE AND IS SITUATED ON A HILL WITHOUT PALISADES OR ANY DEFENSE.
THERE WERE ONLY SEVEN MEN AT HOME AND A GROUP OF OLD WOMEN AND CHILDREN.

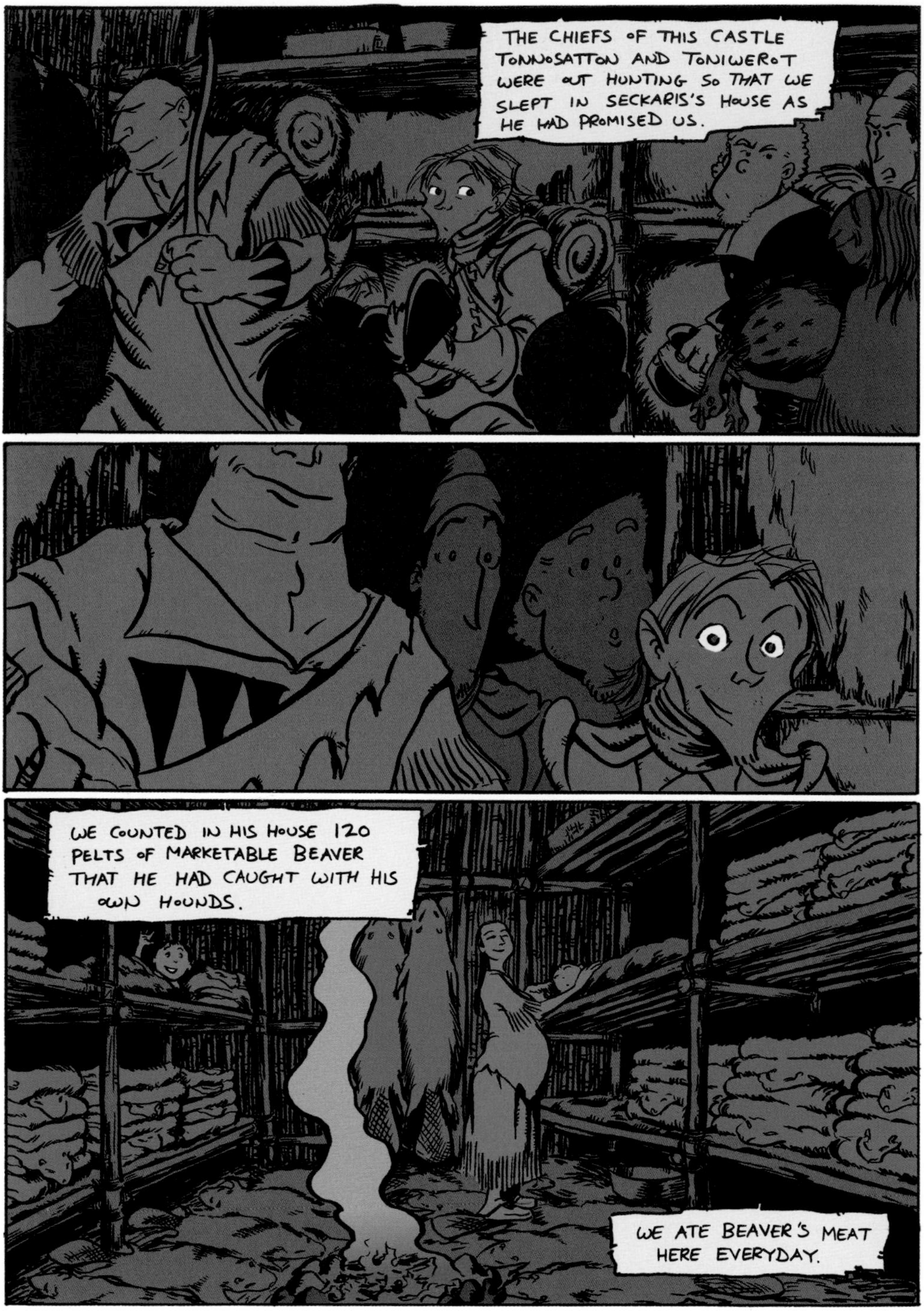
THE CHIEFS OF THIS CASTLE TONNOSATTON AND TONIWEROT WERE OUT HUNTING SO THAT WE SLEPT IN SECKARIS'S HOUSE AS HE HAD PROMISED US.
WE COUNTED IN HIS HOUSE 120 PELTS OF MARKETABLE BEAVER THAT HE HAD CAUGHT WITH HIS OWN HOUNDS.
WE ATE BEAVER'S MEAT HERE EVERYDAY.

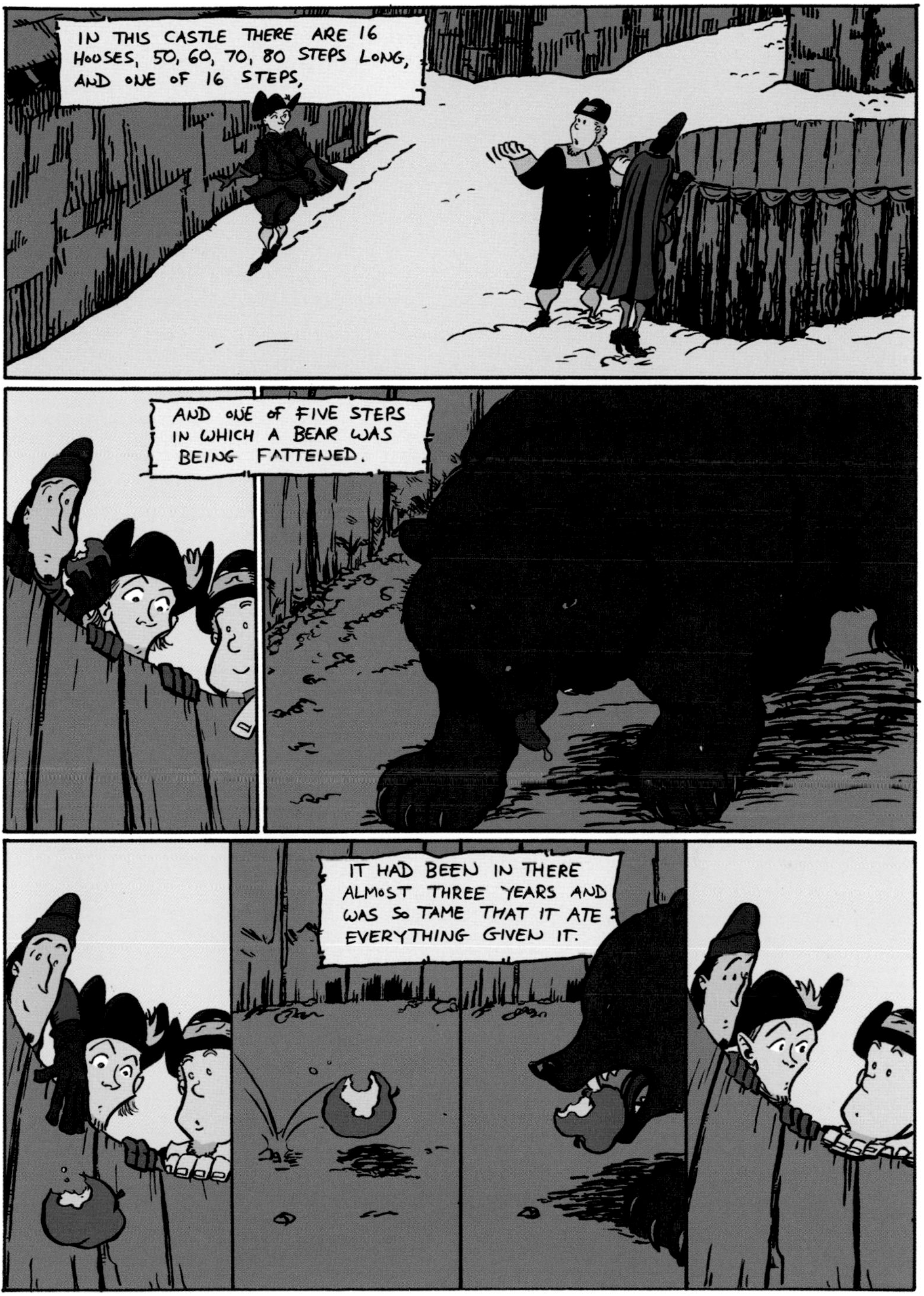
IN THIS CASTLE THERE ARE 16 HOUSES, 50, 60, 70, 80 STEPS LONG, AND ONE OF 16 STEPS,
AND ONE OF FIVE STEPS IN WHICH A BEAR WAS BEING FATTENED.
IT HAD BEEN IN THERE ALMOST THREE YEARS AND WAS SO TAME THAT IT ATE EVERYTHING GIVEN IT.

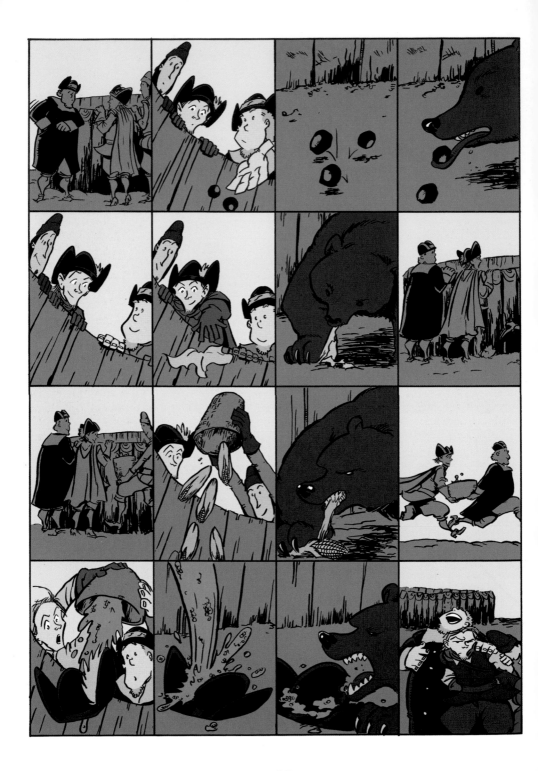

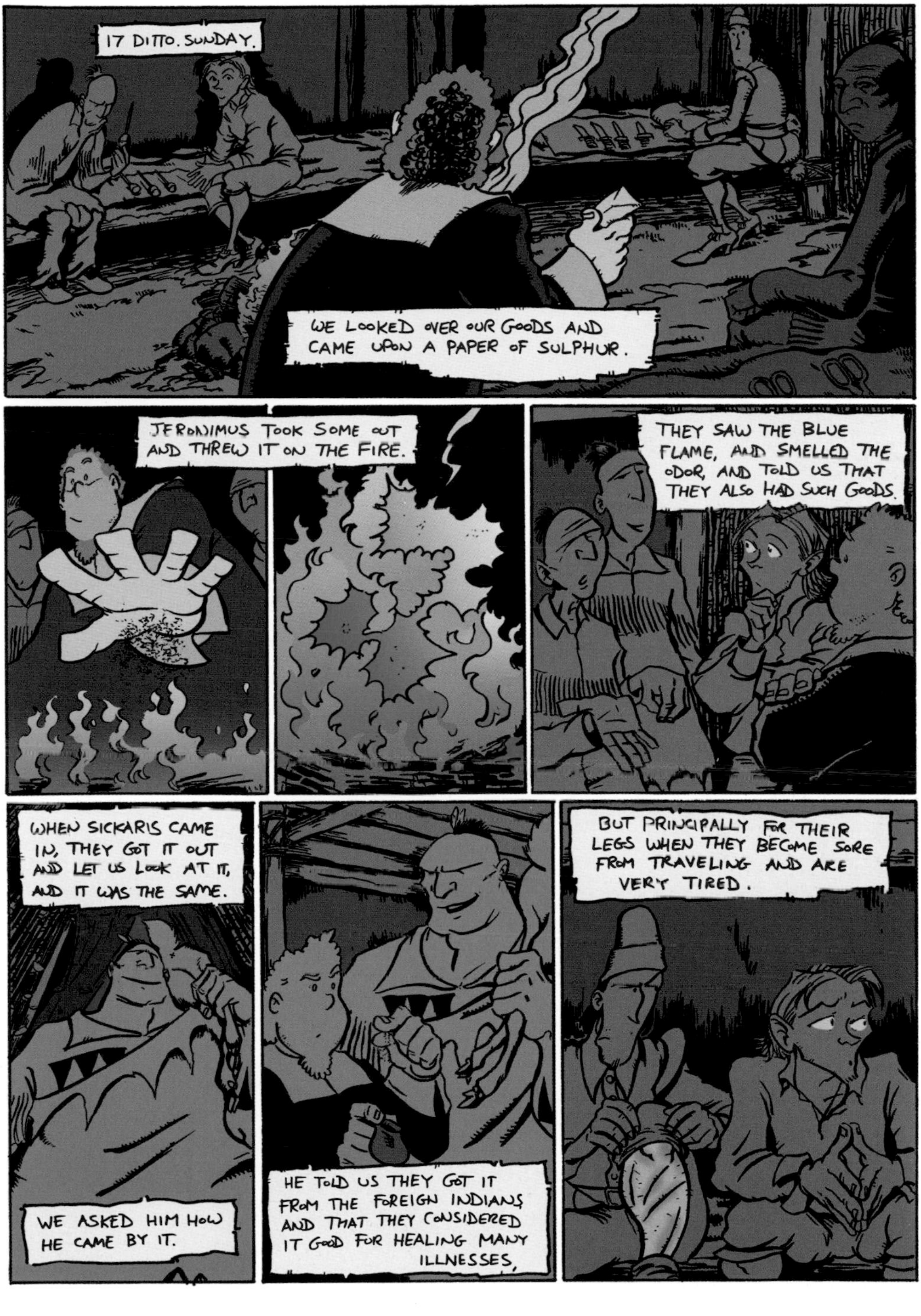
17 DITTO. SUNDAY.
WE LOOKED OVER OUR GOODS AND CAME UPON A PAPER OF SULPHUR.
JERONIMUS TOOK SOME OUT AND THREW IT ON THE FIRE.
THEY SAW THE BLUE FLAME, AND SMELLED THE ODOR, AND TOLD US THAT THEY ALSO HAD SUCH GOODS.
WHEN SICKARIS CAME IN, THEY GOT IT OUT AND LET US LOOK AT IT, AND IT WAS THE SAME.
WE ASKED HIM HOW HE CAME BY IT.
HE TOLD US THEY GOT IT FROM THE FOREIGN INDIANS AND THAT THEY CONSIDERED IT GOOD FOR HEALING MANY ILLNESSES,
BUT PRINCIPALLY FOR THEIR LEGS WHEN THEY BECOME SORE FROM TRAVELING AND ARE VERY TIRED.

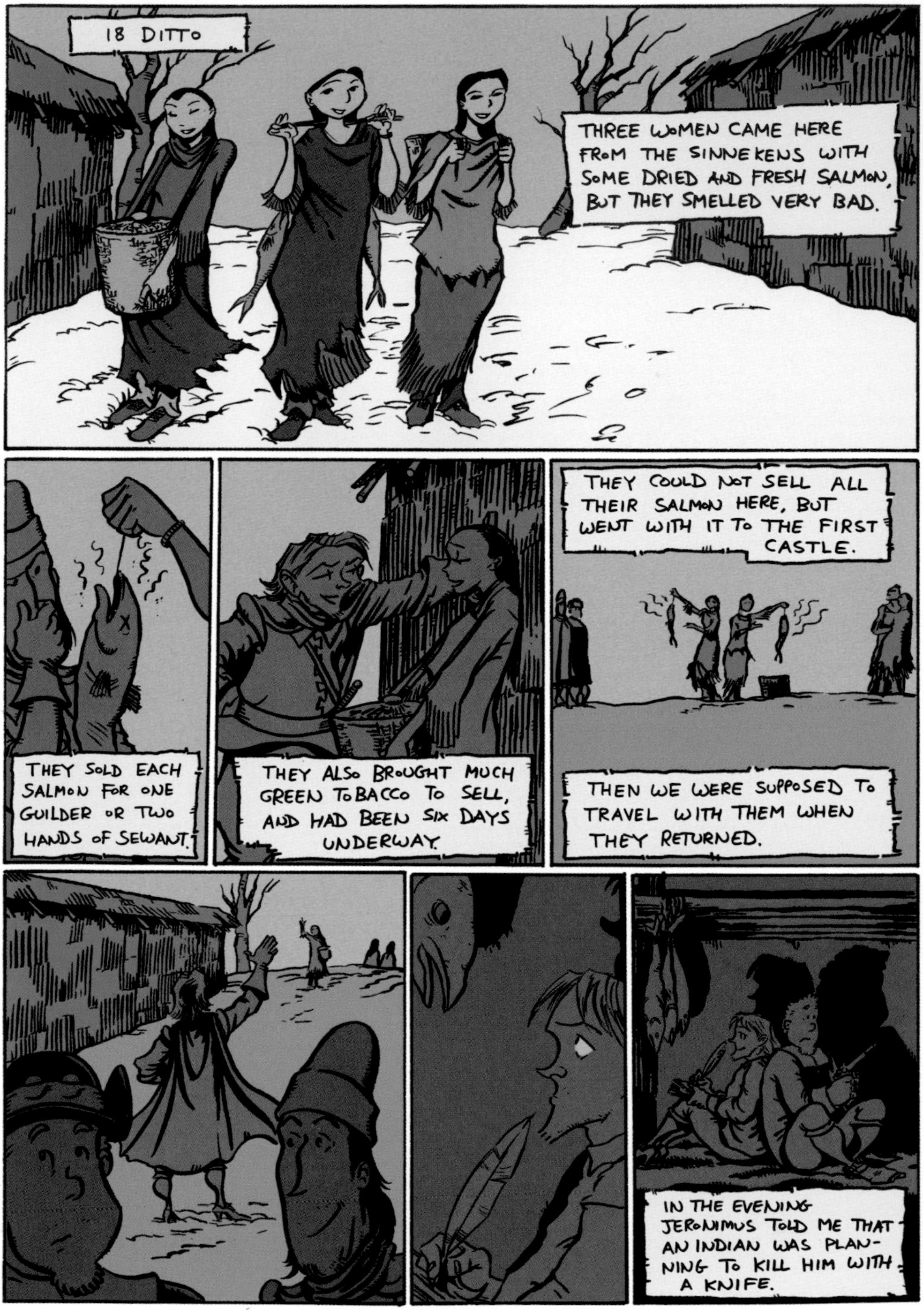
18 DITTO
THREE WOMEN CAME HERE FROM THE SINNEKENS WITH SOME DRIED AND FRESH SALMON, BUT THEY SMELLED VERY BAD.
THEY SOLD EACH SALMON FOR ONE GUILDER OR TWO HANDS OF SEWANT.
THEY ALSO BROUGHT MUCH GREEN TOBACCO TO SELL, AND HAD BEEN SIX DAYS UNDERWAY.
THEY COULD NOT SELL ALL THEIR SALMON HERE, BUT WENT WITH IT TO THE FIRST CASTLE.
THEN WE WERE SUPPOSED TO TRAVEL WITH THEM WHEN THEY RETURNED.
IN THE EVENING JERONIMUS TOLD ME THAT AN INDIAN WAS PLANNING TO KILL HIM WITH A KNIFE.

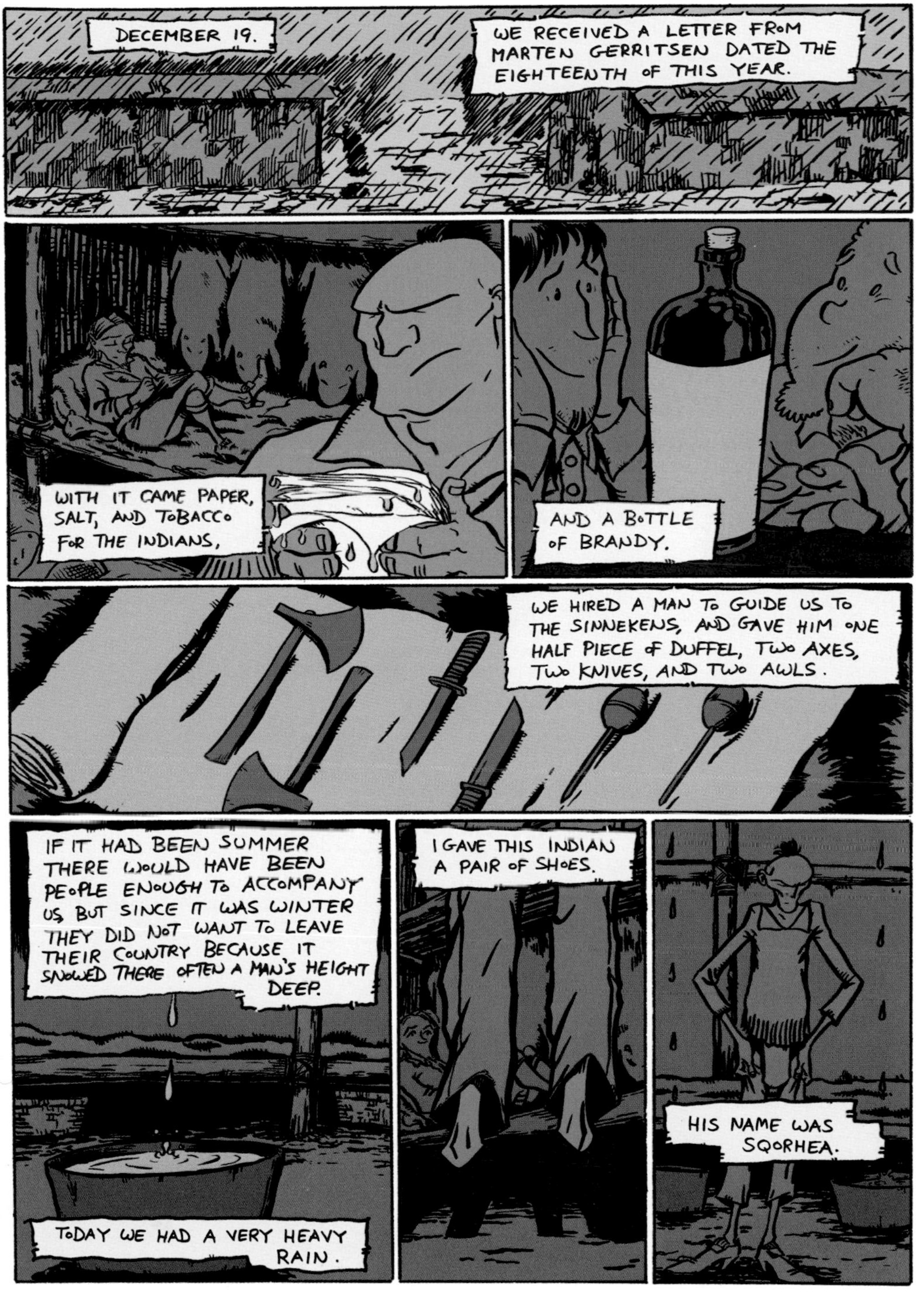
DECEMBER 19.
WE RECEIVED A LETTER FROM MARTEN GERRITSEN DATED THE EIGHTEENTH OF THIS YEAR.
WITH IT CAME PAPER, SALT, AND TOBACCO FOR THE INDIANS,
AND A BOTTLE OF BRANDY.
WE HIRED A MAN TO GUIDE US TO THE SINNEKENS, AND GAVE HIM ONE HALF PIECE OF DUFFEL, TWO AXES, TWO KNIVES, AND TWO AWLS.
IF IT HAD BEEN SUMMER THERE WOULD HAVE BEEN PEOPLE ENOUGH TO ACCOMPANY US, BUT SINCE IT WAS WINTER THEY DID NOT WANT TO LEAVE THEIR COUNTRY BECAUSE IT SNOWED THERE OFTEN A MAN'S HEIGHT DEEP.
TODAY WE HAD A VERY HEAVY RAIN.
I GAVE THIS INDIAN A PAIR OF SHOES.
HIS NAME WAS SQORHEA.

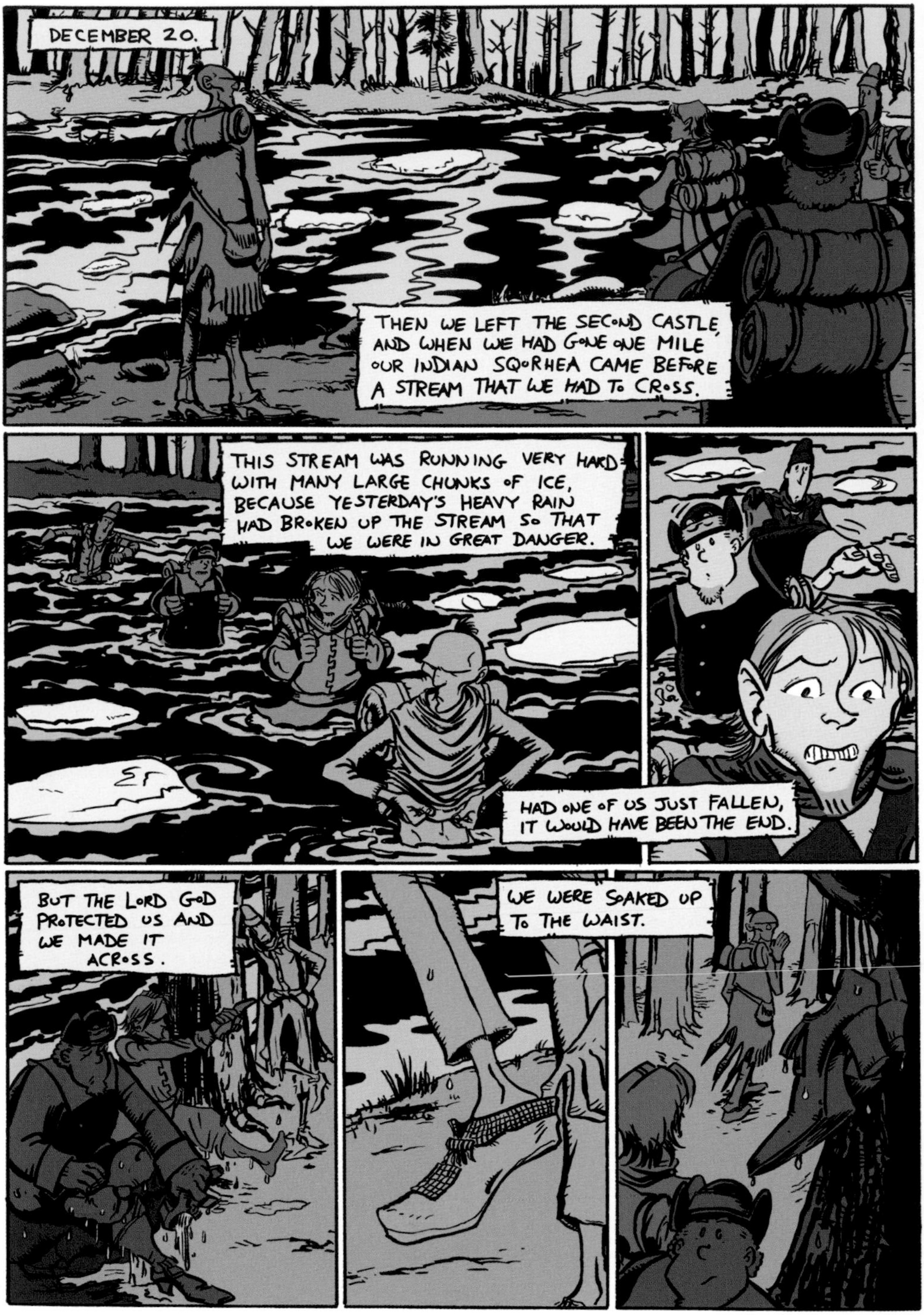
DECEMBER 20.
THEN WE LEFT THE SECOND CASTLE, AND WHEN WE HAD GONE ONE MILE OUR INDIAN SQORHEA CAME BEFORE A STREAM THAT WE HAD TO CROSS.
THIS STREAM WAS RUNNING VERY HARD WITH MANY LARGE CHUNKS OF ICE, BECAUSE YESTERDAY'S HEAVY RAIN HAD BROKEN UP THE STREAM SO THAT WE WERE IN GREAT DANGER.
HAD ONE OF US JUST FALLEN, IT WOULD HAVE BEEN THE END.
BUT THE LORD GOD PROTECTED US AND WE MADE IT ACROSS.
WE WERE SOAKED UP TO THE WAIST.

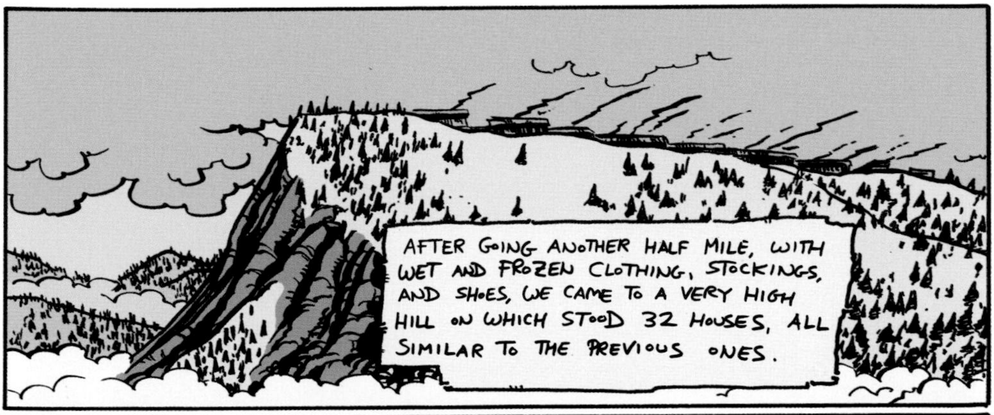
AFTER GOING ANOTHER HALF MILE, WITH WET AND FROZEN CLOTHING, STOCKINGS, AND SHOES, WE CAME TO A VERY HIGH HILL ON WHICH STOOD 32 HOUSES, ALL SIMILAR TO THE PREVIOUS ONES.

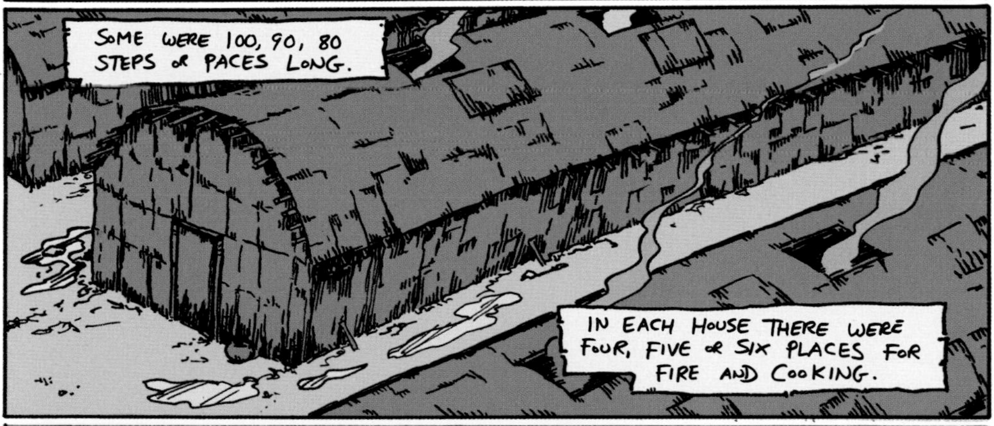
SOME WERE 100, 90, 80 STEPS OR PACES LONG.
IN EACH HOUSE THERE WERE FOUR, FIVE OR SIX PLACES FOR FIRE AND COOKING.

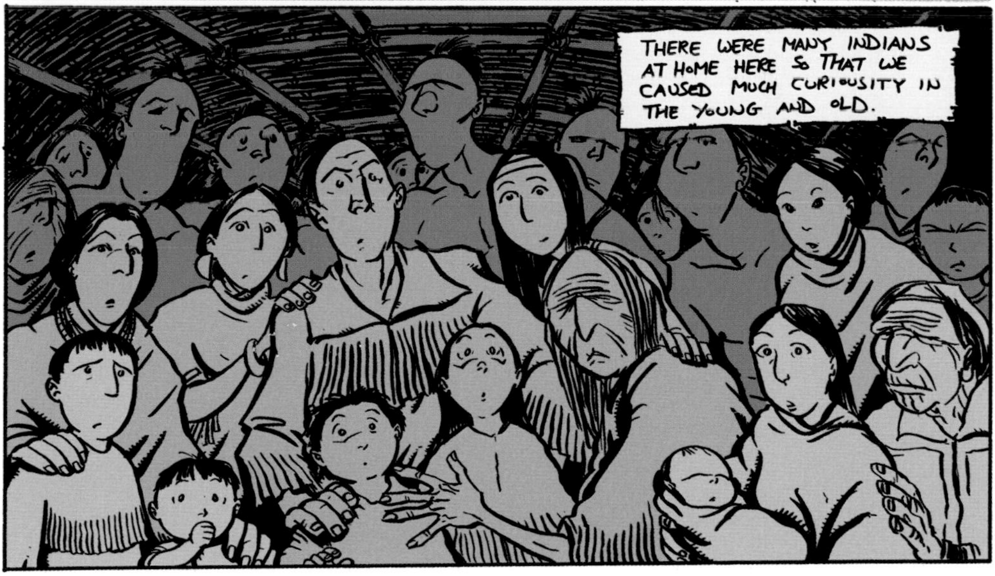
THERE WERE MANY INDIANS AT HOME HERE SO THAT WE CAUSED MUCH CURIOUSITY IN THE YOUNG AND OLD.

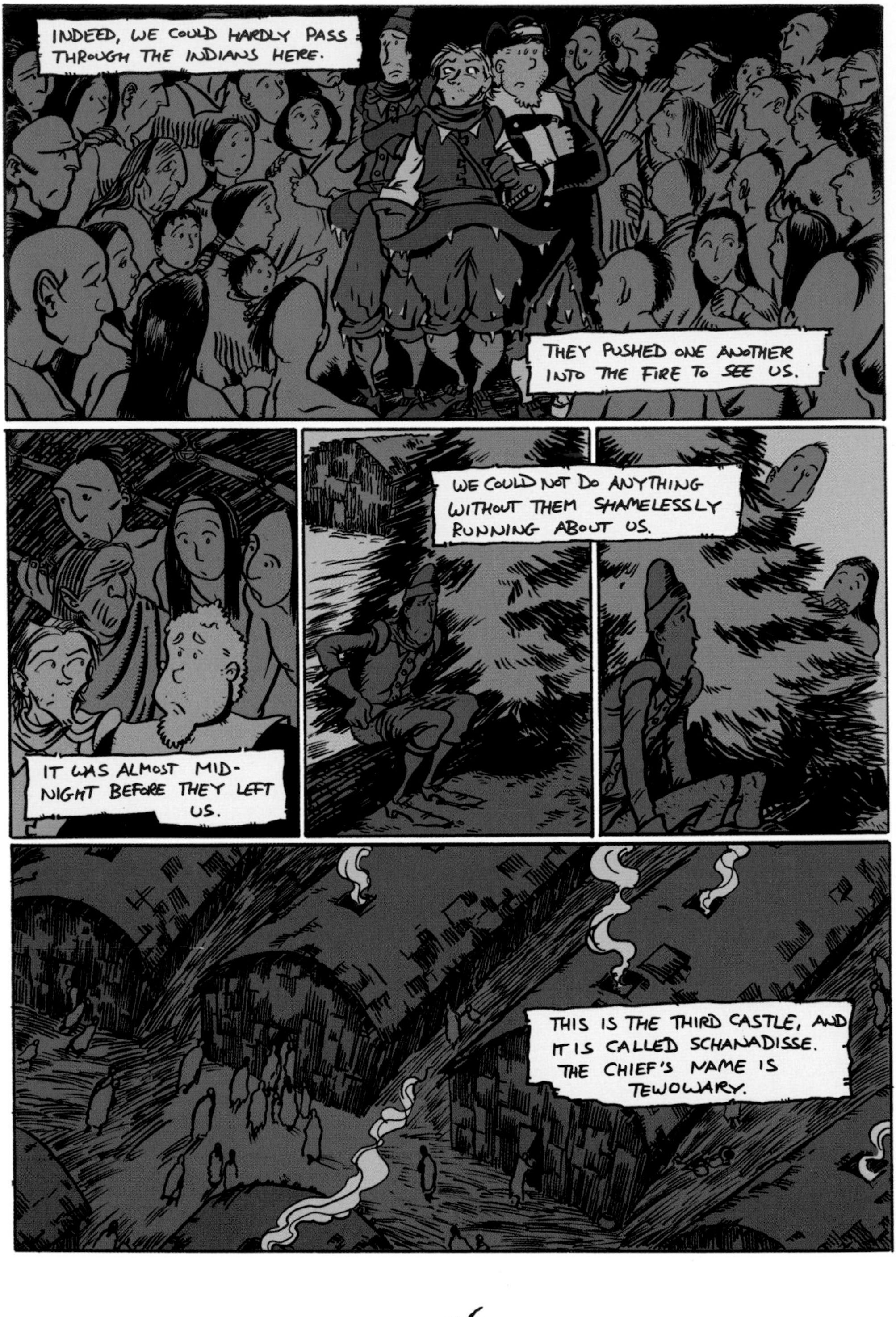
INDEED, WE COULD HARDLY PASS THROUGH THE INDIANS HERE.
THEY PUSHED ONE ANOTHER INTO THE FIRE TO SEE US.
IT WAS ALMOST MID-NIGHT BEFORE THEY LEFT US.
WE COULD NOT DO ANYTHING WITHOUT THEM SHAMELESSLY RUNNING ABOUT US.
THIS IS THE THIRD CASTLE, AND IT IS CALLED SCHANADISSE. THE CHIEF'S NAME IS TEWOWARY.

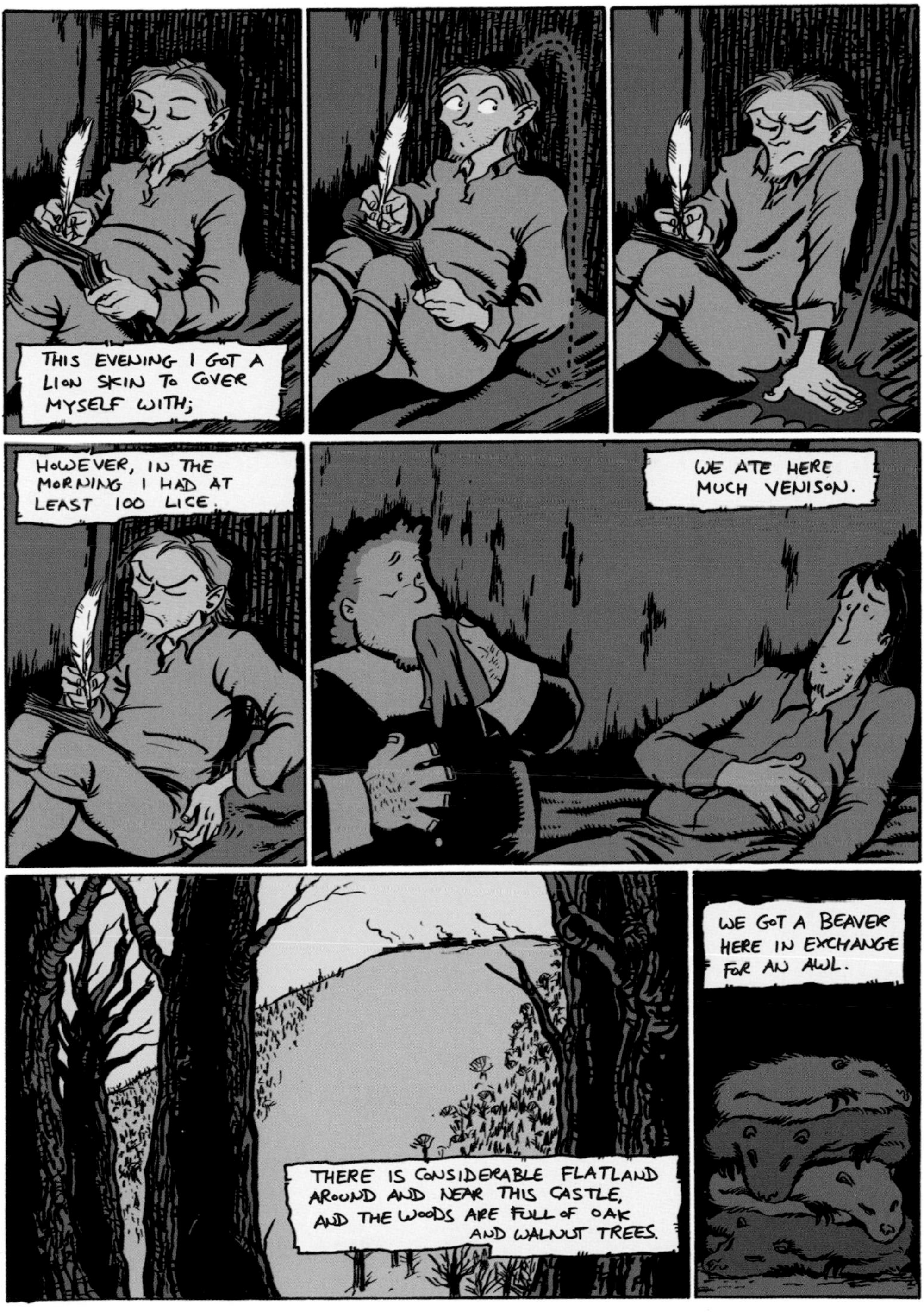
THIS EVENING I GOT A LION SKIN TO COVER MYSELF WITH;
HOWEVER, IN THE MORNING I HAD AT LEAST 100 LICE.
WE ATE HERE MUCH VENISON.
THERE IS CONSIDERABLE FLATLAND AROUND AND NEAR THIS CASTLE, AND THE WOODS ARE FULL OF OAK AND WALNUT TREES.
WE GOT A BEAVER HERE IN EXCHANGE FOR AN AWL.

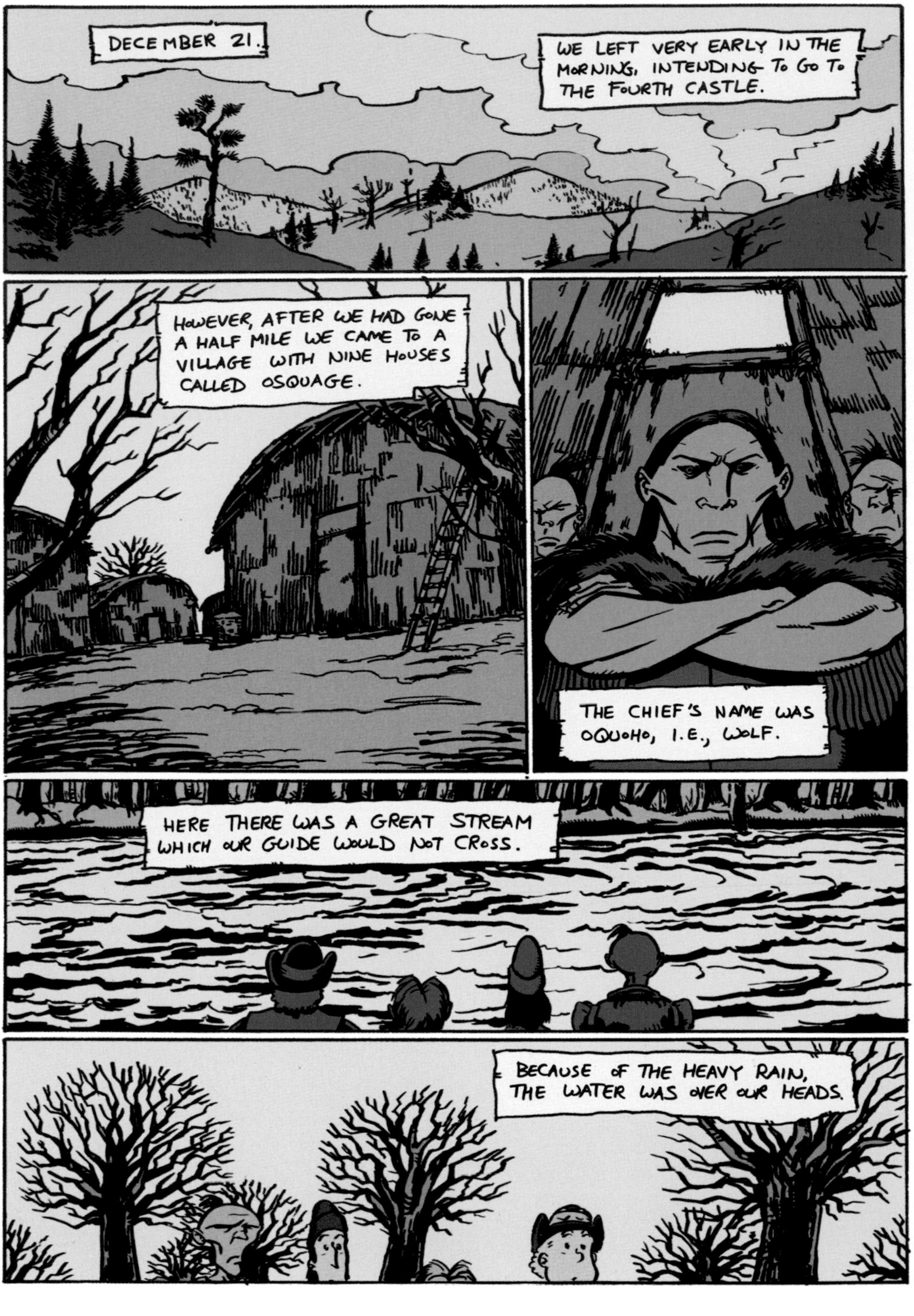
DECEMBER 21.
WE LEFT VERY EARLY IN THE MORNING, INTENDING TO GO TO THE FOURTH CASTLE.
HOWEVER, AFTER WE HAD GONE A HALF MILE WE CAME TO A VILLAGE WITH NINE HOUSES CALLED OSQUAGE.
THE CHIEF'S NAME WAS OQUOHO, I.E., WOLF.
HERE THERE WAS A GREAT STREAM WHICH OUR GUIDE WOULD NOT CROSS.
BECAUSE OF THE HEAVY RAIN, THE WATER WAS OVER OUR HEADS.

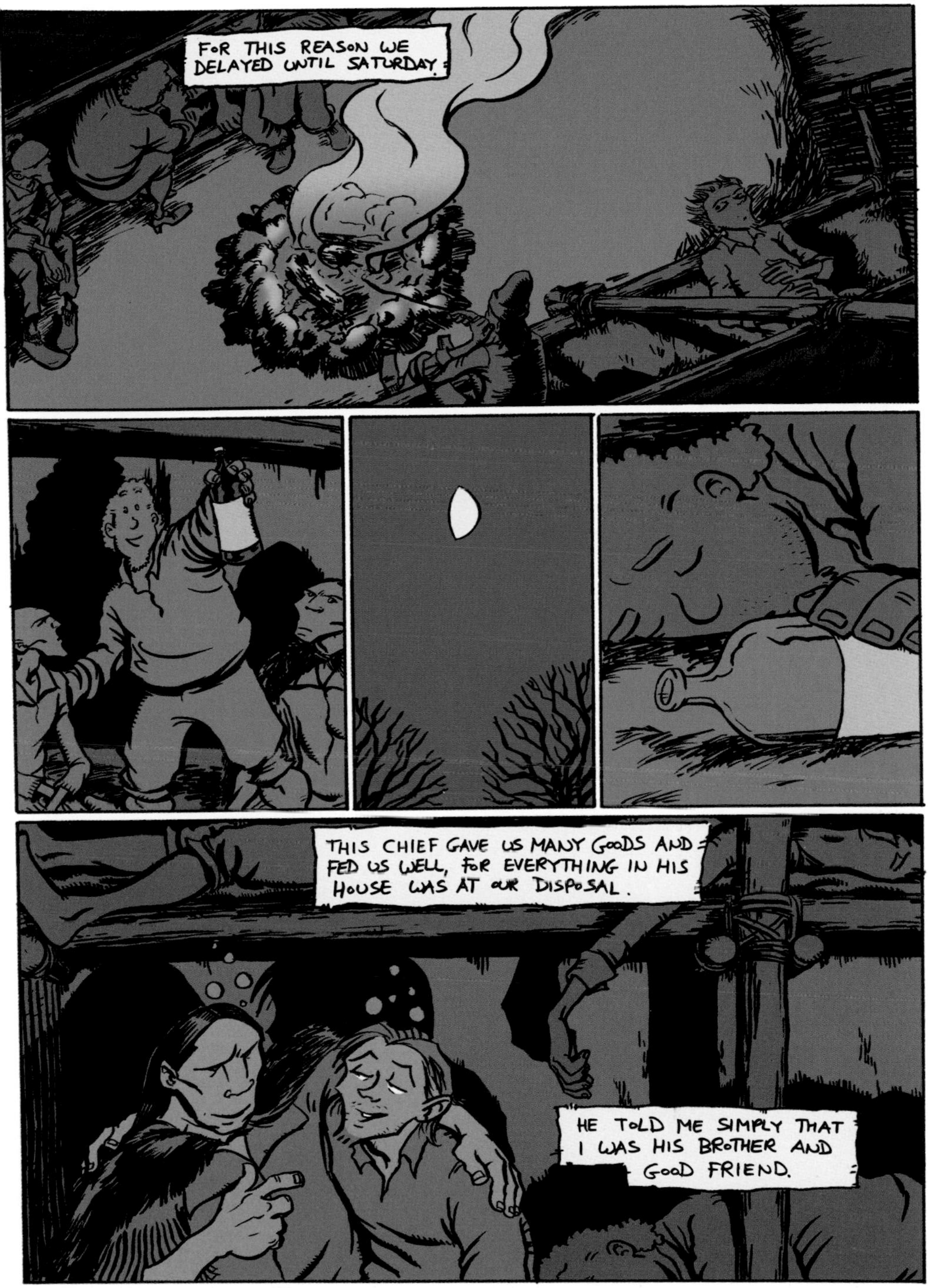
FOR THIS REASON WE DELAYED UNTIL SATURDAY.
THIS CHIEF GAVE US MANY GOODS AND FED US WELL, FOR EVERYTHING IN HIS HOUSE WAS AT OUR DISPOSAL.
HE TOLD ME SIMPLY THAT I WAS HIS BROTHER AND GOOD FRIEND.

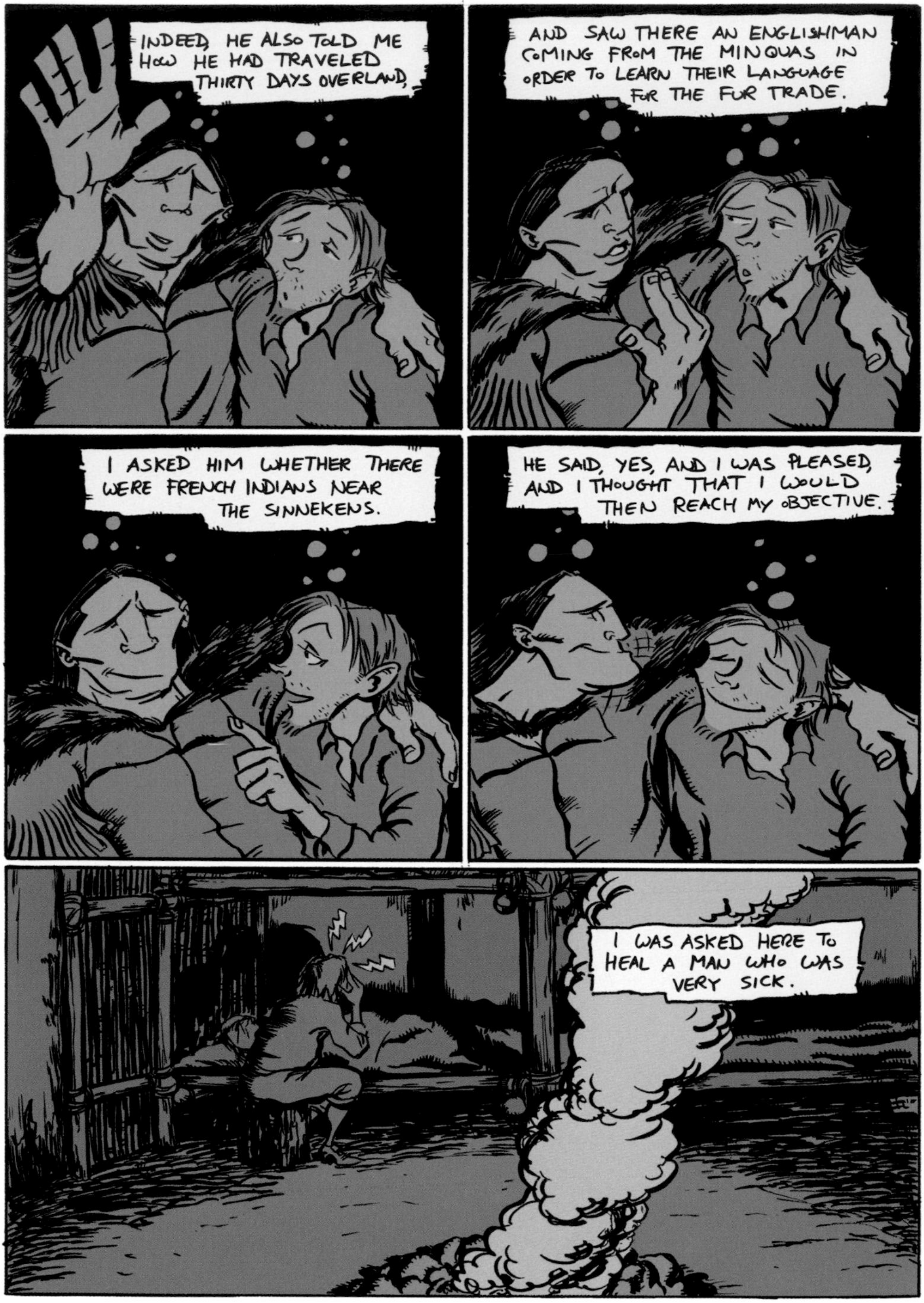
INDEED, HE ALSO TOLD ME HOW HE HAD TRAVELED THIRTY DAYS OVERLAND,
AND SAW THERE AN ENGLISHMAN COMING FROM THE MINQUAS IN ORDER TO LEARN THEIR LANGUAGE FOR THE FUR TRADE.
I ASKED HIM WHETHER THERE WERE FRENCH INDIANS NEAR THE SINNEKENS.
HE SAID, YES, AND I WAS PLEASED, AND I THOUGHT THAT I WOULD THEN REACH MY OBJECTIVE.
I WAS ASKED HERE TO HEAL A MAN WHO WAS VERY SICK.

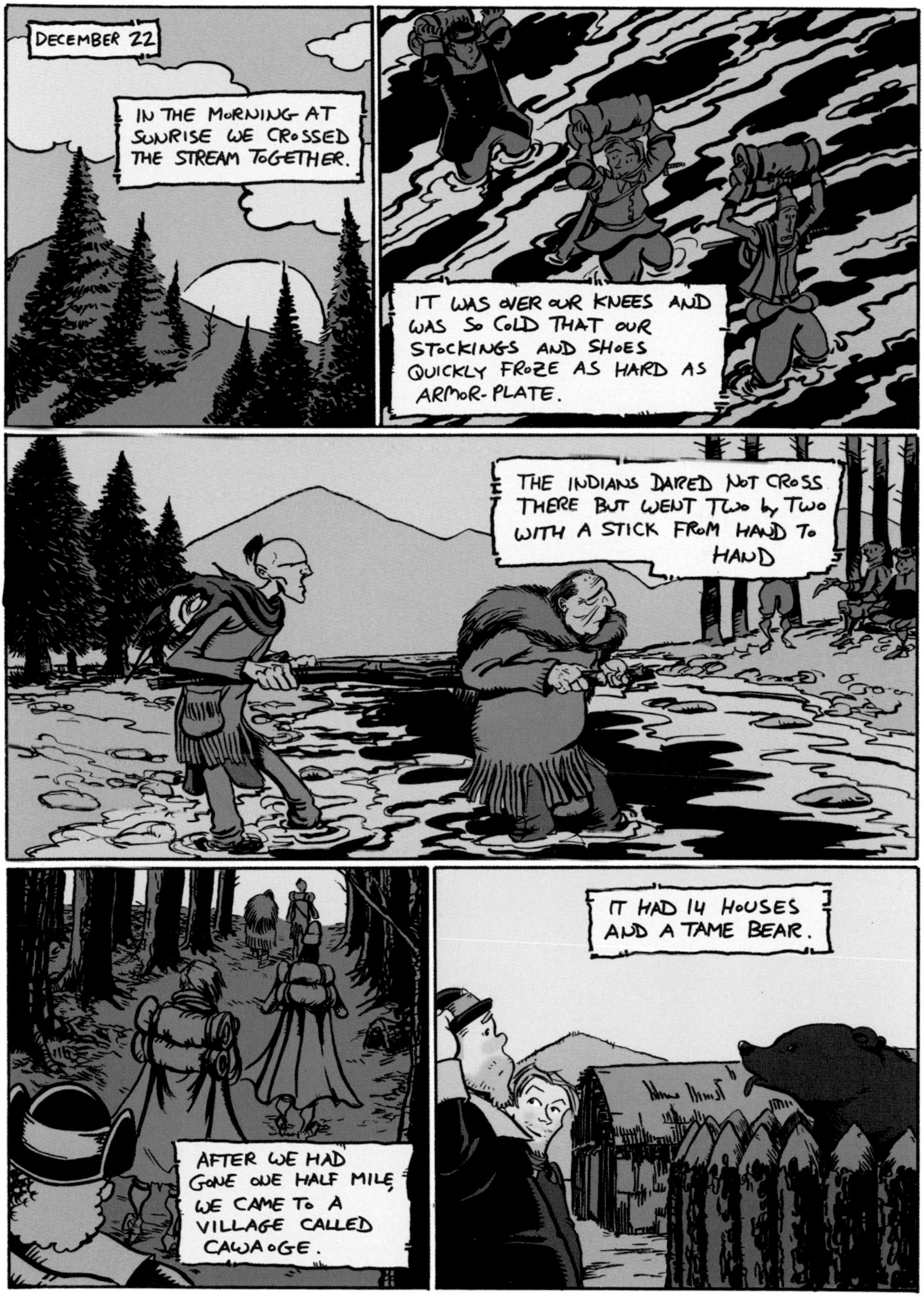
DECEMBER 22
IN THE MORNING AT SUNRISE WE CROSSED THE STREAM TOGETHER.
IT WAS OVER OUR KNEES AND WAS SO COLD THAT OUR STOCKINGS AND SHOES QUICKLY FROZE AS HARD AS ARMOR-PLATE.
THE INDIANS DARED NOT CROSS THERE BUT WENT TWO BY TWO WITH A STICK FROM HAND TO HAND
AFTER WE HAD GONE ONE HALF MILE, WE CAME TO A VILLAGE CALLED CAWAOGE.
IT HAD 14 HOUSES AND A TAME BEAR.

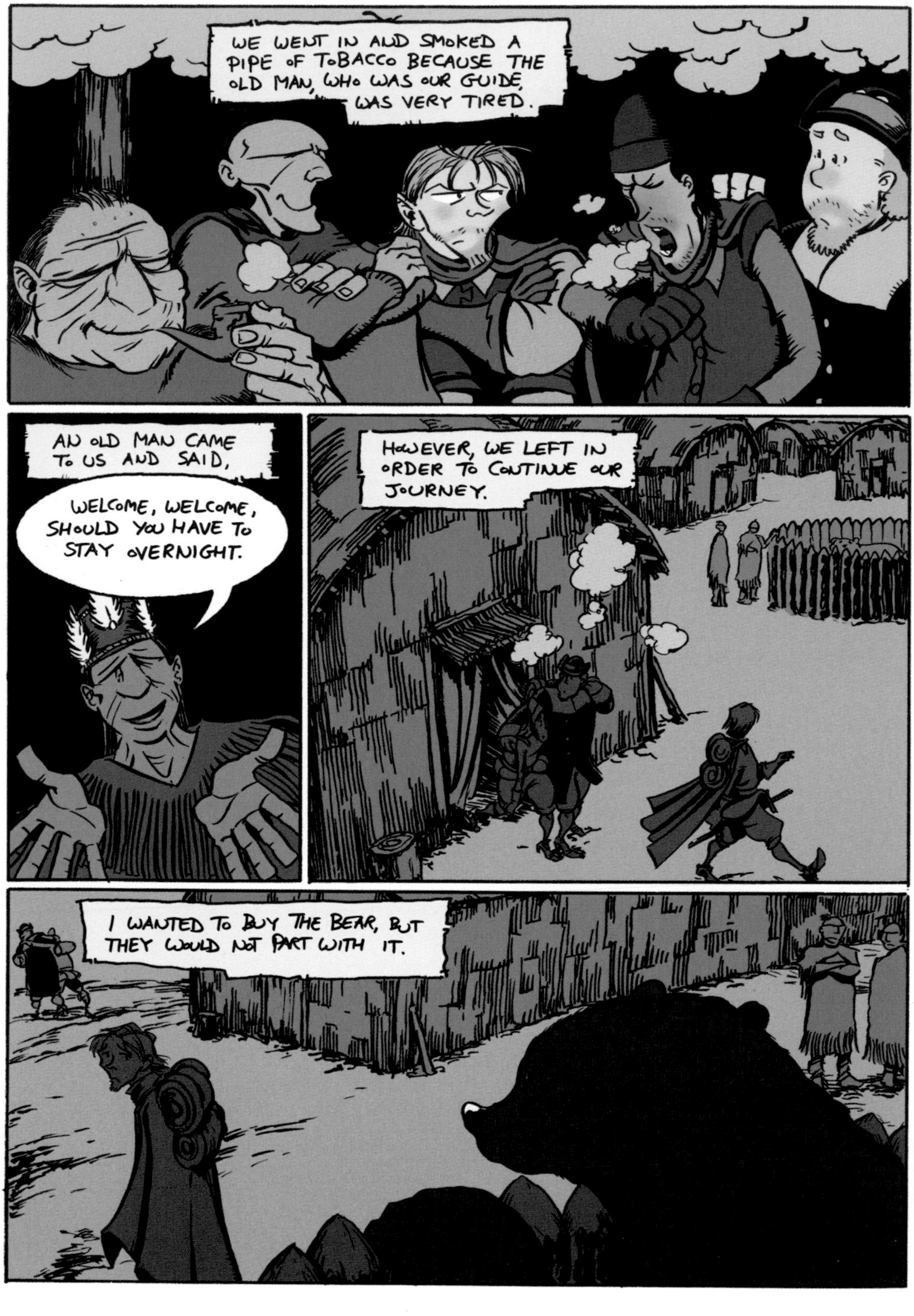
WE WENT IN AND SMOKED A PIPE OF TOBACCO BECAUSE THE OLD MAN, WHO WAS OUR GUIDE, WAS VERY TIRED.
AN OLD MAN CAME TO US AND SAID,
WELCOME, WELCOME, SHOULD YOU HAVE TO STAY OVERNIGHT.
HOWEVER, WE LEFT IN ORDER TO CONTINUE OUR JOURNEY.
I WANTED TO BUY THE BEAR, BUT THEY WOULD NOT PART WITH IT.

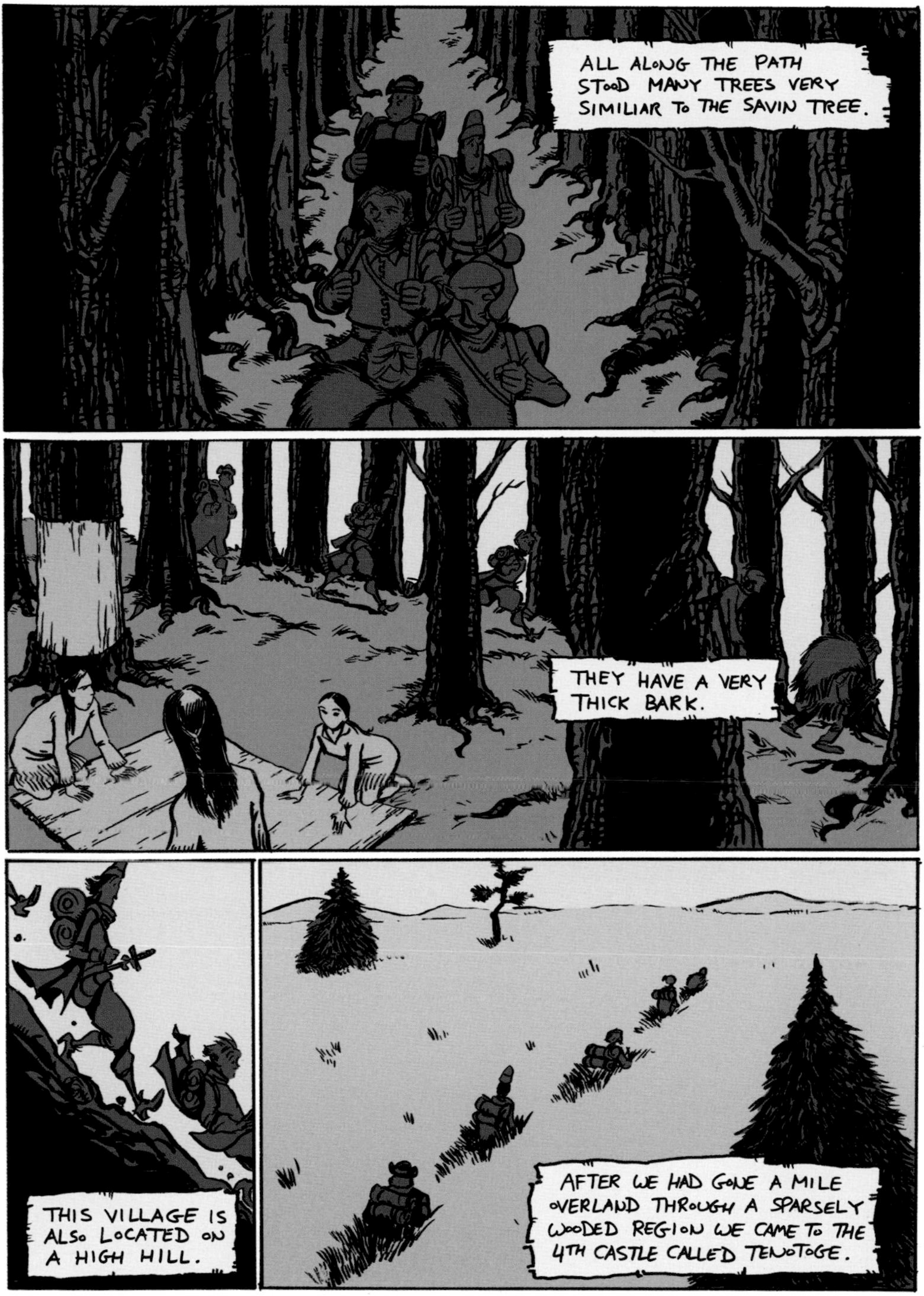
ALL ALONG THE PATH STOOD MANY TREES VERY SIMILIAR TO THE SAVIN TREE.
THEY HAVE A VERY THICK BARK.
THIS VILLAGE IS ALSO LOCATED ON A HIGH HILL.
AFTER WE HAD GONE A MILE OVERLAND THROUGH A SPARSELY WOODED REGION WE CAME TO THE 4TH CASTLE CALLED TENOTOGE.

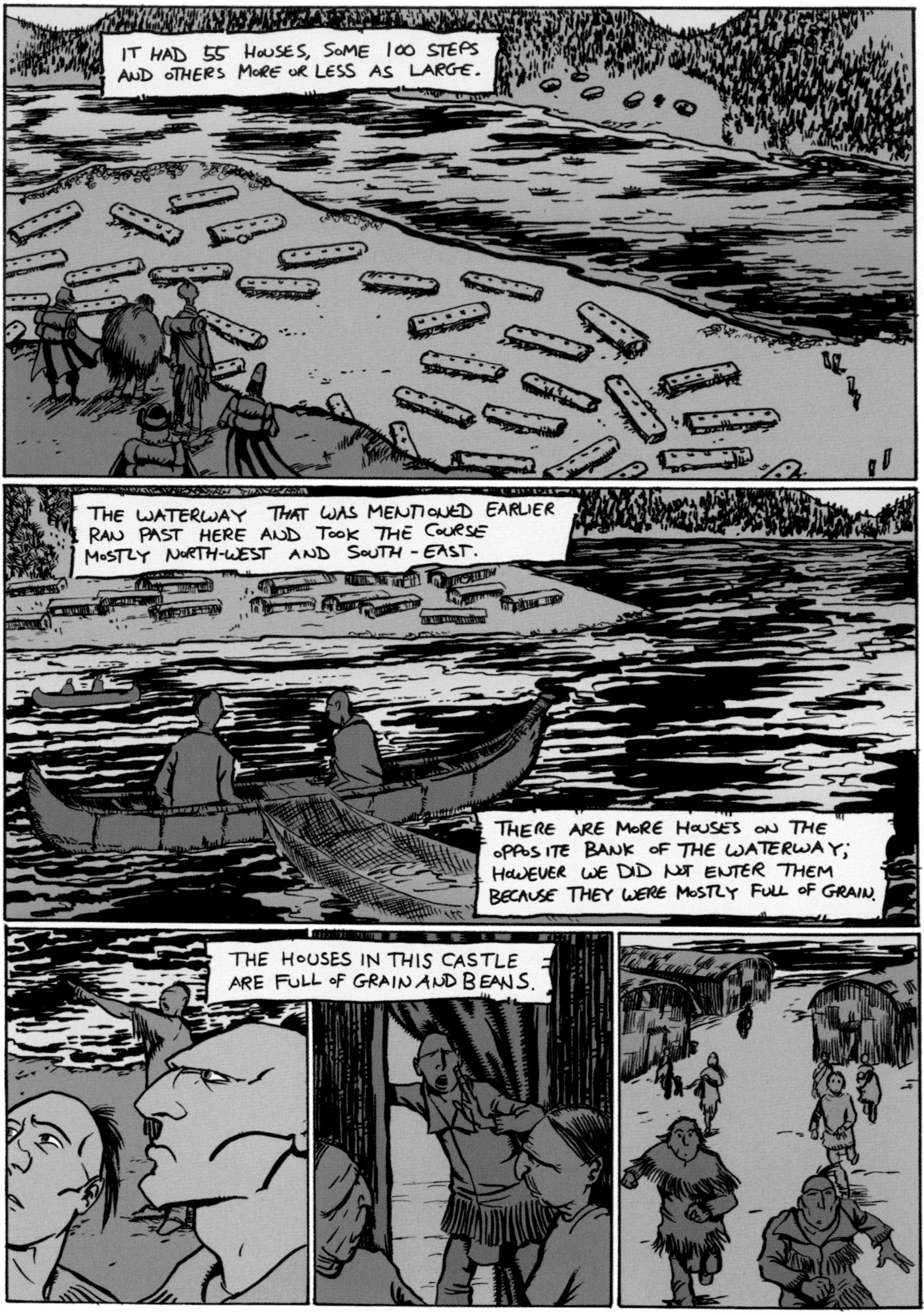
IT HAD 55 HOUSES, SOME 100 STEPS AND OTHERS MORE OR LESS AS LARGE.
THE WATERWAY THAT WAS MENTIONED EARLIER RAN PAST HERE AND TOOK THE COURSE MOSTLY NORTH-WEST AND SOUTH-EAST.
THERE ARE MORE HOUSES ON THE OPPOSITE BANK OF THE WATERWAY; HOWEVER WE DID NOT ENTER THEM BECAUSE THEY WERE MOSTLY FULL OF GRAIN.
THE HOUSES IN THIS CASTLE ARE FULL OF GRAIN AND BEANS.

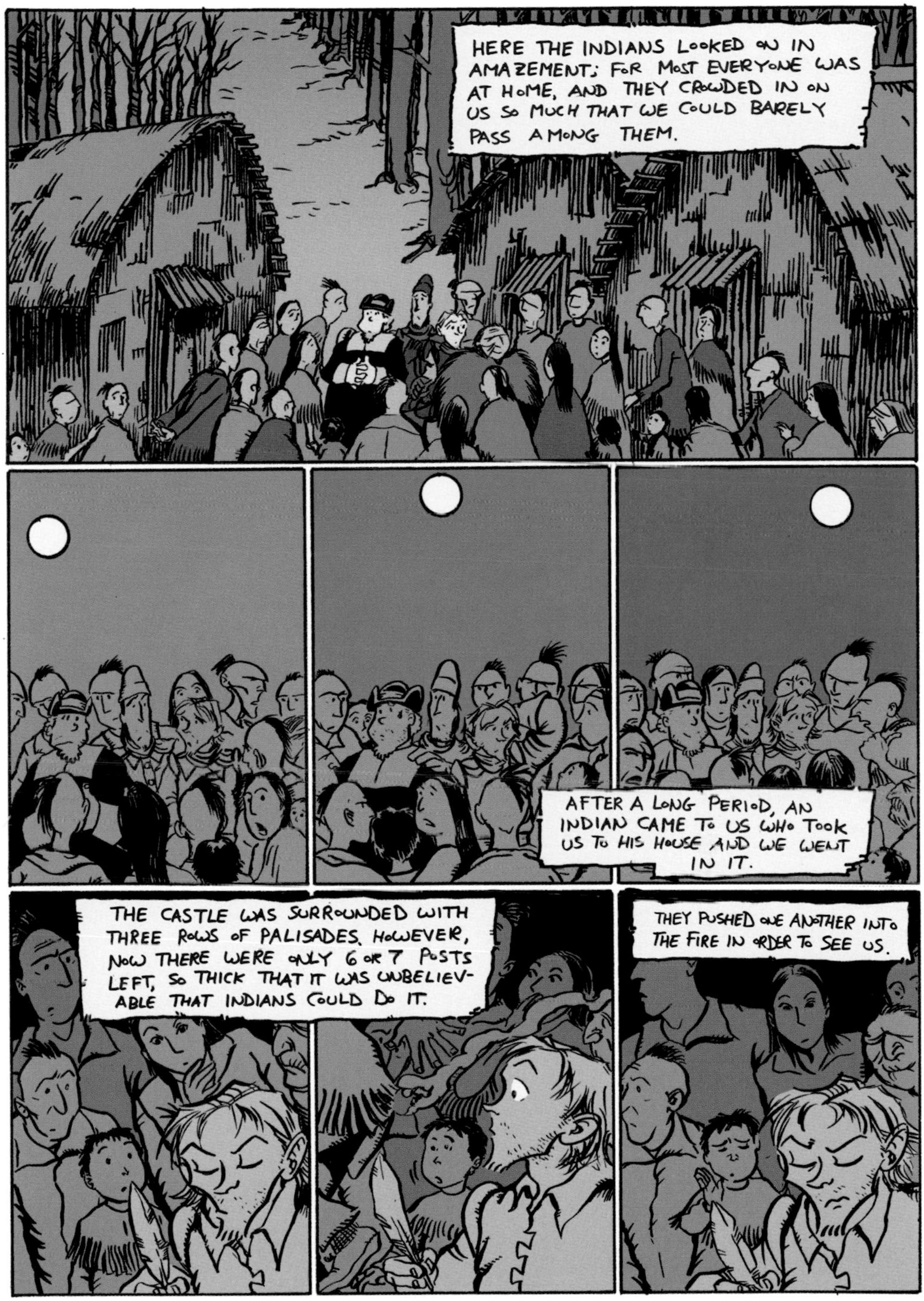
HERE THE INDIANS LOOKED ON IN AMAZEMENT; FOR MOST EVERYONE WAS AT HOME, AND THEY CROWDED IN ON US SO MUCH THAT WE COULD BARELY PASS AMONG THEM.
AFTER A LONG PERIOD, AN INDIAN CAME TO US WHO TOOK US TO HIS HOUSE AND WE WENT IN IT.
THE CASTLE WAS SURROUNDED WITH THREE ROWS OF PALISADES. HOWEVER, NOW THERE WERE ONLY 6 OR 7 POSTS LEFT, SO THICK THAT IT WAS UNBELIEVABLE THAT INDIANS COULD DO IT.
THEY PUSHED ONE ANOTHER INTO THE FIRE IN ORDER TO SEE US.

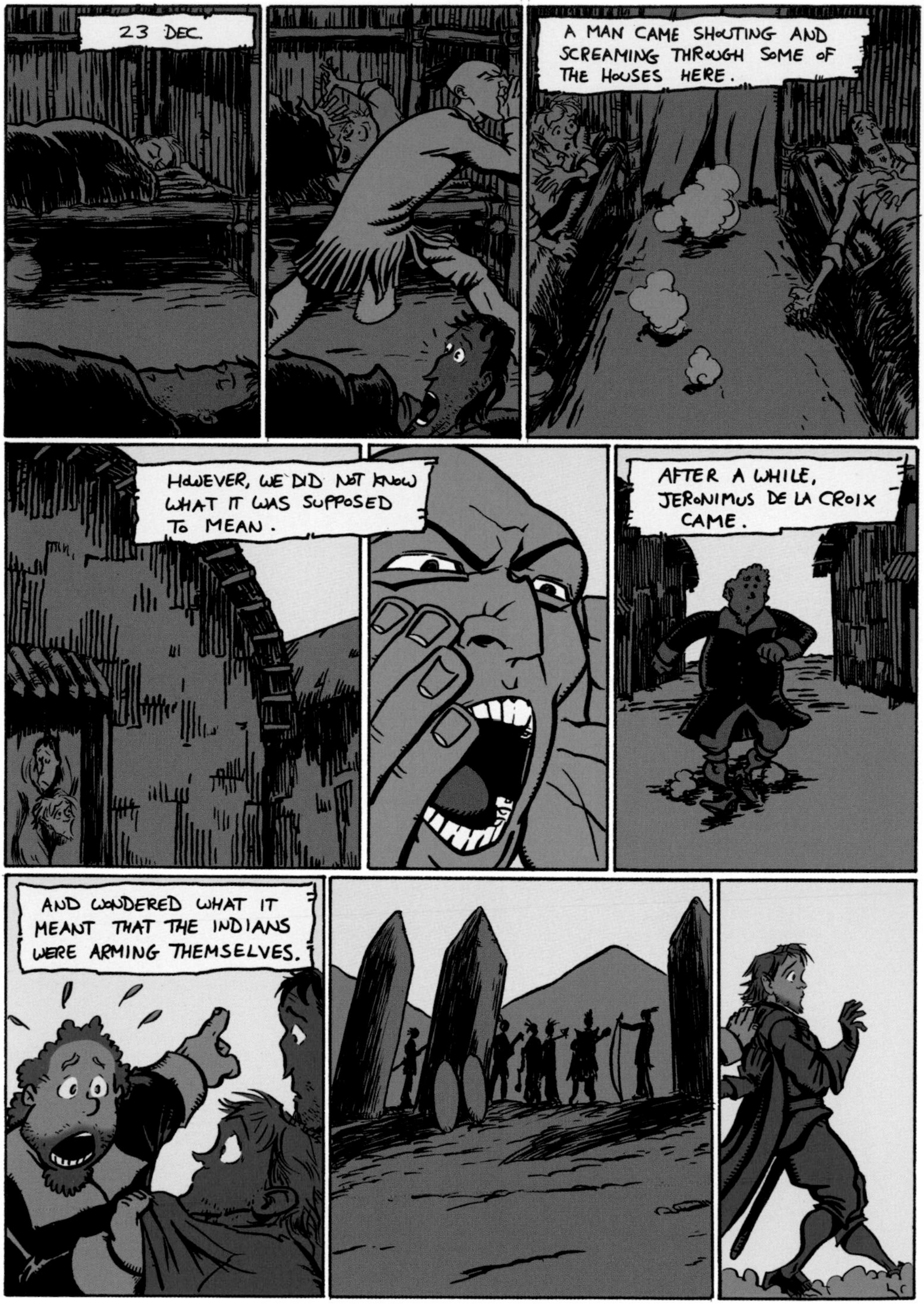
23 DEC.
A MAN CAME SHOUTING AND SCREAMING THROUGH SOME OF THE HOUSES HERE.
HOWEVER, WE DID NOT KNOW WHAT IT WAS SUPPOSED TO MEAN.
AFTER A WHILE, JERONIMUS DE LA CROIX CAME.
AND WONDERED WHAT IT MEANT THAT THE INDIANS WERE ARMING THEMSELVES.

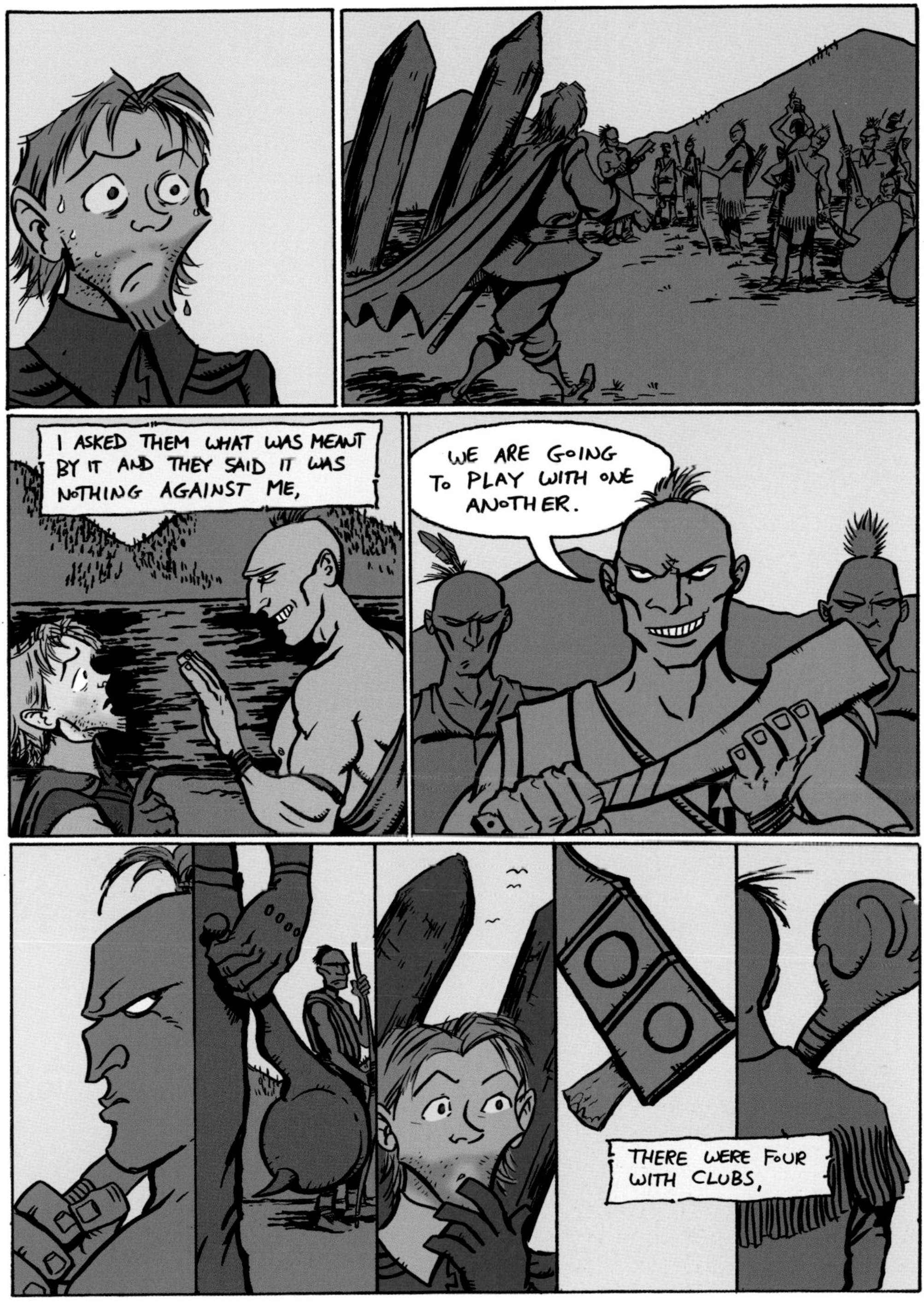
I ASKED THEM WHAT WAS MEANT BY IT AND THEY SAID IT WAS NOTHING AGAINST ME,
WE ARE GOING TO PLAY WITH ONE ANOTHER.
THERE WERE FOUR WITH CLUBS,

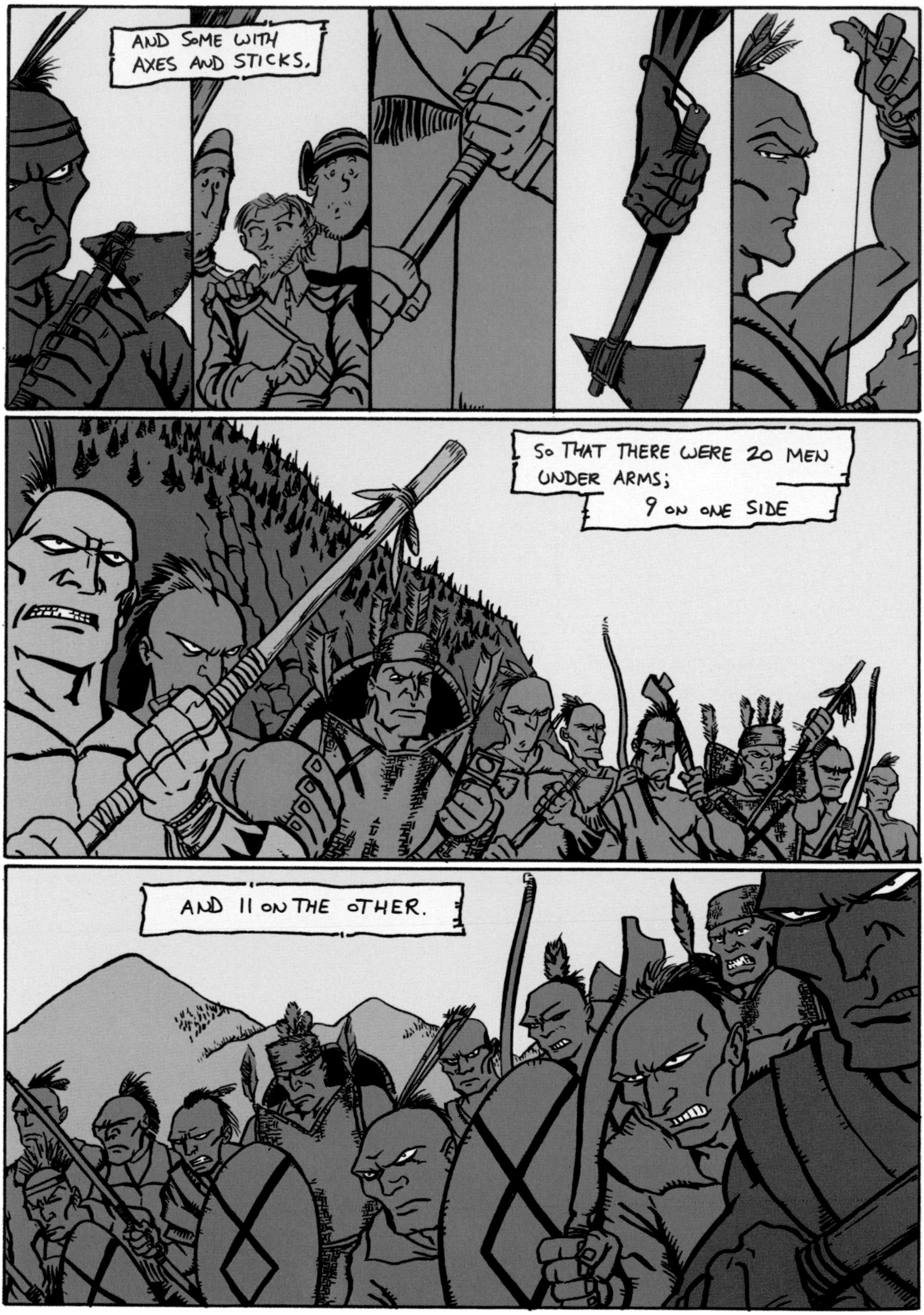
AND SOME WITH AXES AND STICKS.
SO THAT THERE WERE 20 MEN UNDER ARMS;
9 ON ONE SIDE
AND 11 ON THE OTHER.

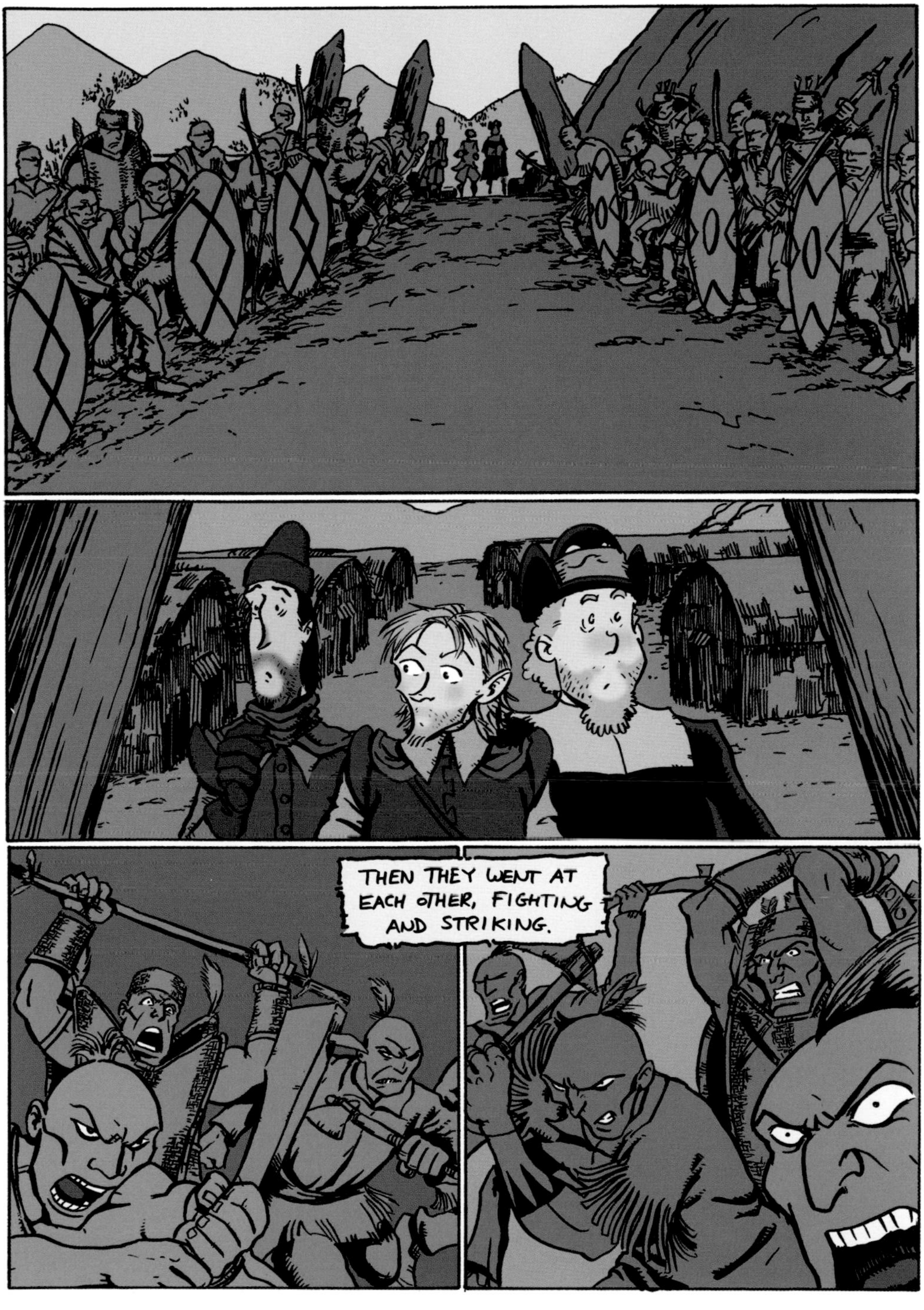
THEN THEY WENT AT EACH OTHER, FIGHTING AND STRIKING.

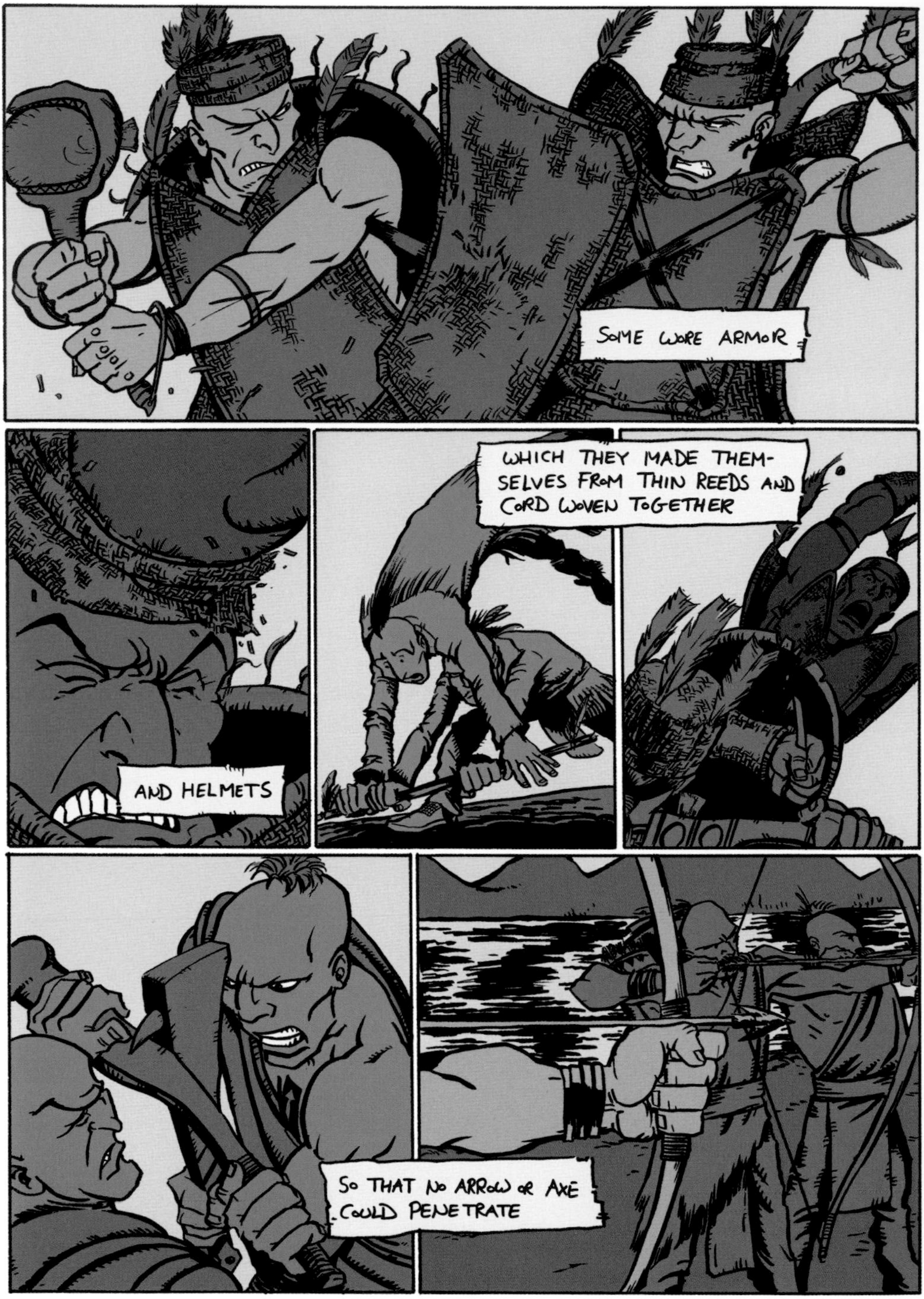
SOME WORE ARMOR
AND HELMETS
WHICH THEY MADE THEMSELVES FROM THIN REEDS AND CORD WOVEN TOGETHER
SO THAT NO ARROW OR AXE COULD PENETRATE

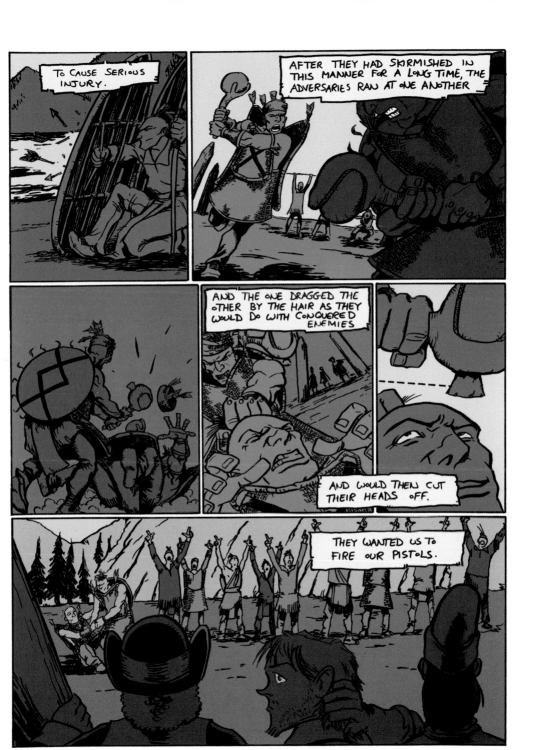

TO CAUSE SERIOUS INJURY.

AFTER THEY HAD SKIRMISHED IN THIS MANNER FOR A LONG TIME, THE ADVERSARIES RAN AT ONE ANOTHER

AND THE ONE DRAGGED THE OTHER BY THE HAIR AS THEY WOULD DO WITH CONQUERED ENEMIES

AND WOULD THEN CUT THEIR HEADS OFF.

THEY WANTED US TO FIRE OUR PISTOLS.

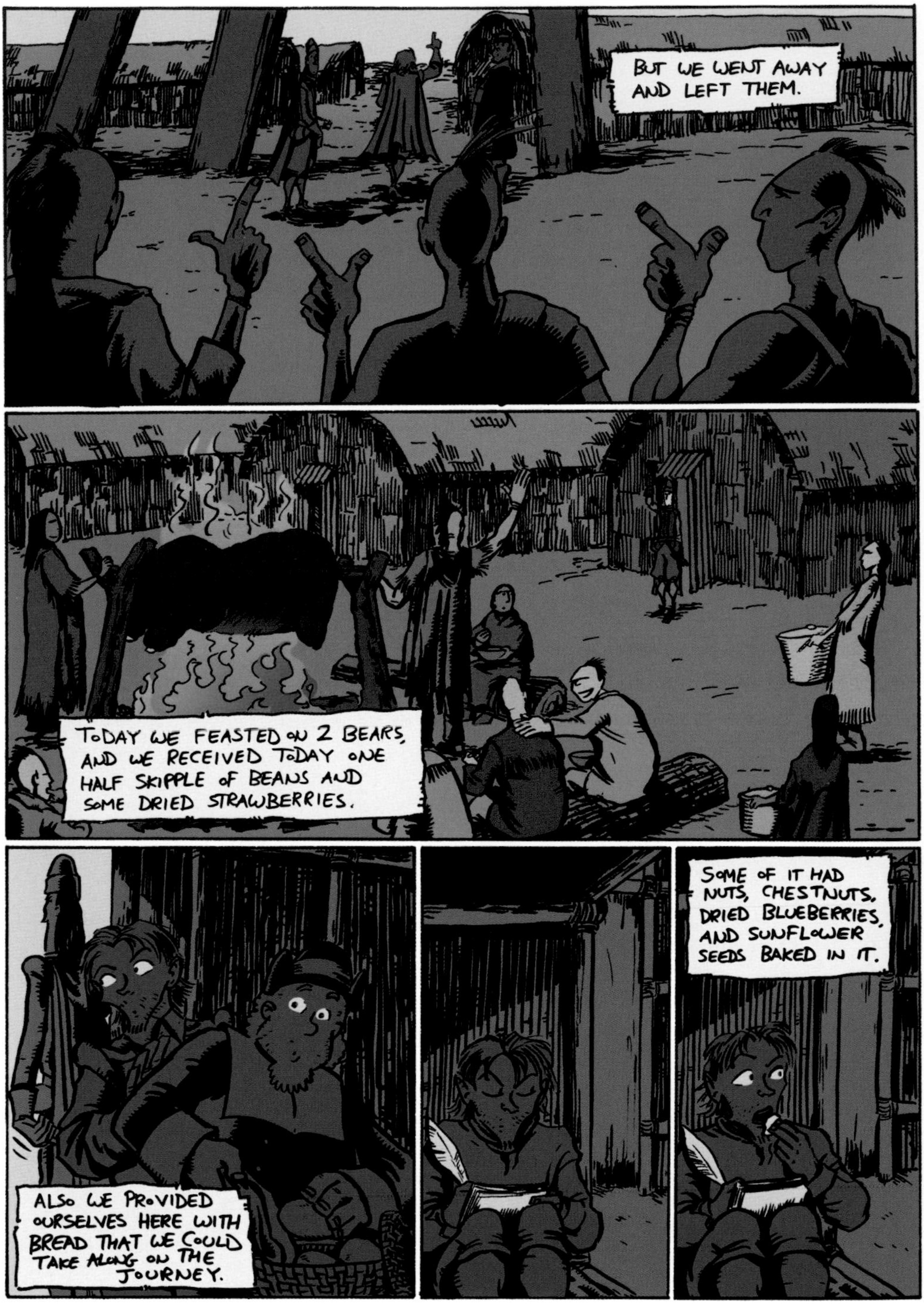
BUT WE WENT AWAY AND LEFT THEM.
TODAY WE FEASTED ON 2 BEARS, AND WE RECEIVED TODAY ONE HALF SKIPPLE OF BEANS AND SOME DRIED STRAWBERRIES.
ALSO WE PROVIDED OURSELVES HERE WITH BREAD THAT WE COULD TAKE ALONG ON THE JOURNEY.
SOME OF IT HAD NUTS, CHESTNUTS, DRIED BLUEBERRIES, AND SUNFLOWER SEEDS BAKED IN IT.

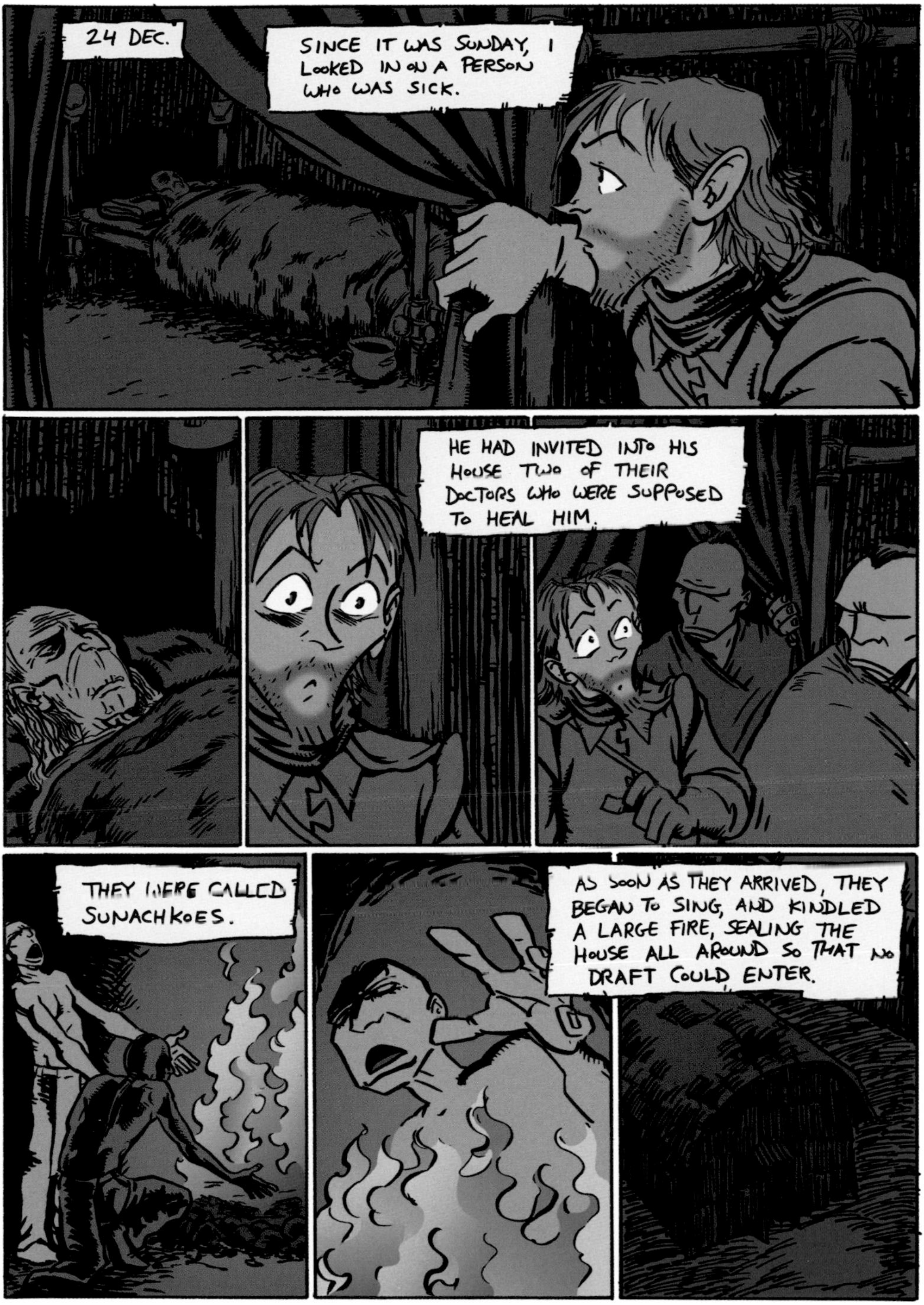
24 DEC.
SINCE IT WAS SUNDAY, I LOOKED IN ON A PERSON WHO WAS SICK.
HE HAD INVITED INTO HIS HOUSE TWO OF THEIR DOCTORS WHO WERE SUPPOSED TO HEAL HIM.
THEY WERE CALLED SUNACHKOES.
AS SOON AS THEY ARRIVED, THEY BEGAN TO SING, AND KINDLED A LARGE FIRE, SEALING THE HOUSE ALL AROUND SO THAT NO DRAFT COULD ENTER.

THEN BOTH OF THEM PUT A SNAKESKIN AROUND THEIR HEADS AND WASHED THEIR HANDS AND FACES.

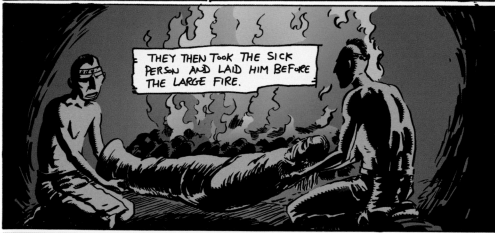

THEY THEN TOOK THE SICK PERSON AND LAID HIM BEFORE THE LARGE FIRE.

TAKING A BUCKET OF WATER IN WHICH THEY HAD PUT SOME MEDICINE, THEY WASHED A STICK IN IT ½ ELL LONG.

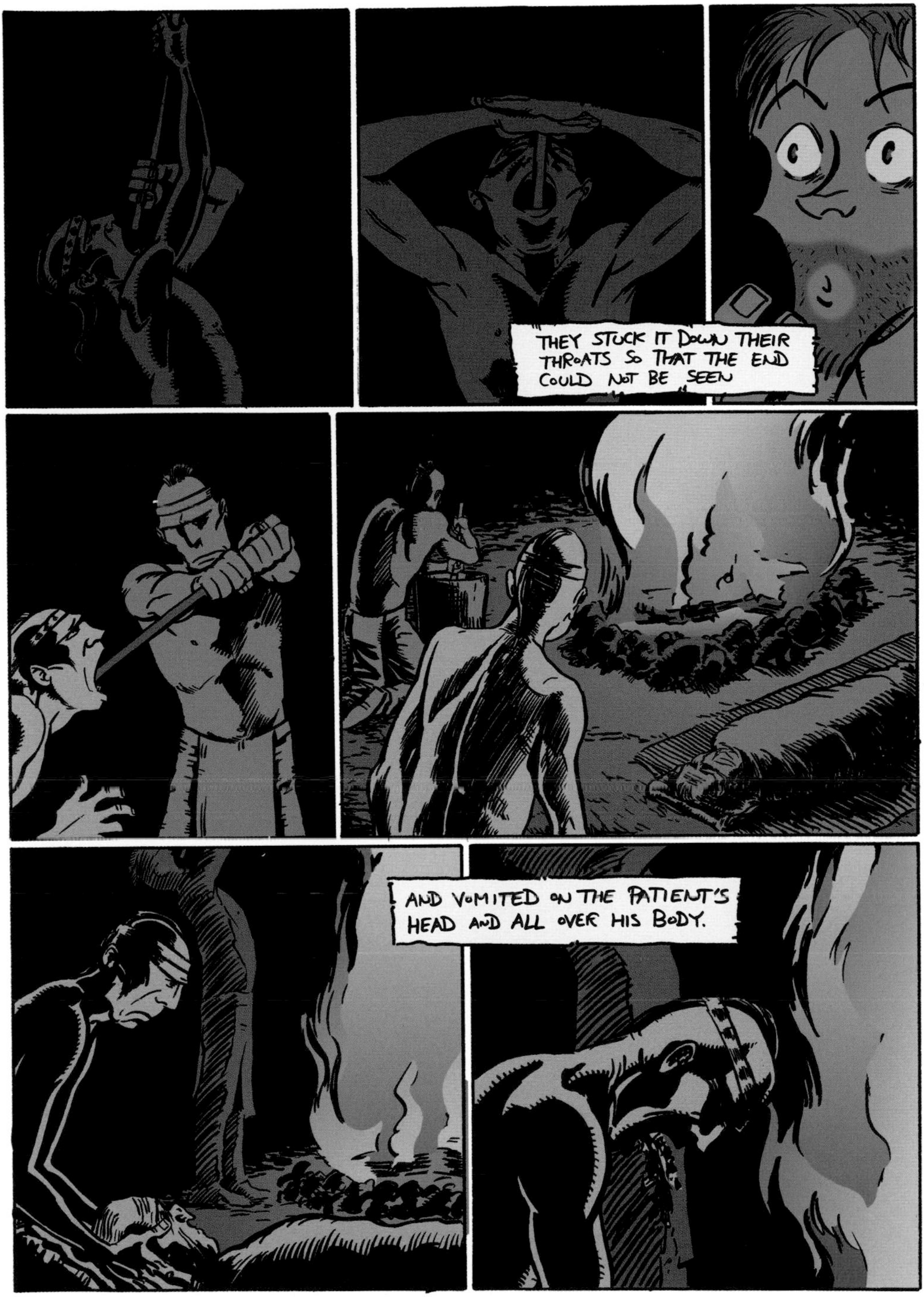
THEY STUCK IT DOWN THEIR THROATS SO THAT THE END COULD NOT BE SEEN
AND VOMITED ON THE PATIENT'S HEAD AND ALL OVER HIS BODY.

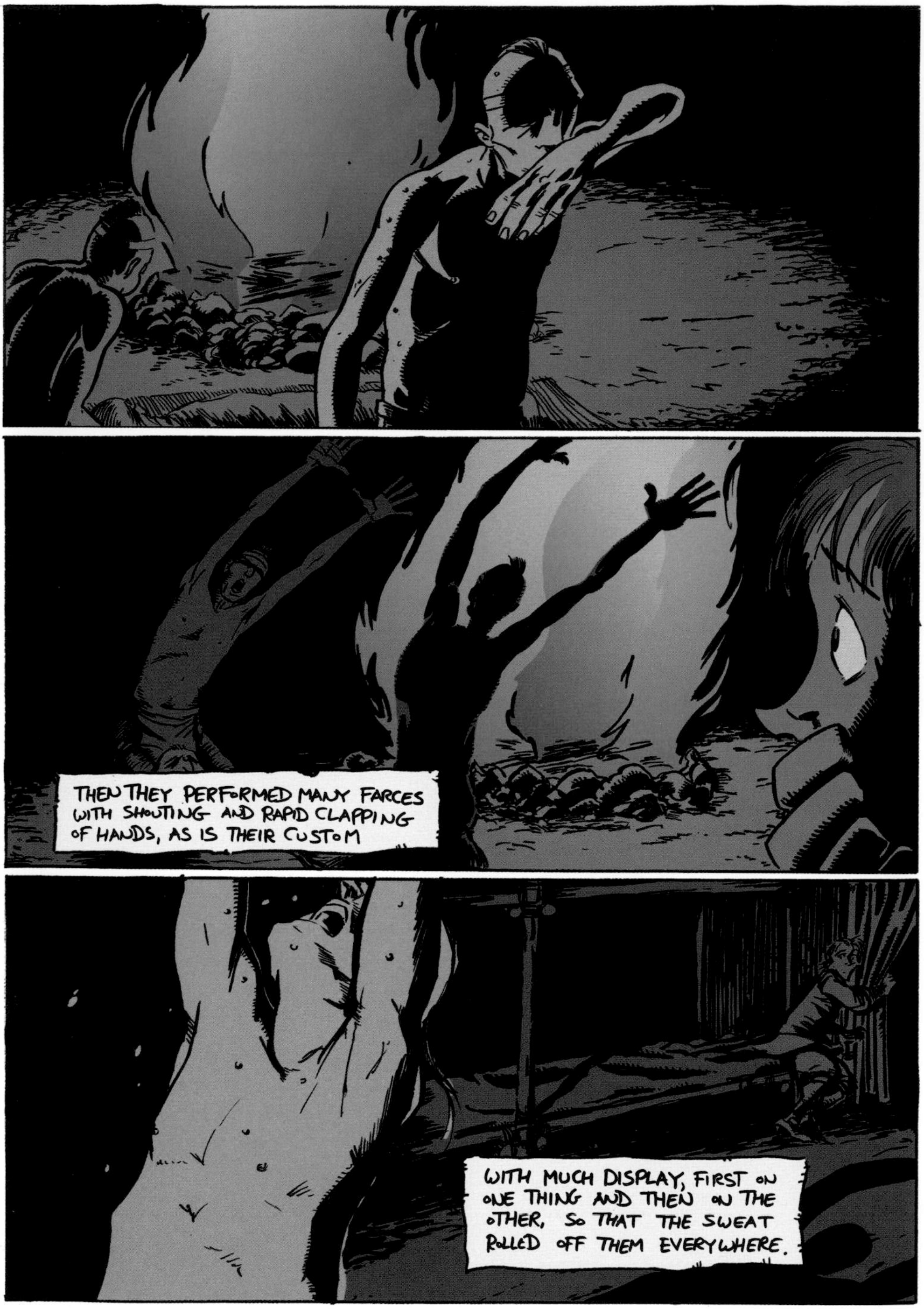
THEN THEY PERFORMED MANY FARCES WITH SHOUTING AND RAPID CLAPPING OF HANDS, AS IS THEIR CUSTOM
WITH MUCH DISPLAY, FIRST ON ONE THING AND THEN ON THE OTHER, SO THAT THE SWEAT ROLLED OFF THEM EVERYWHERE.

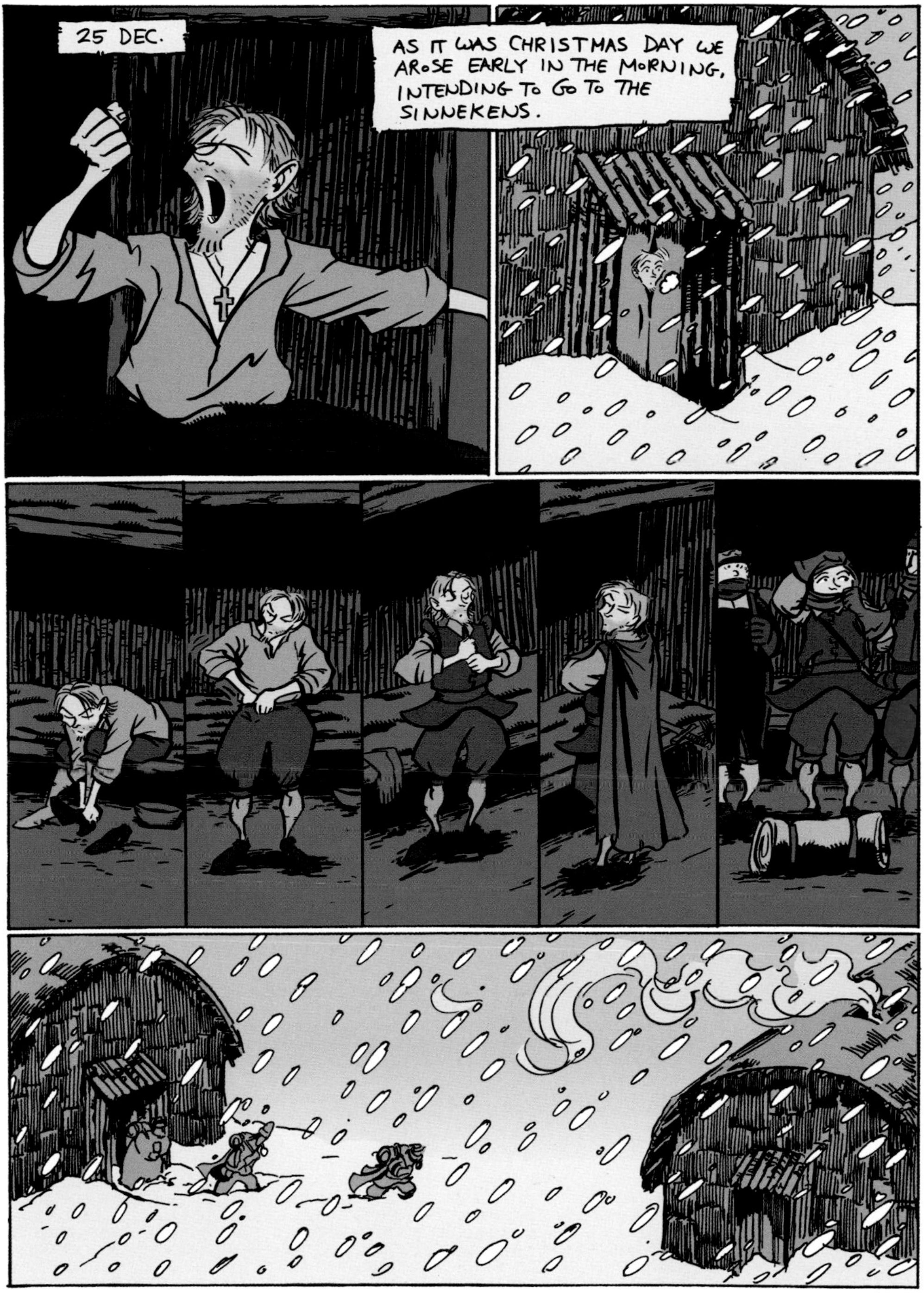
25 DEC.
AS IT WAS CHRISTMAS DAY WE AROSE EARLY IN THE MORNING, INTENDING TO GO TO THE SINNEKENS.

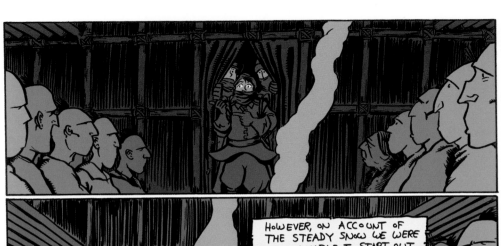

HOWEVER, ON ACCOUNT OF THE STEADY SNOW WE WERE UNABLE TO START OUT

BECAUSE NO ONE WOULD GO WITH US TO CARRY OUR GOODS.

I ASKED THEM HOW MANY CHIEFS THERE WERE AND THEY TOLD ME 30 PERSONS.

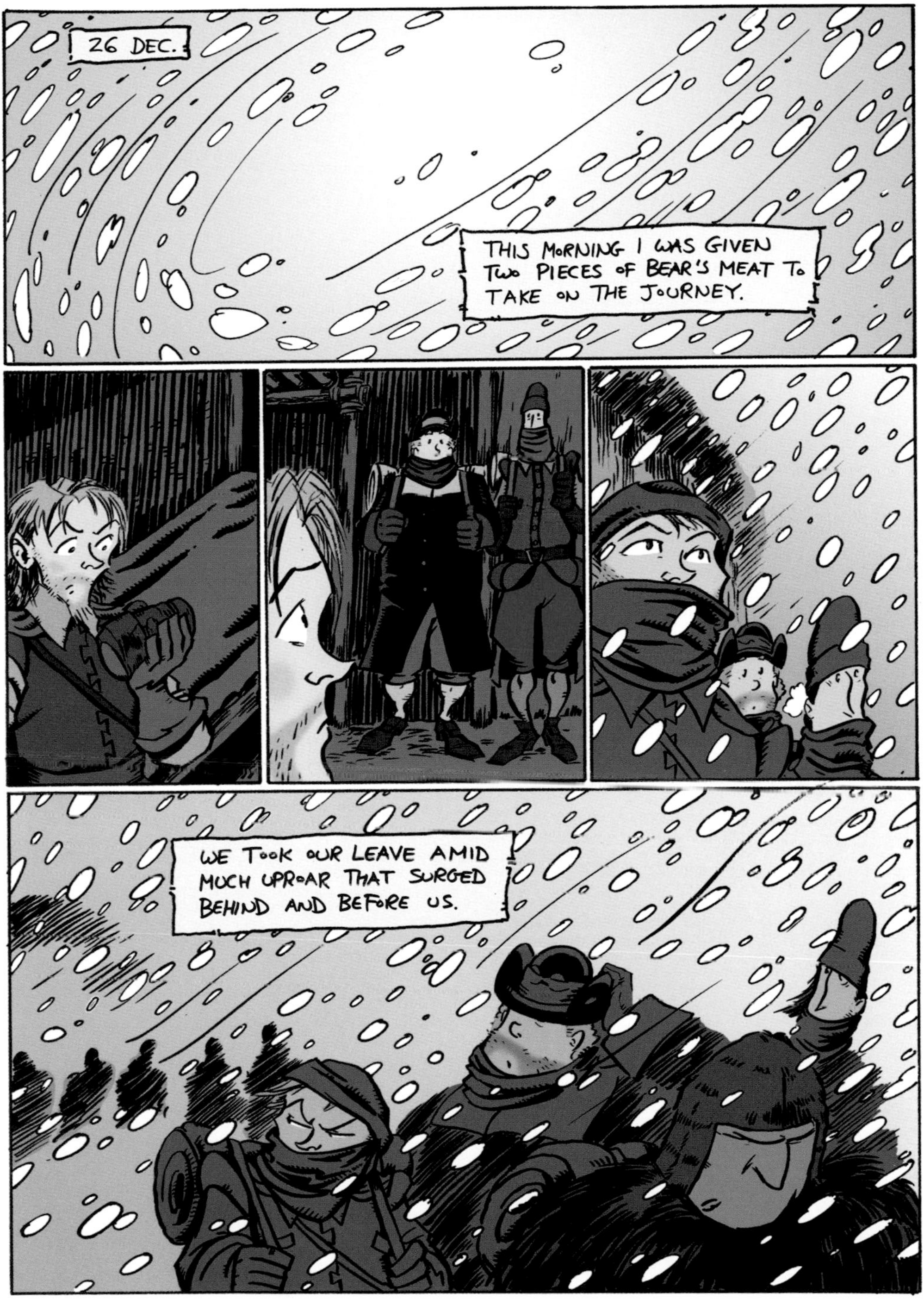
26 DEC.
THIS MORNING I WAS GIVEN TWO PIECES OF BEAR'S MEAT TO TAKE ON THE JOURNEY.
WE TOOK OUR LEAVE AMID MUCH UPROAR THAT SURGED BEHIND AND BEFORE US.

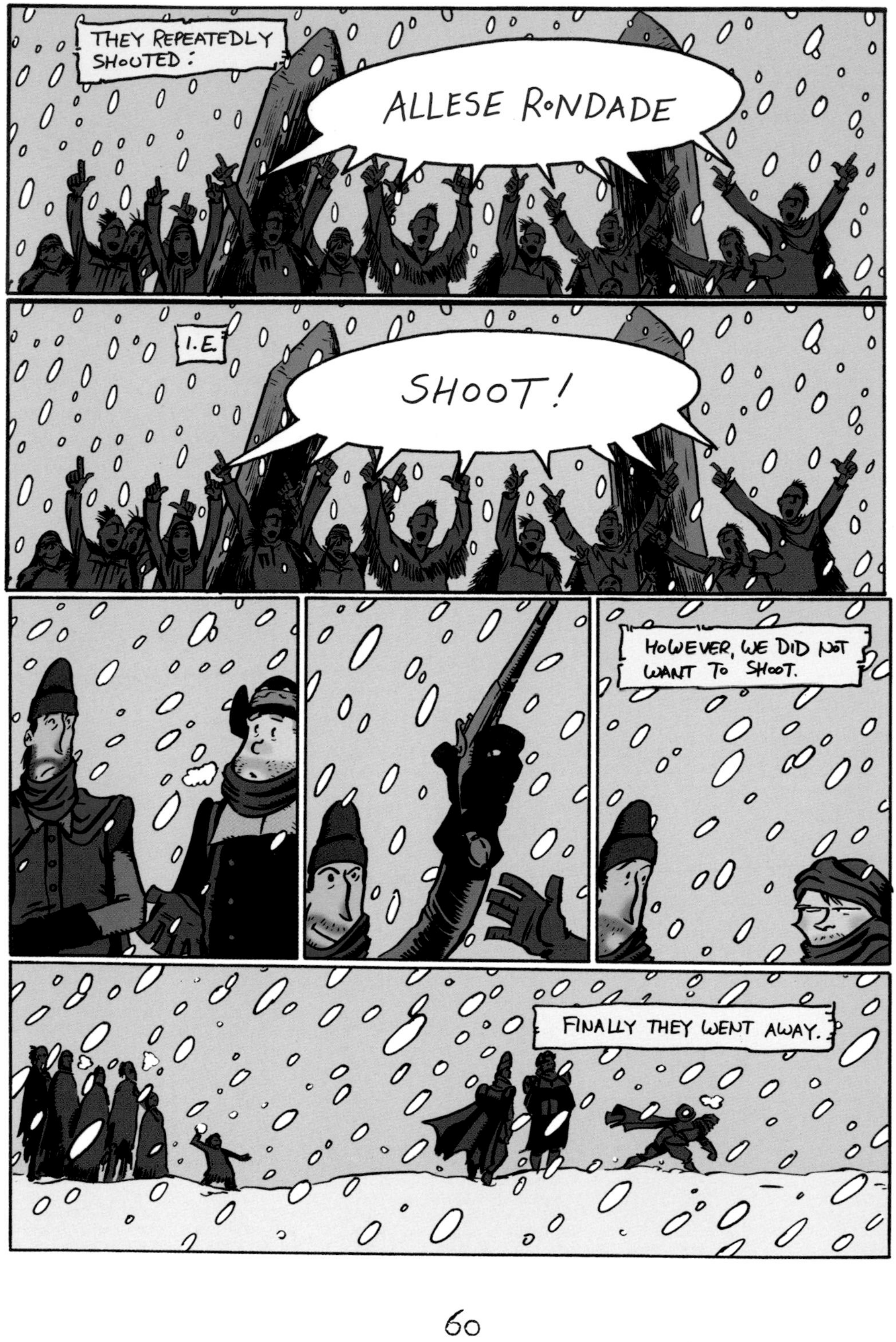
THEY REPEATEDLY SHOUTED:
ALLESE RONDADE
I.E.
SHOOT!
HOWEVER, WE DID NOT WANT TO SHOOT.
FINALLY THEY WENT AWAY.

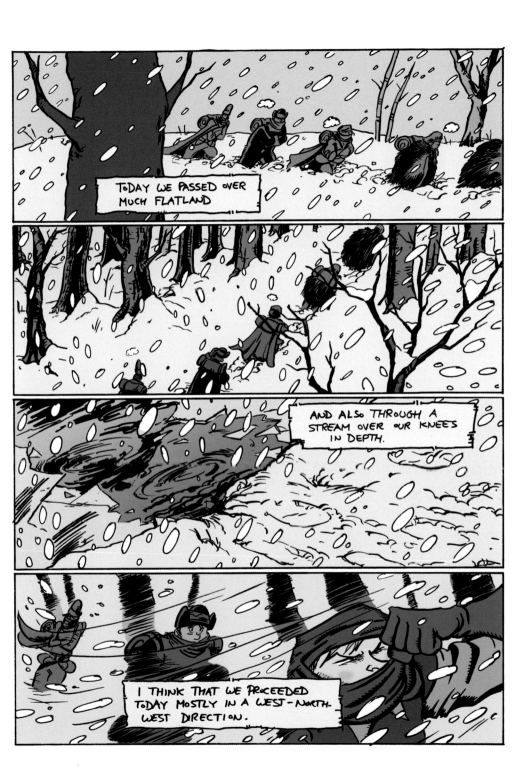

TODAY WE PASSED OVER MUCH FLATLAND

AND ALSO THROUGH A STREAM OVER OUR KNEES IN DEPTH.

I THINK THAT WE PROCEEDED TODAY MOSTLY IN A WEST-NORTH-WEST DIRECTION.

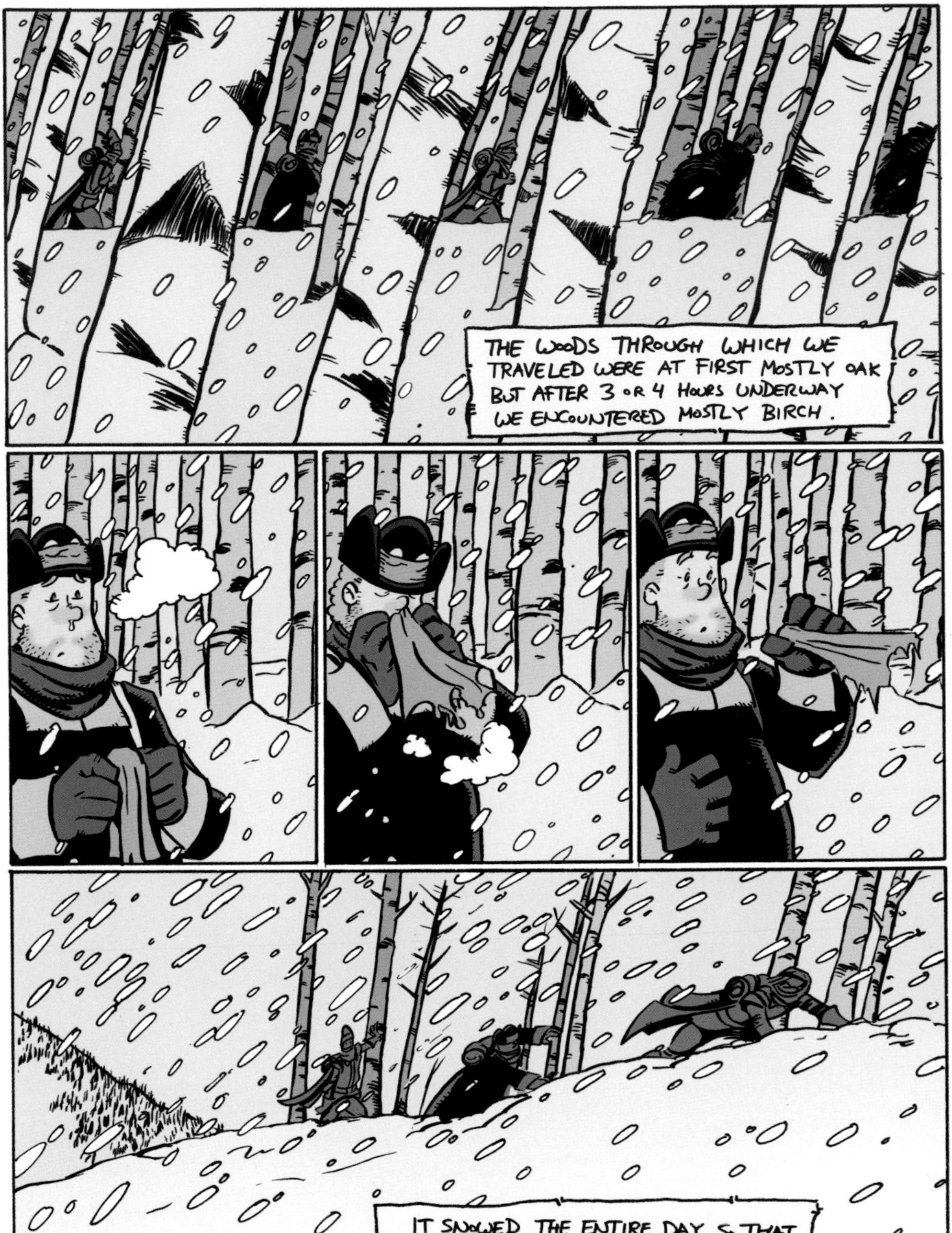
THE WOODS THROUGH WHICH WE TRAVELED WERE AT FIRST MOSTLY OAK BUT AFTER 3 OR 4 HOURS UNDERWAY WE ENCOUNTERED MOSTLY BIRCH.
IT SNOWED THE ENTIRE DAY SO THAT IT WAS VERY DIFFICULT TO CLIMB OVER THE HILLS.

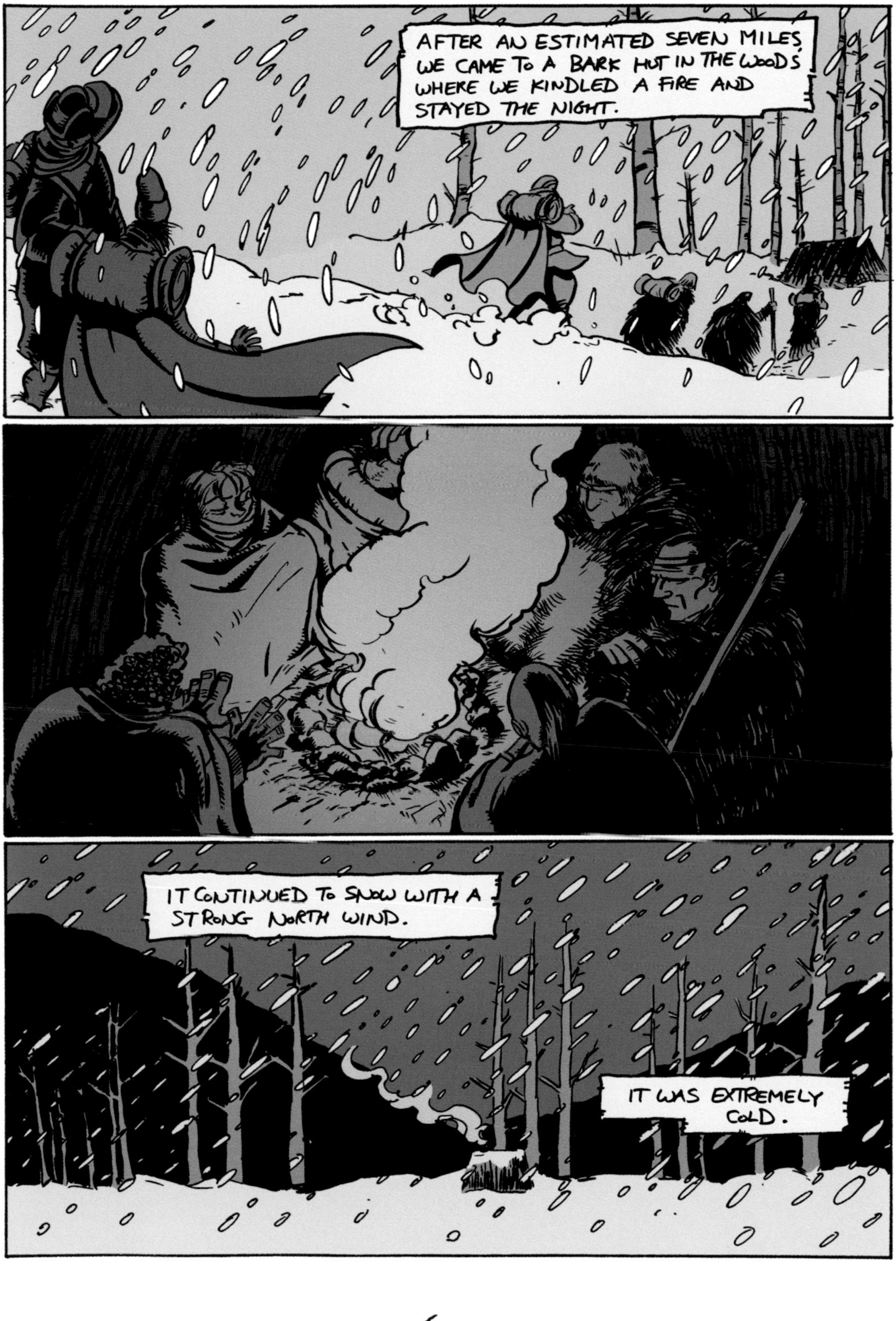
AFTER AN ESTIMATED SEVEN MILES WE CAME TO A BARK HUT IN THE WOODS WHERE WE KINDLED A FIRE AND STAYED THE NIGHT.
IT CONTINUED TO SNOW WITH A STRONG NORTH WIND.
IT WAS EXTREMELY COLD.

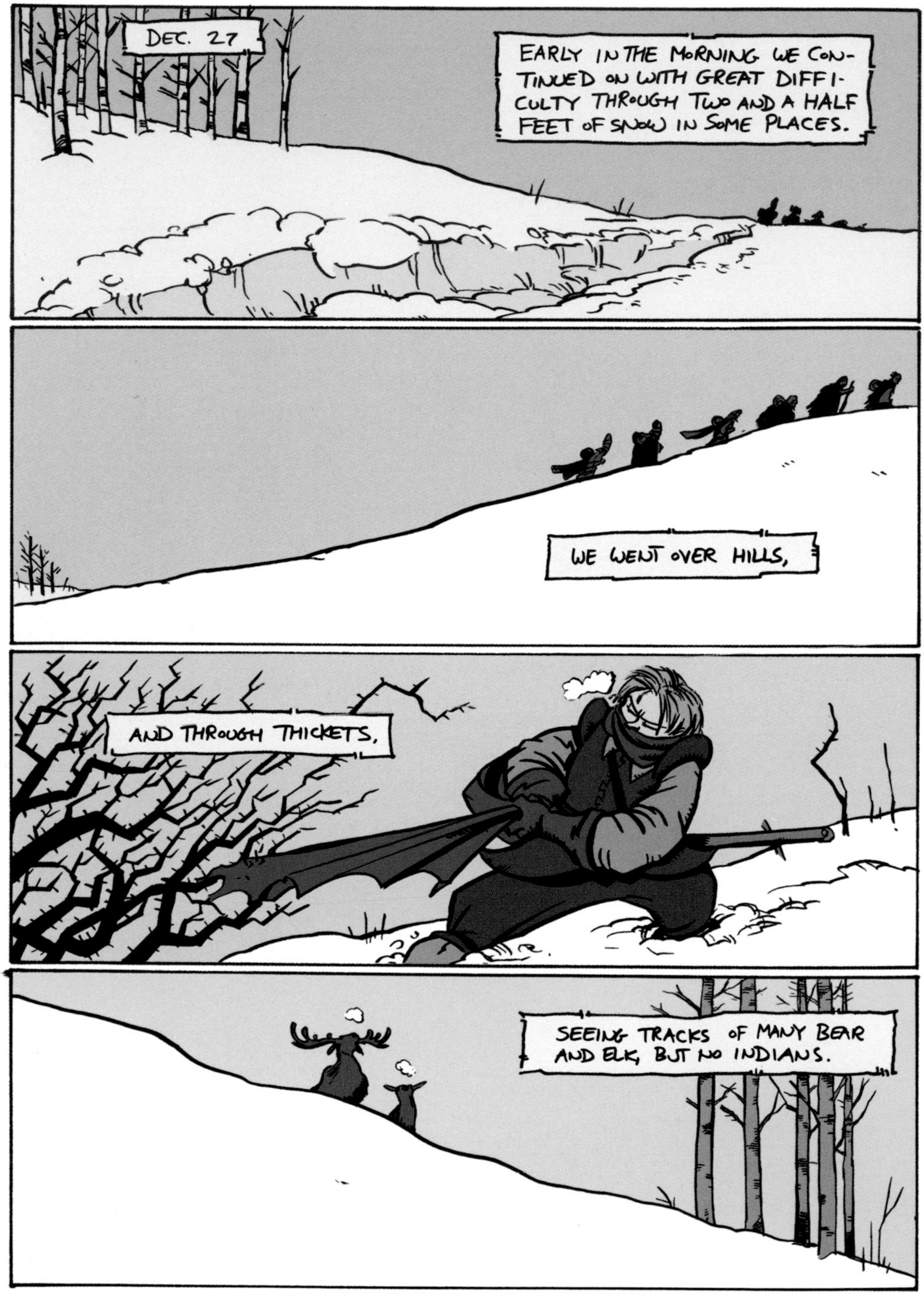
DEC. 27
EARLY IN THE MORNING WE CONTINUED ON WITH GREAT DIFFICULTY THROUGH TWO AND A HALF FEET OF SNOW IN SOME PLACES.
WE WENT OVER HILLS,
AND THROUGH THICKETS,
SEEING TRACKS OF MANY BEAR AND ELK, BUT NO INDIANS.

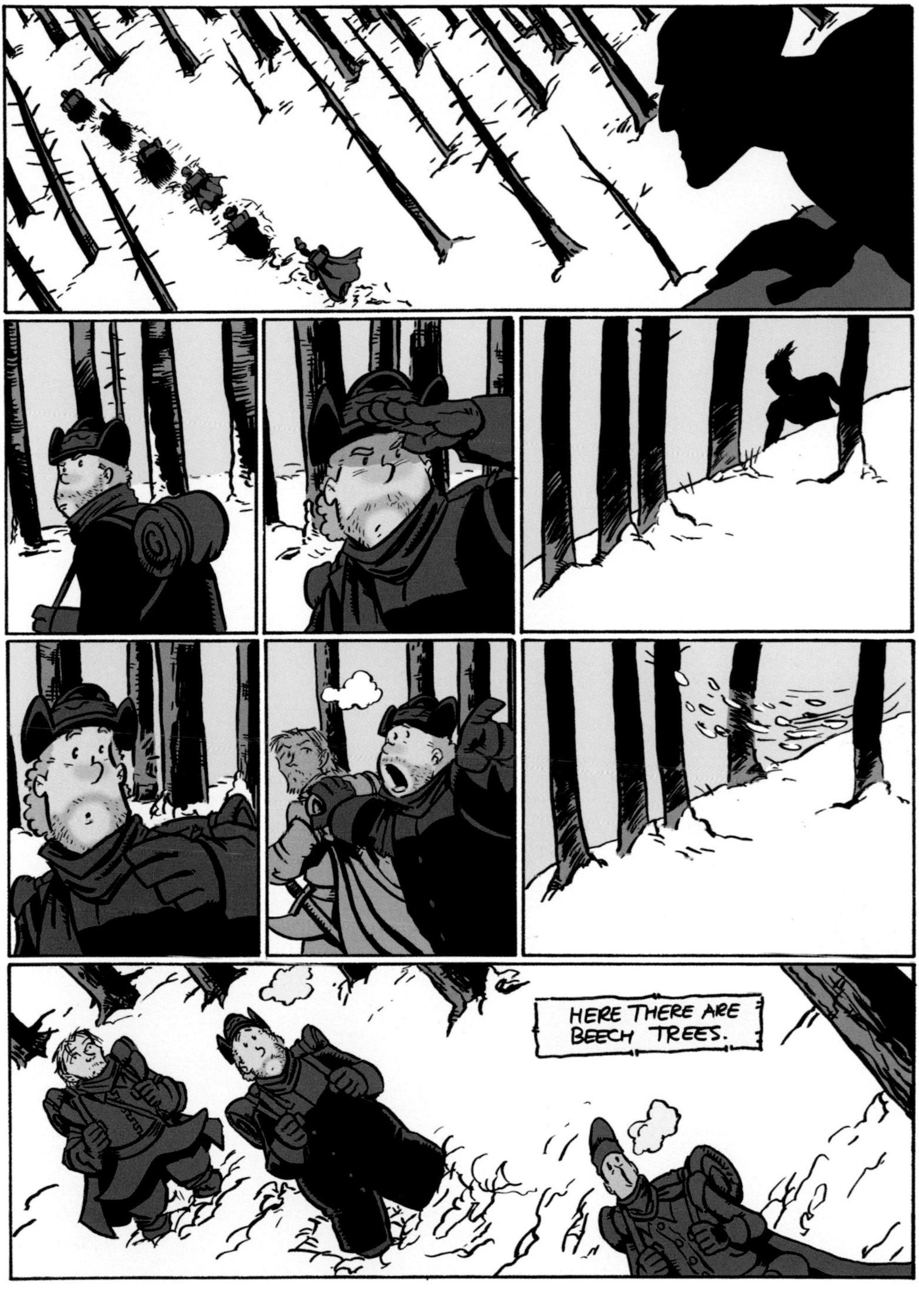
HERE THERE ARE BEECH TREES.

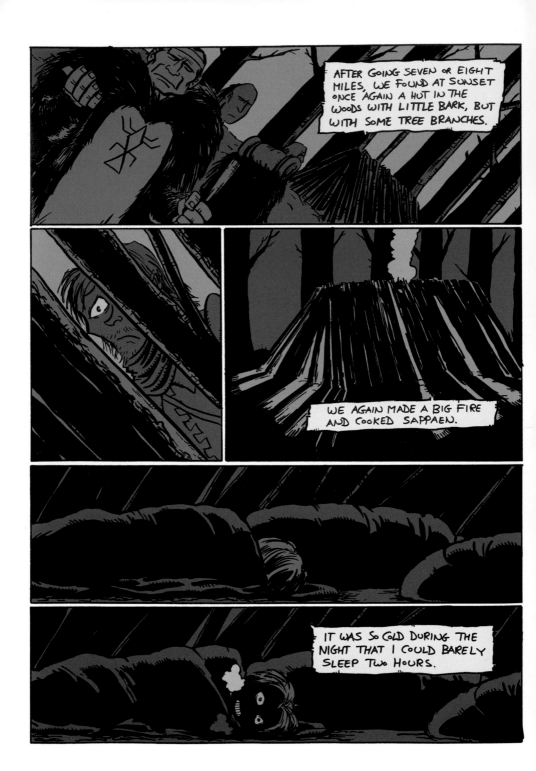

AFTER GOING SEVEN OR EIGHT MILES, WE FOUND AT SUNSET ONCE AGAIN A HUT IN THE WOODS WITH LITTLE BARK, BUT WITH SOME TREE BRANCHES.

WE AGAIN MADE A BIG FIRE AND COOKED SAPPAEN.

IT WAS SO COLD DURING THE NIGHT THAT I COULD BARELY SLEEP TWO HOURS.

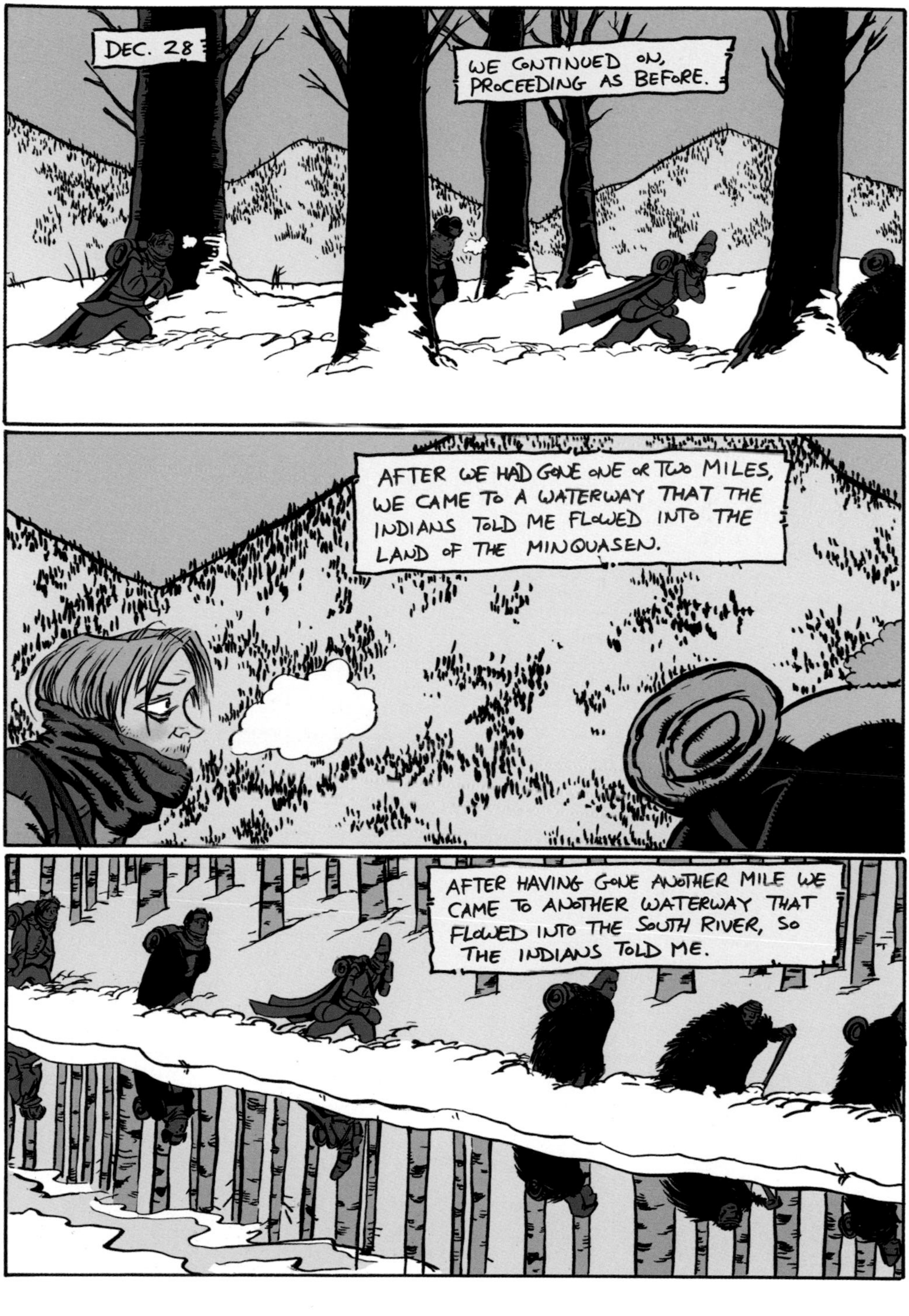
DEC. 28
WE CONTINUED ON, PROCEEDING AS BEFORE.
AFTER WE HAD GONE ONE OR TWO MILES, WE CAME TO A WATERWAY THAT THE INDIANS TOLD ME FLOWED INTO THE LAND OF THE MINQUASEN.
AFTER HAVING GONE ANOTHER MILE WE CAME TO ANOTHER WATERWAY THAT FLOWED INTO THE SOUTH RIVER, SO THE INDIANS TOLD ME.

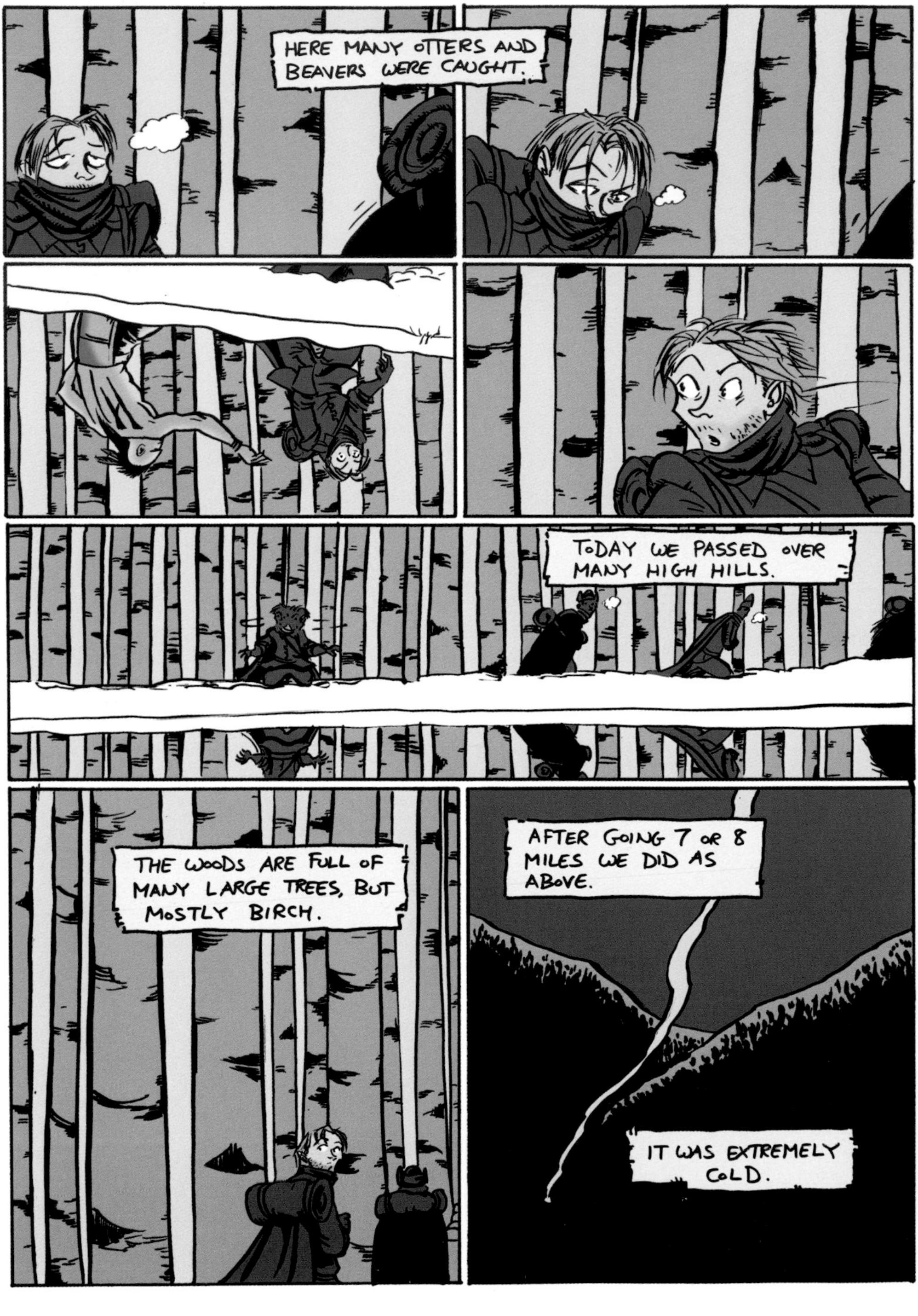
HERE MANY OTTERS AND BEAVERS WERE CAUGHT.
TODAY WE PASSED OVER MANY HIGH HILLS.
THE WOODS ARE FULL OF MANY LARGE TREES, BUT MOSTLY BIRCH.
AFTER GOING 7 OR 8 MILES WE DID AS ABOVE.
IT WAS EXTREMELY COLD.

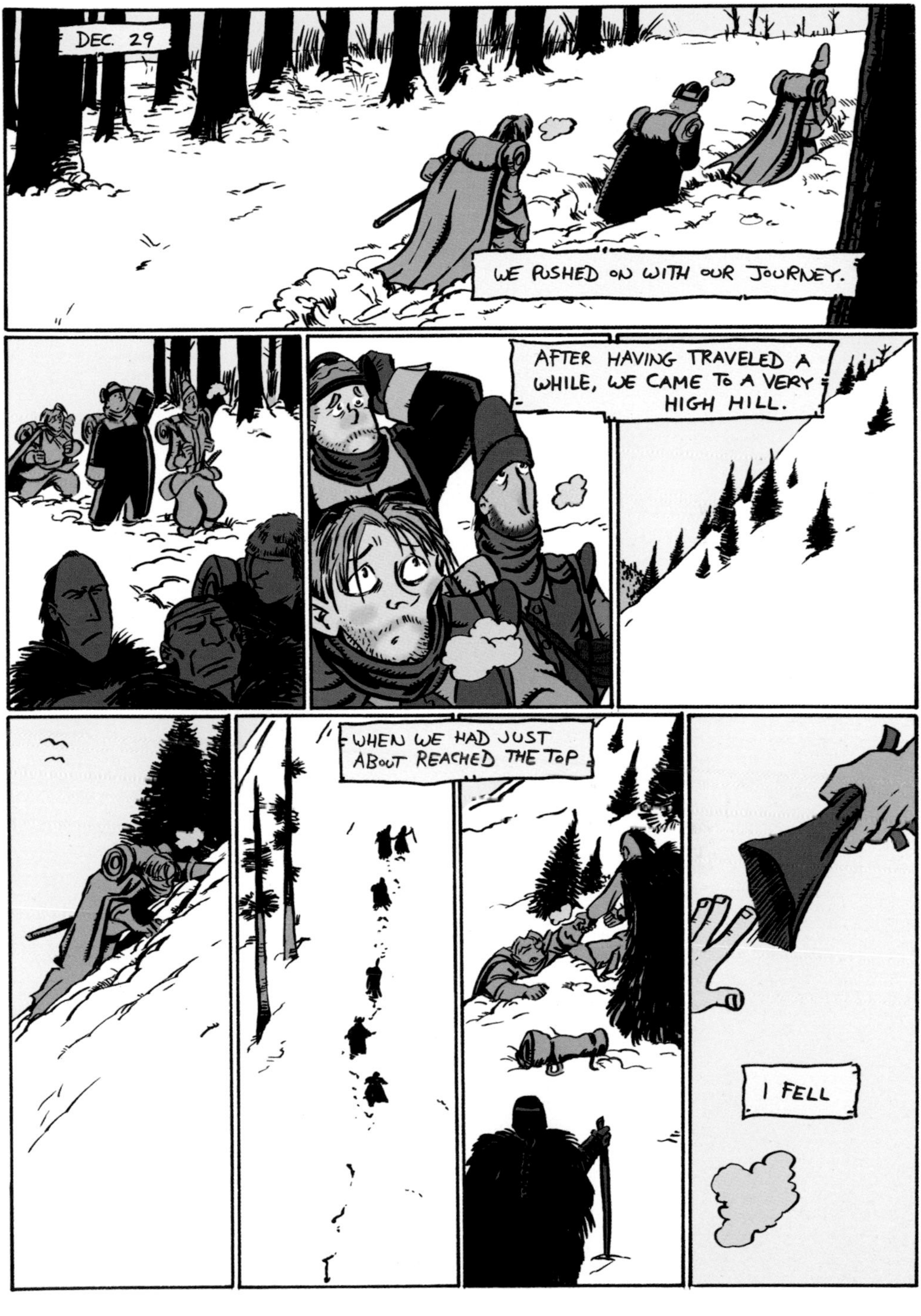

DEC. 29
WE PUSHED ON WITH OUR JOURNEY.
AFTER HAVING TRAVELED A WHILE, WE CAME TO A VERY HIGH HILL.
WHEN WE HAD JUST ABOUT REACHED THE TOP
I FELL

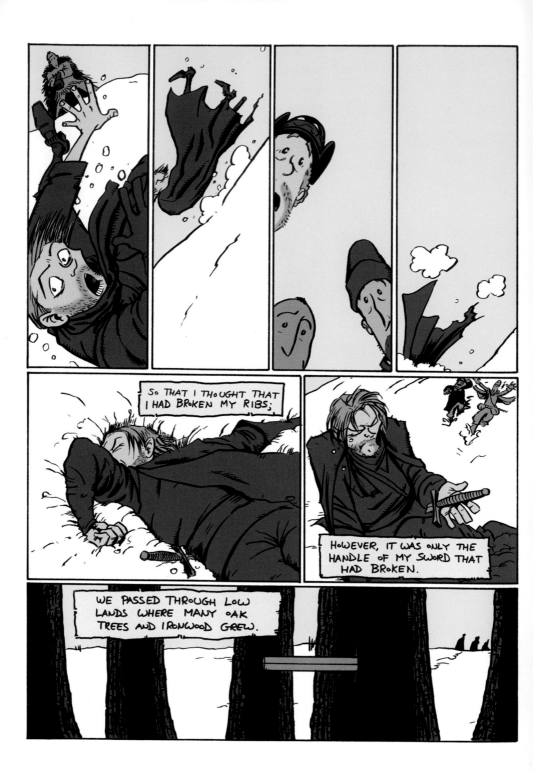

SO THAT I THOUGHT THAT I HAD BROKEN MY RIBS;

HOWEVER, IT WAS ONLY THE HANDLE OF MY SWORD THAT HAD BROKEN.

WE PASSED THROUGH LOW LANDS WHERE MANY OAK TREES AND IRONWOOD GREW.

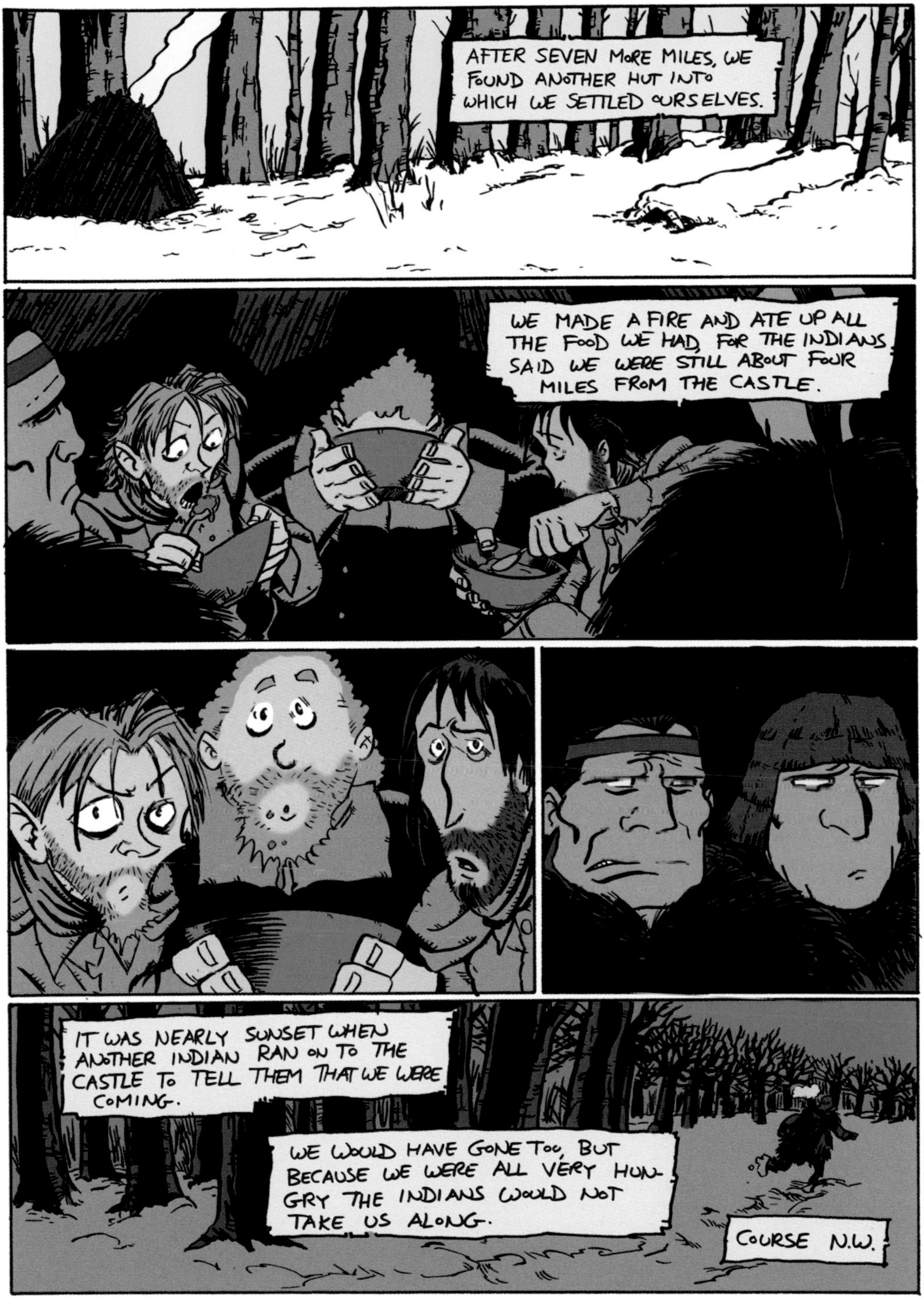
AFTER SEVEN MORE MILES, WE FOUND ANOTHER HUT INTO WHICH WE SETTLED OURSELVES.
WE MADE A FIRE AND ATE UP ALL THE FOOD WE HAD, FOR THE INDIANS SAID WE WERE STILL ABOUT FOUR MILES FROM THE CASTLE.
IT WAS NEARLY SUNSET WHEN ANOTHER INDIAN RAN ON TO THE CASTLE TO TELL THEM THAT WE WERE COMING.
WE WOULD HAVE GONE TOO, BUT BECAUSE WE WERE ALL VERY HUNGRY THE INDIANS WOULD NOT TAKE US ALONG.
COURSE N.W.

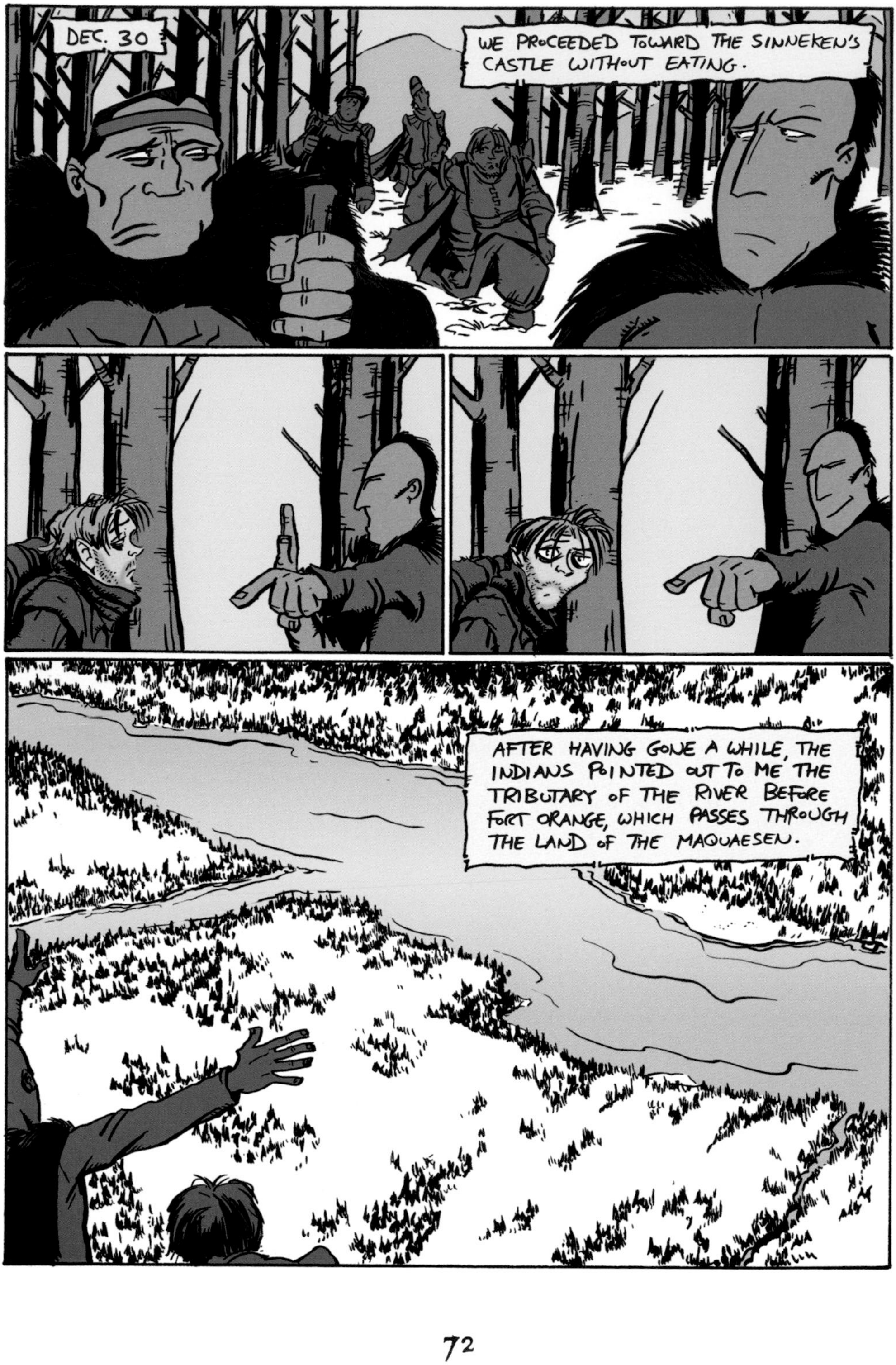
DEC. 30
WE PROCEEDED TOWARD THE SINNEKEN'S CASTLE WITHOUT EATING.
AFTER HAVING GONE A WHILE, THE INDIANS POINTED OUT TO ME THE TRIBUTARY OF THE RIVER BEFORE FORT ORANGE, WHICH PASSES THROUGH THE LAND OF THE MAQUAESEN.

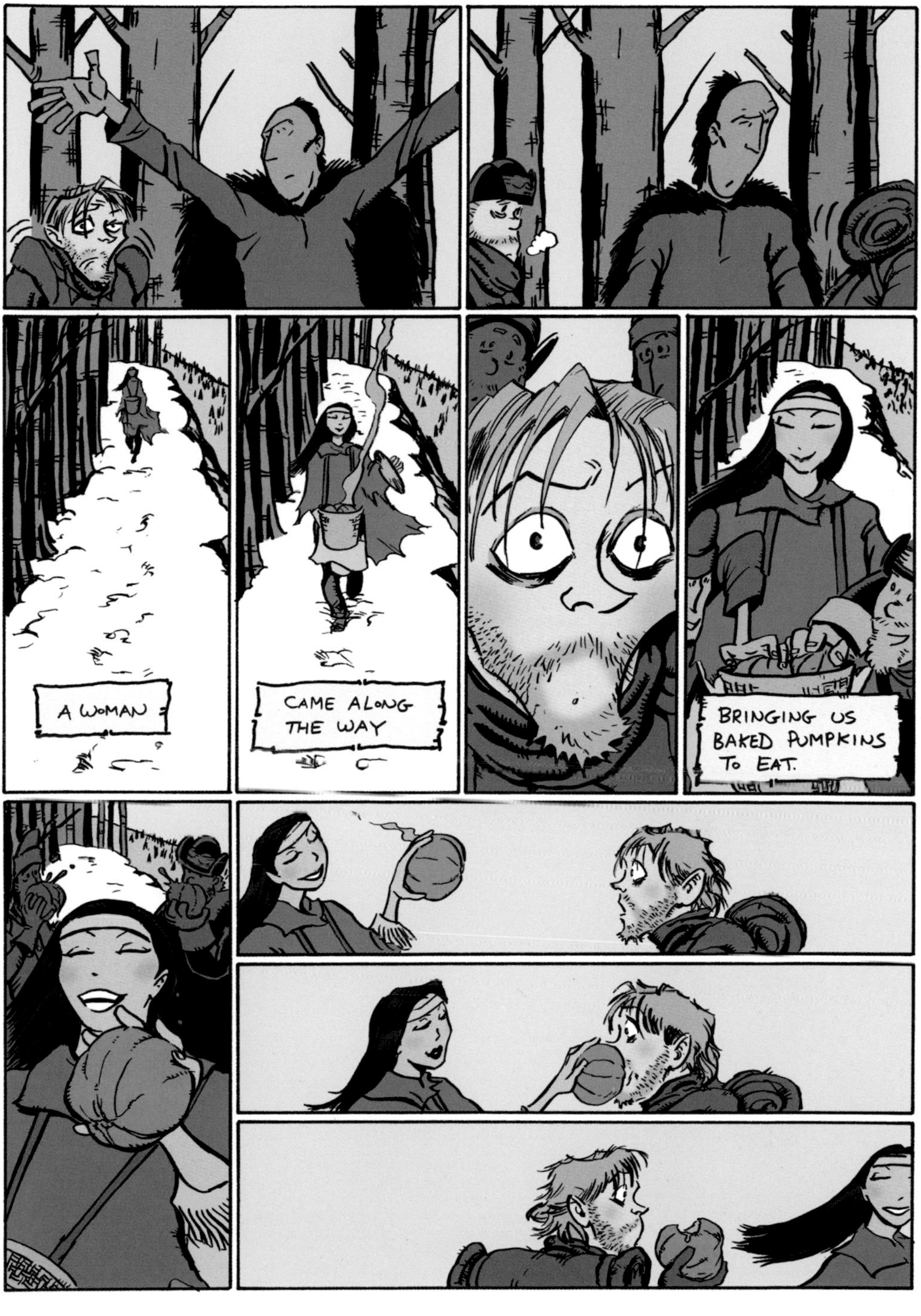
A WOMAN
CAME ALONG THE WAY
BRINGING US BAKED PUMPKINS TO EAT.

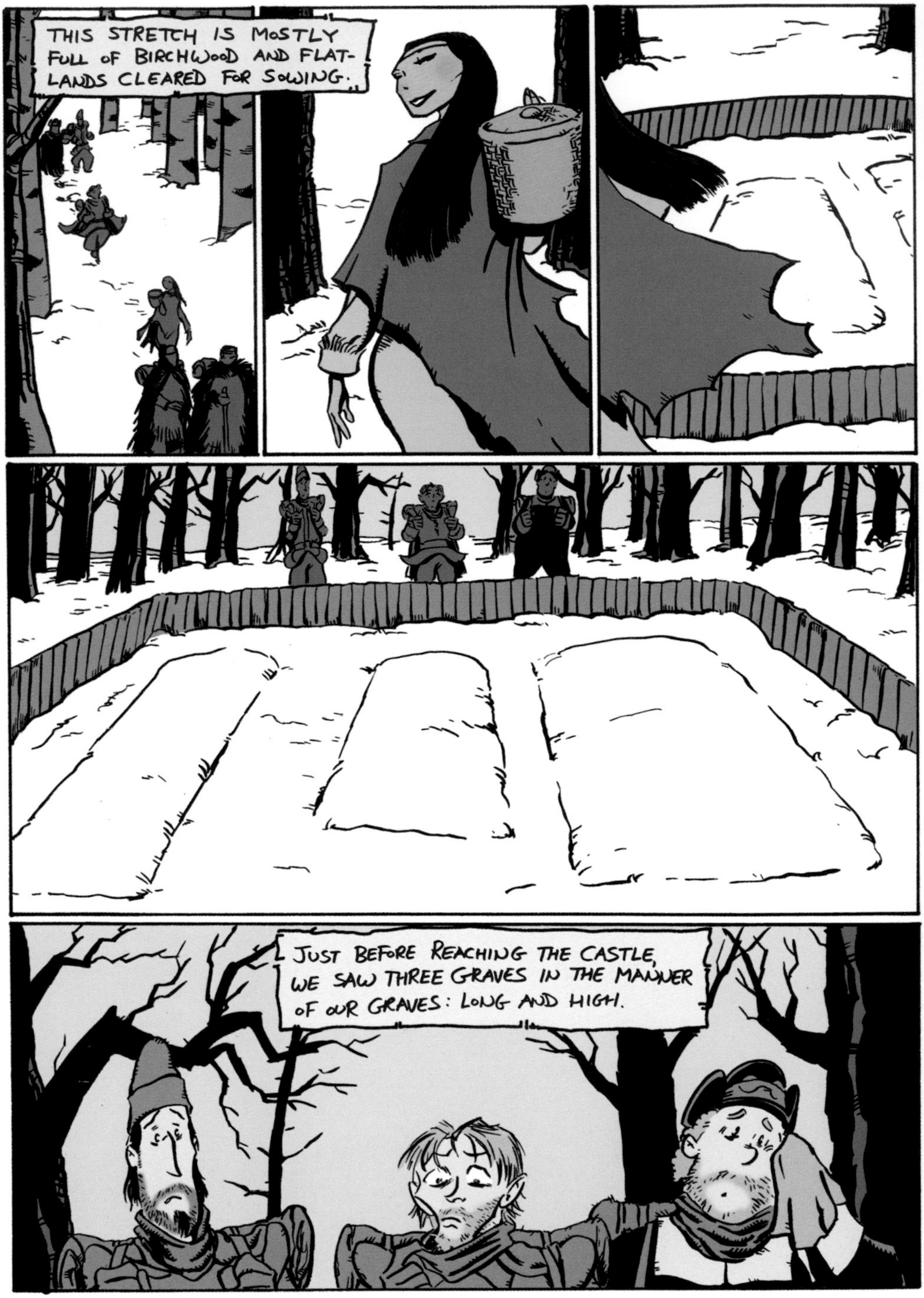
THIS STRETCH IS MOSTLY FULL OF BIRCHWOOD AND FLAT-LANDS CLEARED FOR SOWING.
JUST BEFORE REACHING THE CASTLE, WE SAW THREE GRAVES IN THE MANNER OF OUR GRAVES: LONG AND HIGH.

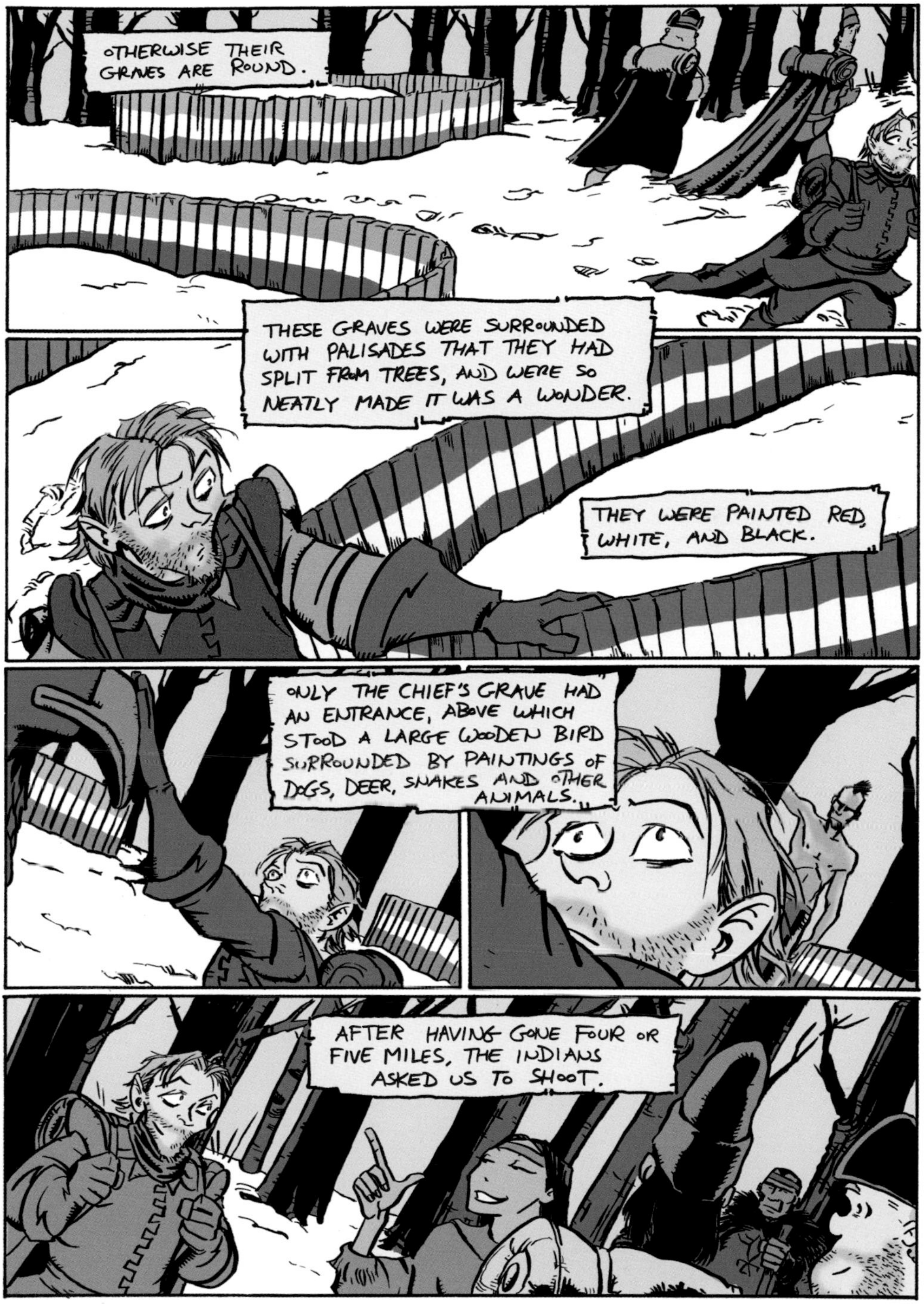
OTHERWISE THEIR GRAVES ARE ROUND.
THESE GRAVES WERE SURROUNDED WITH PALISADES THAT THEY HAD SPLIT FROM TREES, AND WERE SO NEATLY MADE IT WAS A WONDER.
THEY WERE PAINTED RED, WHITE, AND BLACK.
ONLY THE CHIEF'S GRAVE HAD AN ENTRANCE, ABOVE WHICH STOOD A LARGE WOODEN BIRD SURROUNDED BY PAINTINGS OF DOGS, DEER, SNAKES AND OTHER ANIMALS.
AFTER HAVING GONE FOUR OR FIVE MILES, THE INDIANS ASKED US TO SHOOT.

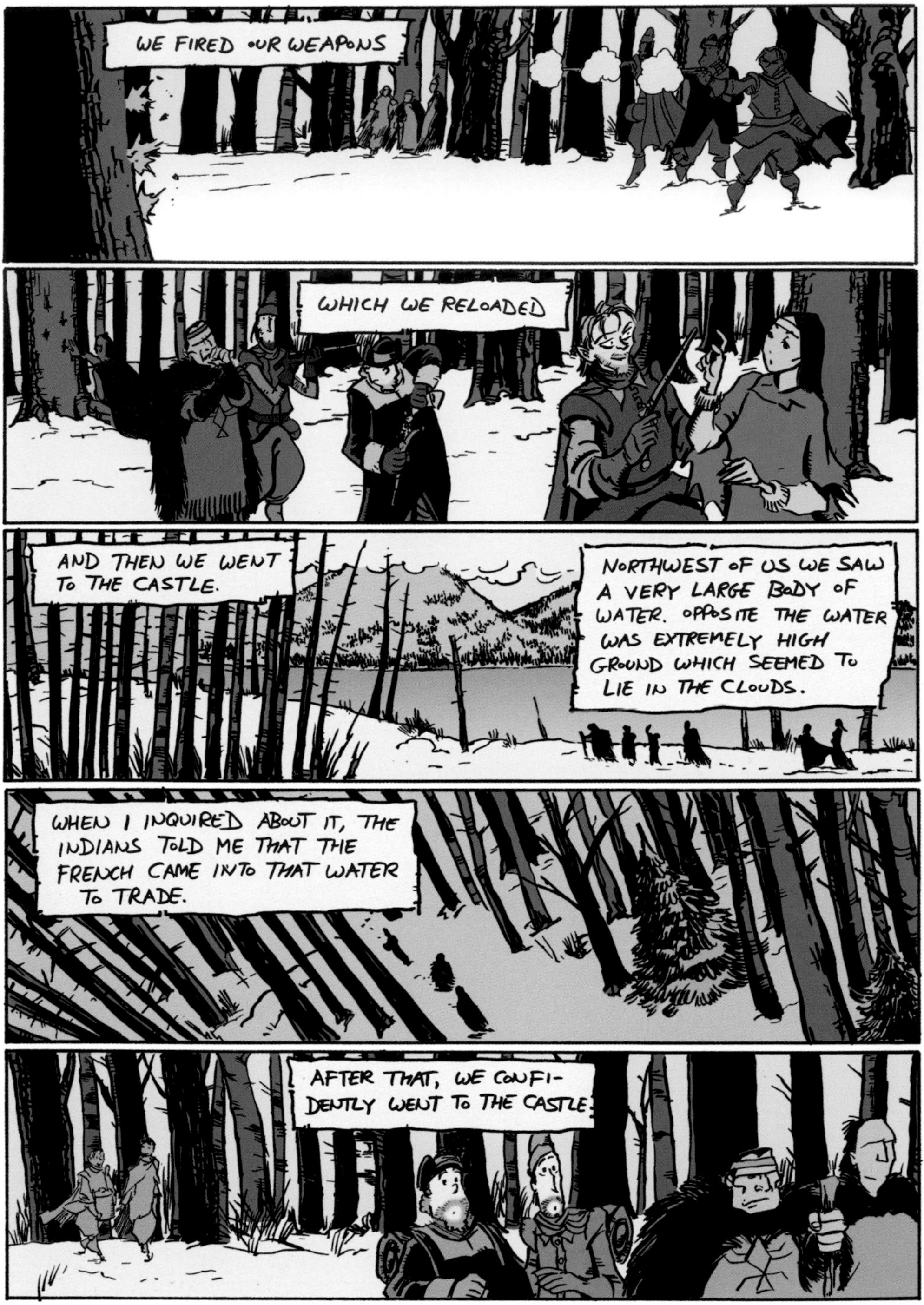
WE FIRED OUR WEAPONS
WHICH WE RELOADED
AND THEN WE WENT TO THE CASTLE.
NORTHWEST OF US WE SAW A VERY LARGE BODY OF WATER. OPPOSITE THE WATER WAS EXTREMELY HIGH GROUND WHICH SEEMED TO LIE IN THE CLOUDS.
WHEN I INQUIRED ABOUT IT, THE INDIANS TOLD ME THAT THE FRENCH CAME INTO THAT WATER TO TRADE.
AFTER THAT, WE CONFIDENTLY WENT TO THE CASTLE.

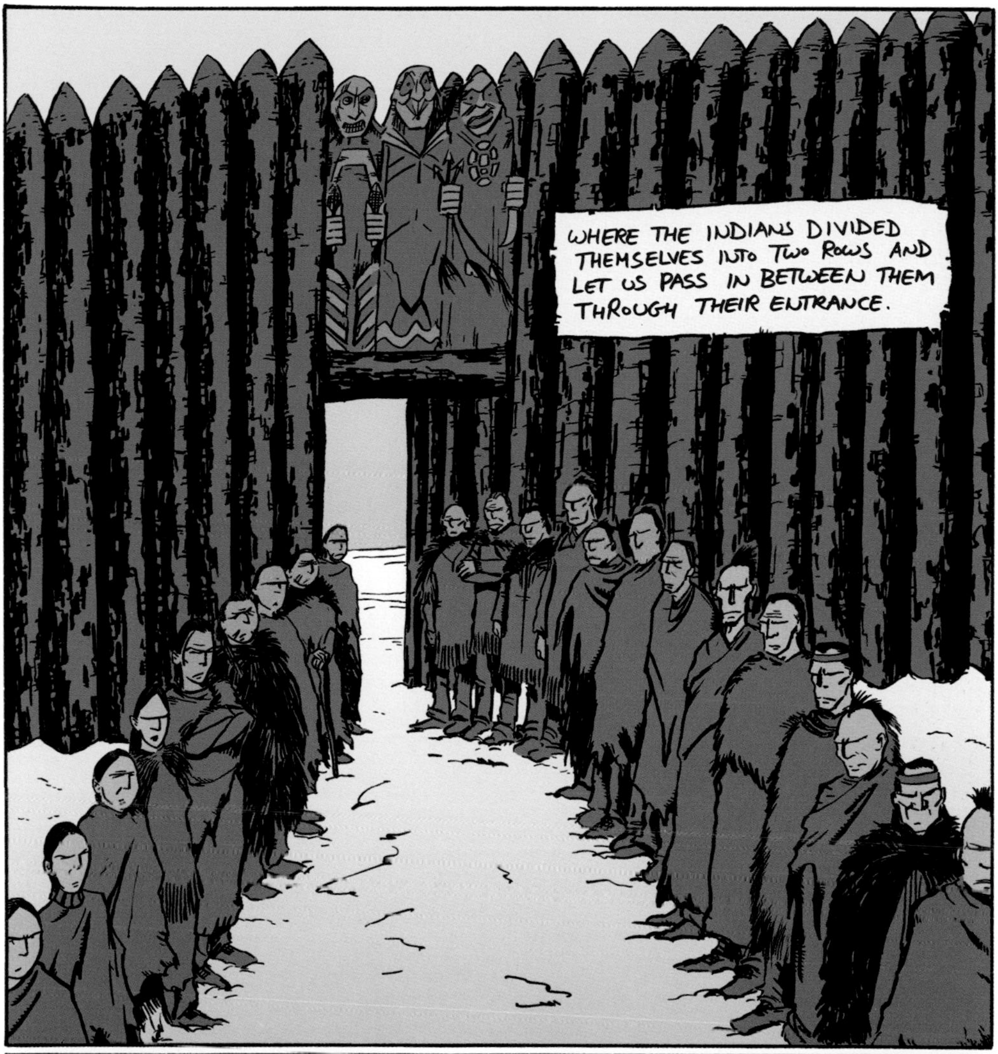
WHERE THE INDIANS DIVIDED THEMSELVES INTO TWO ROWS AND LET US PASS IN BETWEEN THEM THROUGH THEIR ENTRANCE.

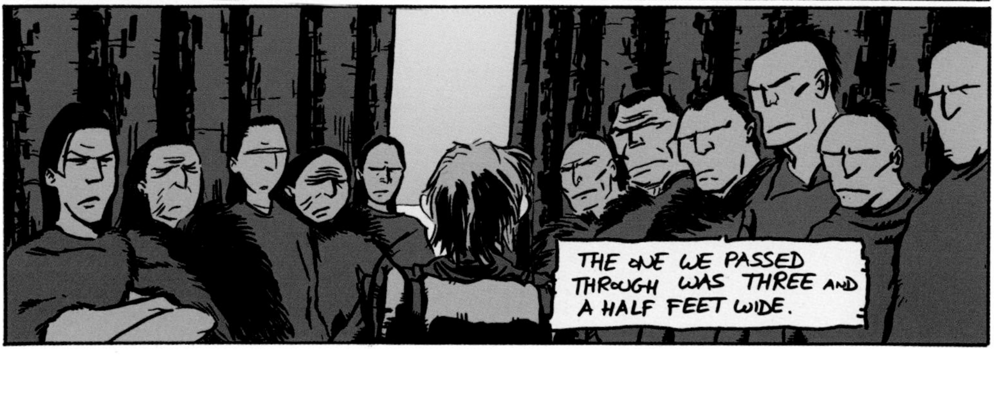
THE ONE WE PASSED THROUGH WAS THREE AND A HALF FEET WIDE.

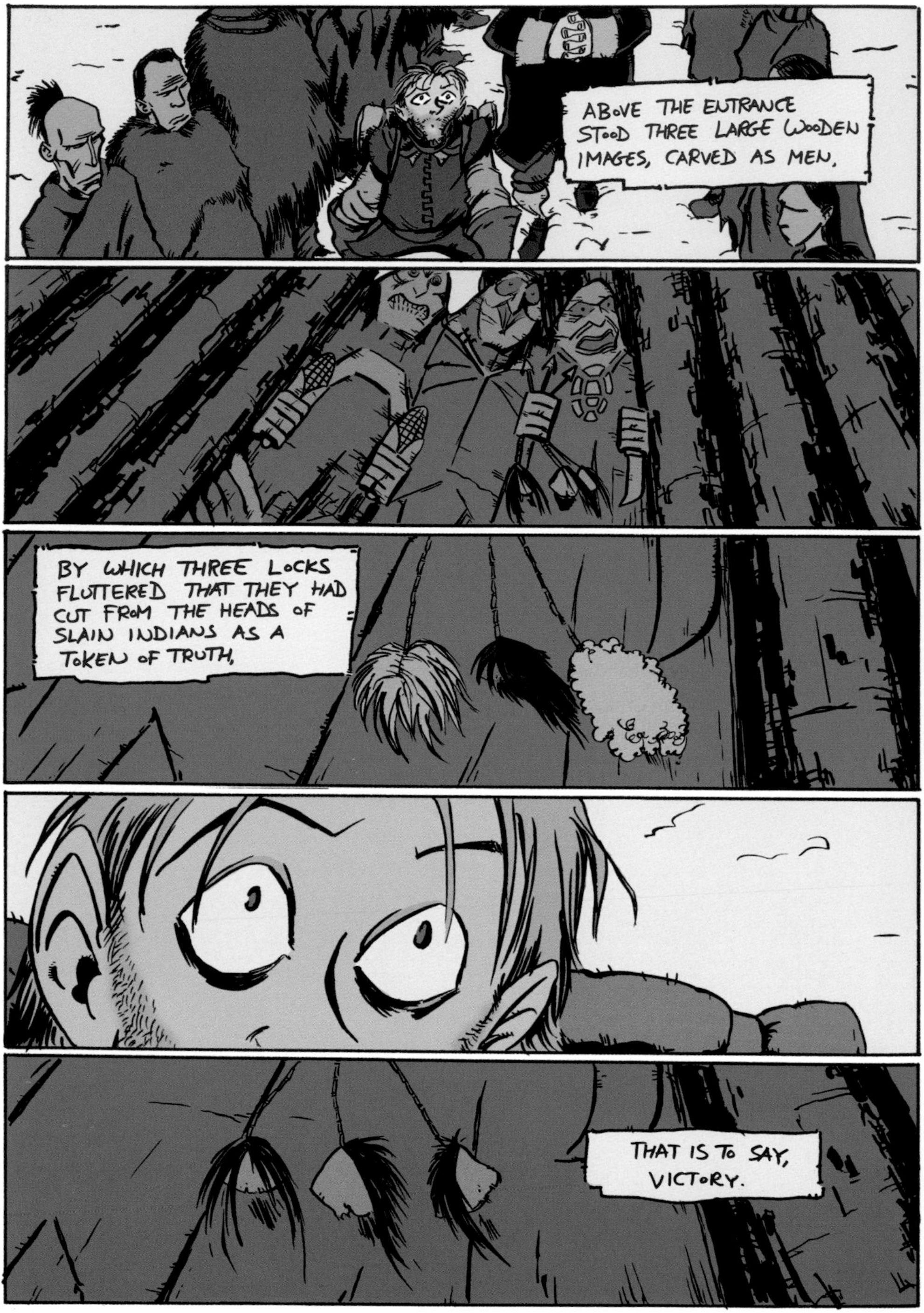
ABOVE THE ENTRANCE STOOD THREE LARGE WOODEN IMAGES, CARVED AS MEN,
BY WHICH THREE LOCKS FLUTTERED THAT THEY HAD CUT FROM THE HEADS OF SLAIN INDIANS AS A TOKEN OF TRUTH,
THAT IS TO SAY, VICTORY.

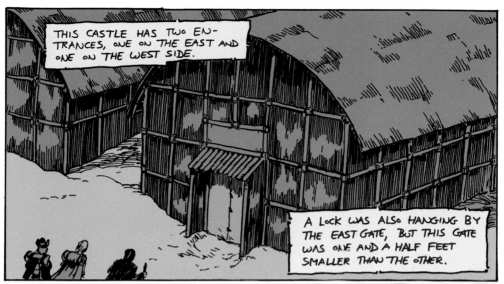

THIS CASTLE HAS TWO EN-
TRANCES, ONE ON THE EAST AND
ONE ON THE WEST SIDE.

A LOCK WAS ALSO HANGING BY
THE EAST GATE, BUT THIS GATE
WAS ONE AND A HALF FEET
SMALLER THAN THE OTHER.

THEN WE WERE FINALLY BROUGHT
INTO THE FARTHEST HOUSE, WHERE
I FOUND MANY ACQUAINTANCES.

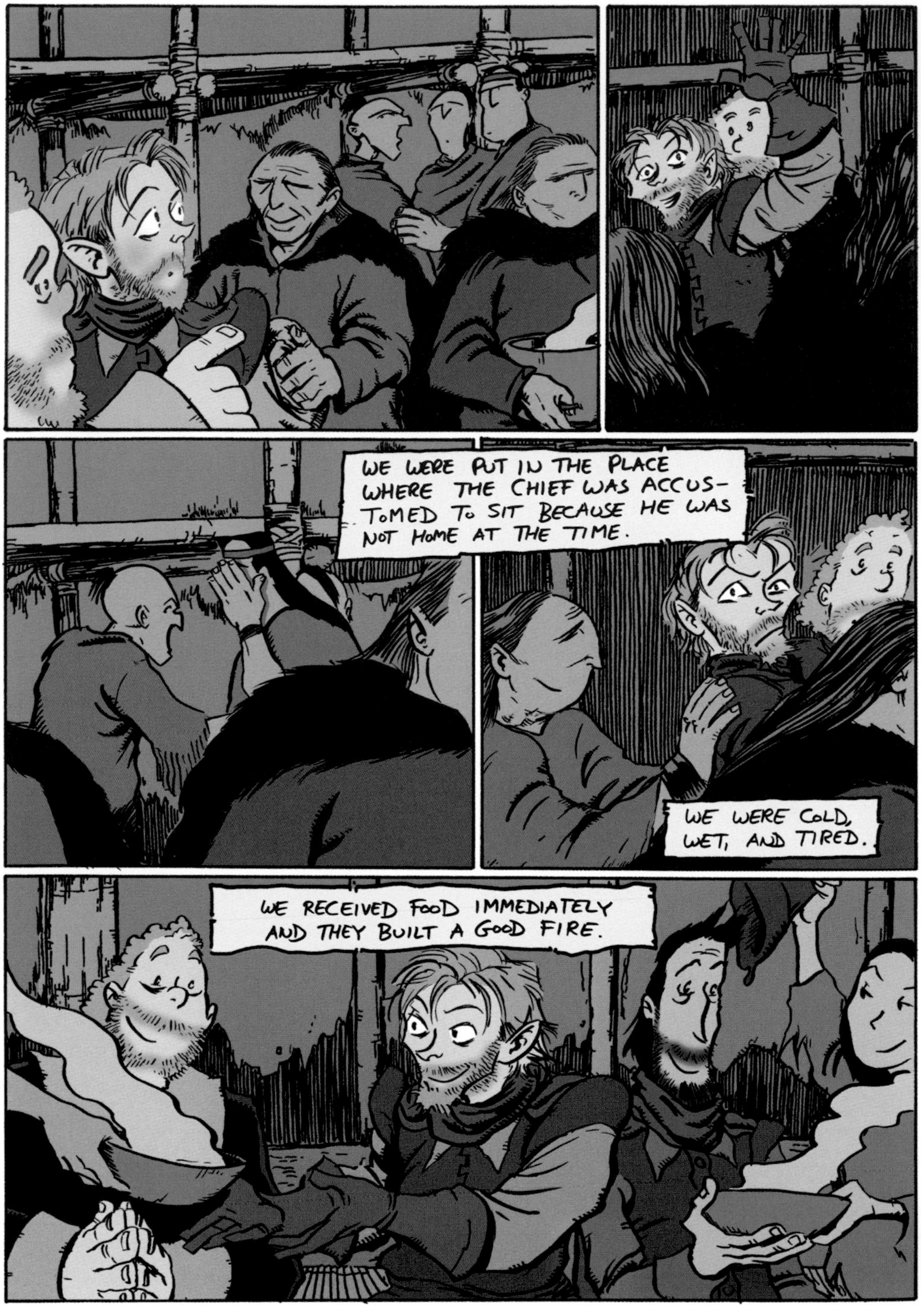
WE WERE PUT IN THE PLACE WHERE THE CHIEF WAS ACCUSTOMED TO SIT BECAUSE HE WAS NOT HOME AT THE TIME.
WE WERE COLD, WET, AND TIRED.
WE RECEIVED FOOD IMMEDIATELY AND THEY BUILT A GOOD FIRE.

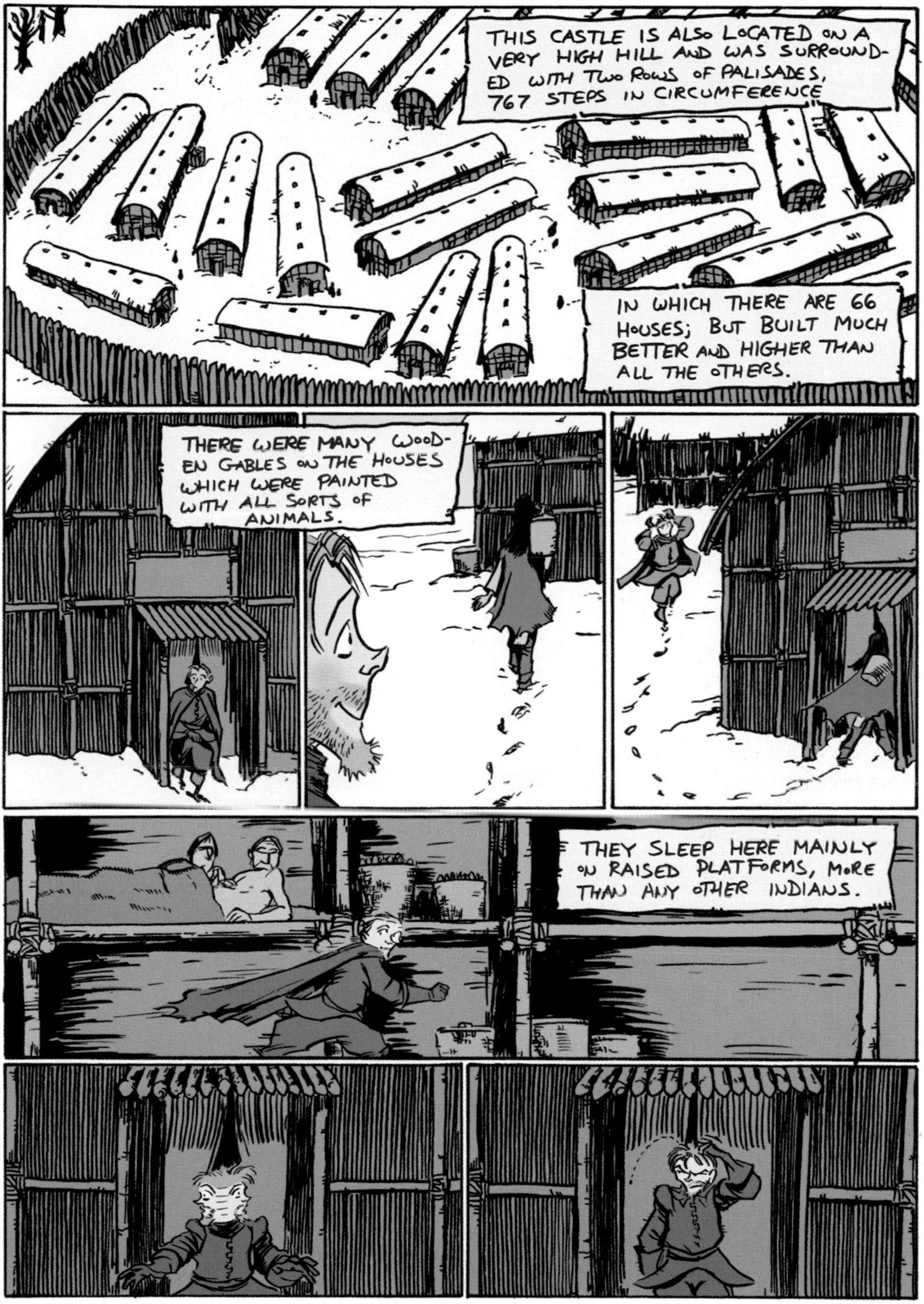
THIS CASTLE IS ALSO LOCATED ON A VERY HIGH HILL AND WAS SURROUNDED WITH TWO ROWS OF PALISADES, 767 STEPS IN CIRCUMFERENCE
IN WHICH THERE ARE 66 HOUSES; BUT BUILT MUCH BETTER AND HIGHER THAN ALL THE OTHERS.
THERE WERE MANY WOODEN GABLES ON THE HOUSES WHICH WERE PAINTED WITH ALL SORTS OF ANIMALS.
THEY SLEEP HERE MAINLY ON RAISED PLATFORMS, MORE THAN ANY OTHER INDIANS.

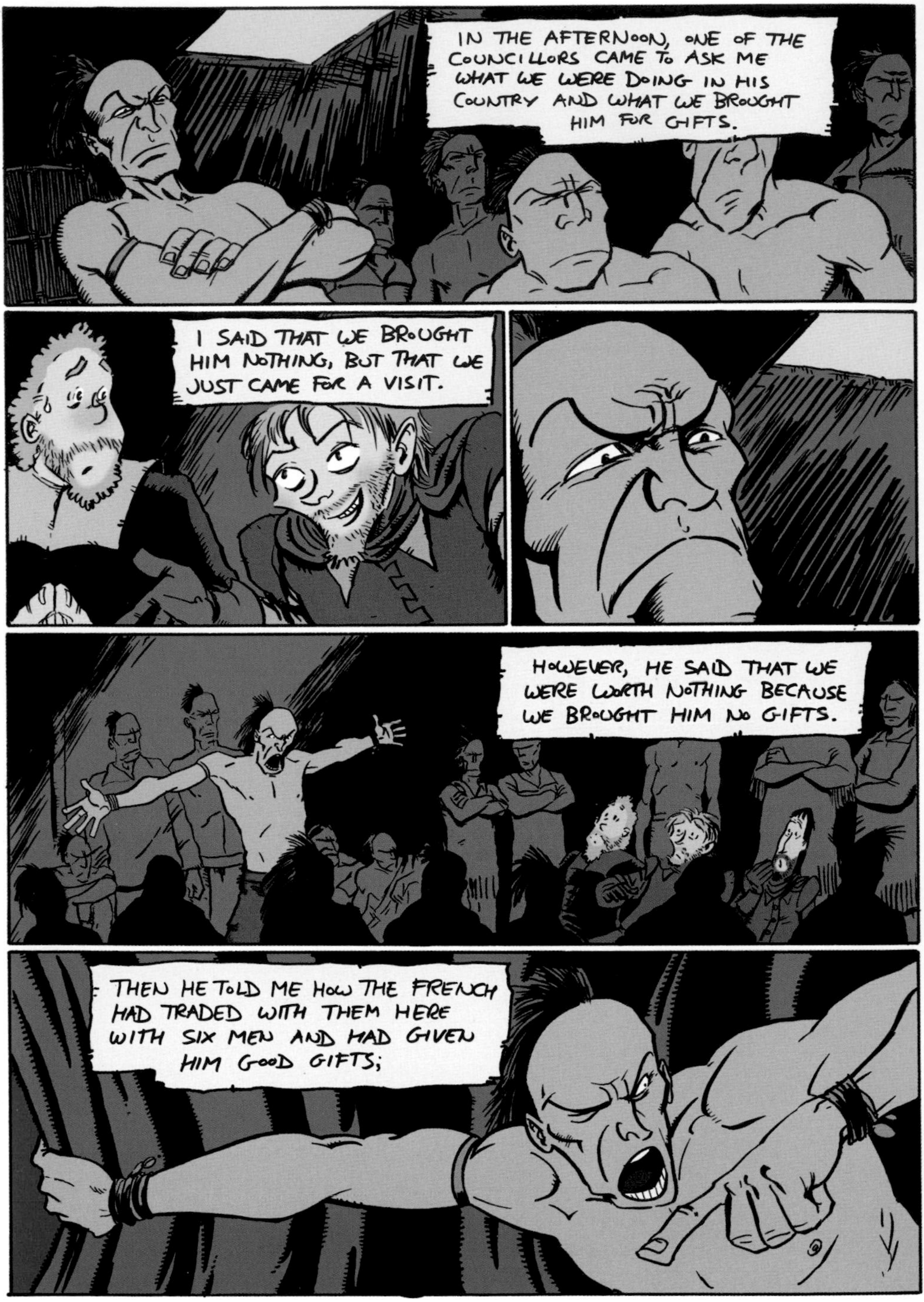
IN THE AFTERNOON, ONE OF THE COUNCILLORS CAME TO ASK ME WHAT WE WERE DOING IN HIS COUNTRY AND WHAT WE BROUGHT HIM FOR GIFTS.
I SAID THAT WE BROUGHT HIM NOTHING, BUT THAT WE JUST CAME FOR A VISIT.
HOWEVER, HE SAID THAT WE WERE WORTH NOTHING BECAUSE WE BROUGHT HIM NO GIFTS.
THEN HE TOLD ME HOW THE FRENCH HAD TRADED WITH THEM HERE WITH SIX MEN AND HAD GIVEN HIM GOOD GIFTS;

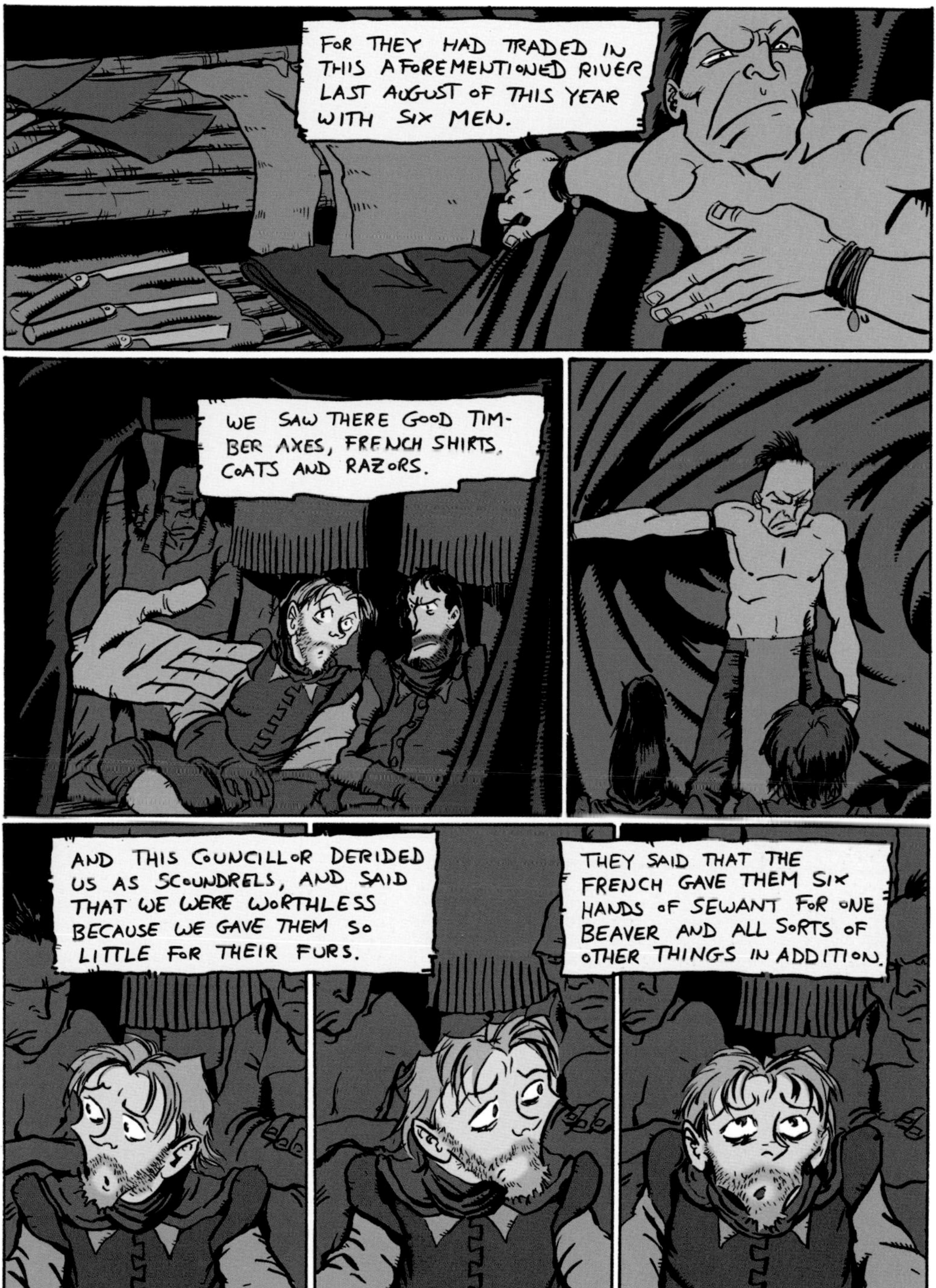
FOR THEY HAD TRADED IN THIS AFOREMENTIONED RIVER LAST AUGUST OF THIS YEAR WITH SIX MEN.
WE SAW THERE GOOD TIMBER AXES, FRENCH SHIRTS, COATS AND RAZORS.
AND THIS COUNCILLOR DERIDED US AS SCOUNDRELS, AND SAID THAT WE WERE WORTHLESS BECAUSE WE GAVE THEM SO LITTLE FOR THEIR FURS.
THEY SAID THAT THE FRENCH GAVE THEM SIX HANDS OF SEWANT FOR ONE BEAVER AND ALL SORTS OF OTHER THINGS IN ADDITION.

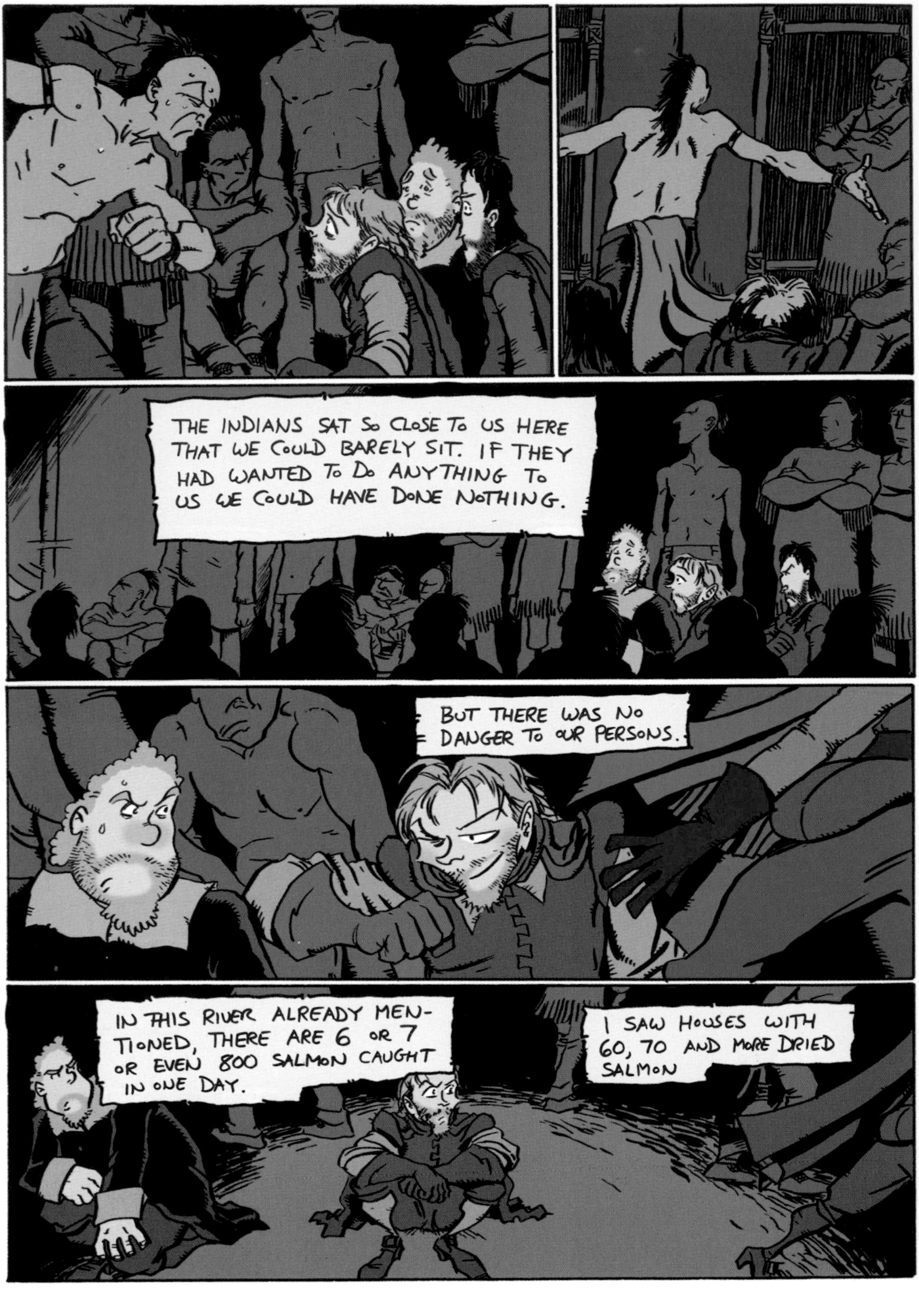
THE INDIANS SAT SO CLOSE TO US HERE THAT WE COULD BARELY SIT. IF THEY HAD WANTED TO DO ANYTHING TO US WE COULD HAVE DONE NOTHING.
BUT THERE WAS NO DANGER TO OUR PERSONS.
IN THIS RIVER ALREADY MEN-TIONED, THERE ARE 6 OR 7 OR EVEN 800 SALMON CAUGHT IN ONE DAY.
I SAW HOUSES WITH 60, 70 AND MORE DRIED SALMON

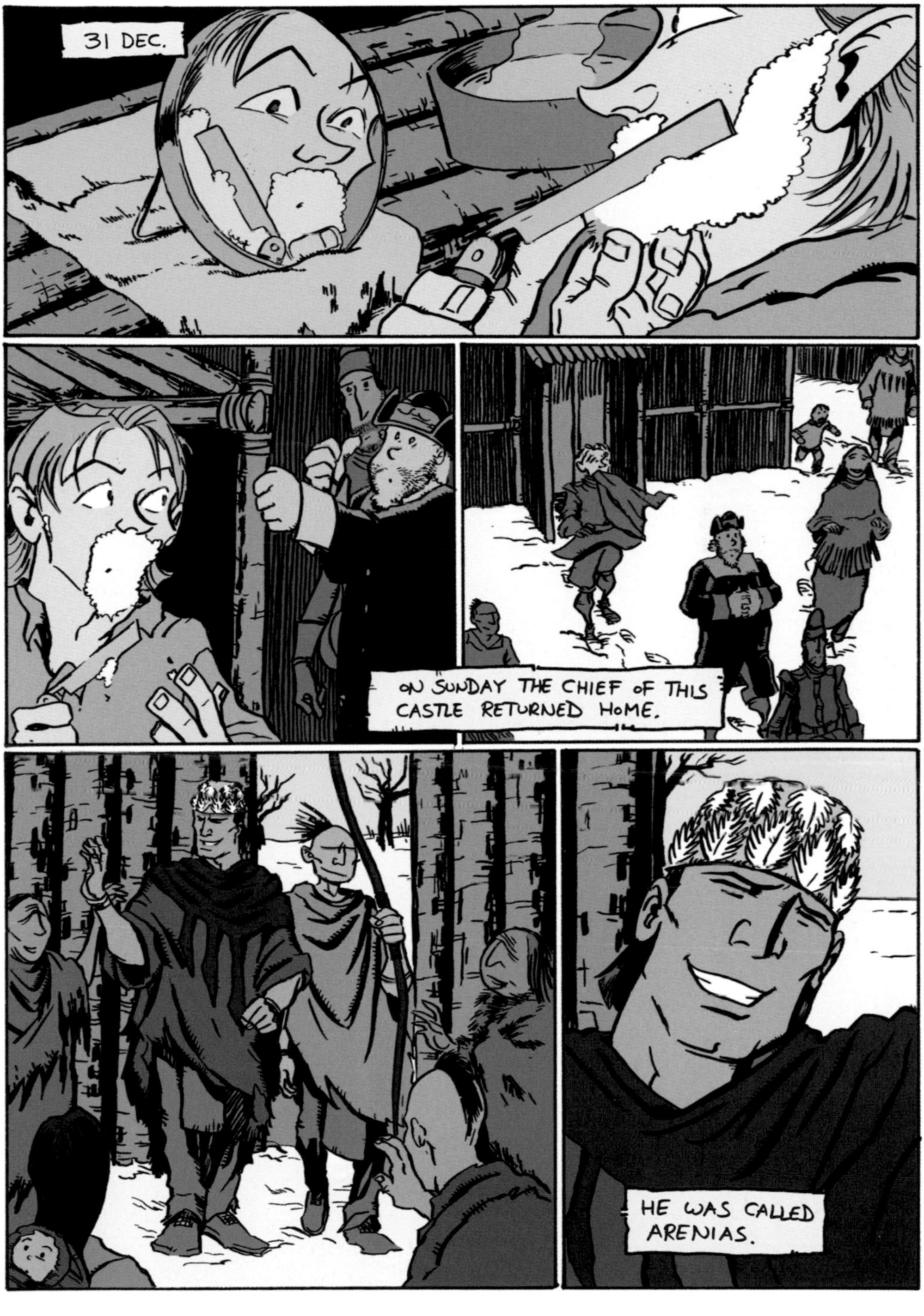
31 DEC.
ON SUNDAY THE CHIEF OF THIS CASTLE RETURNED HOME.
HE WAS CALLED ARENIAS.

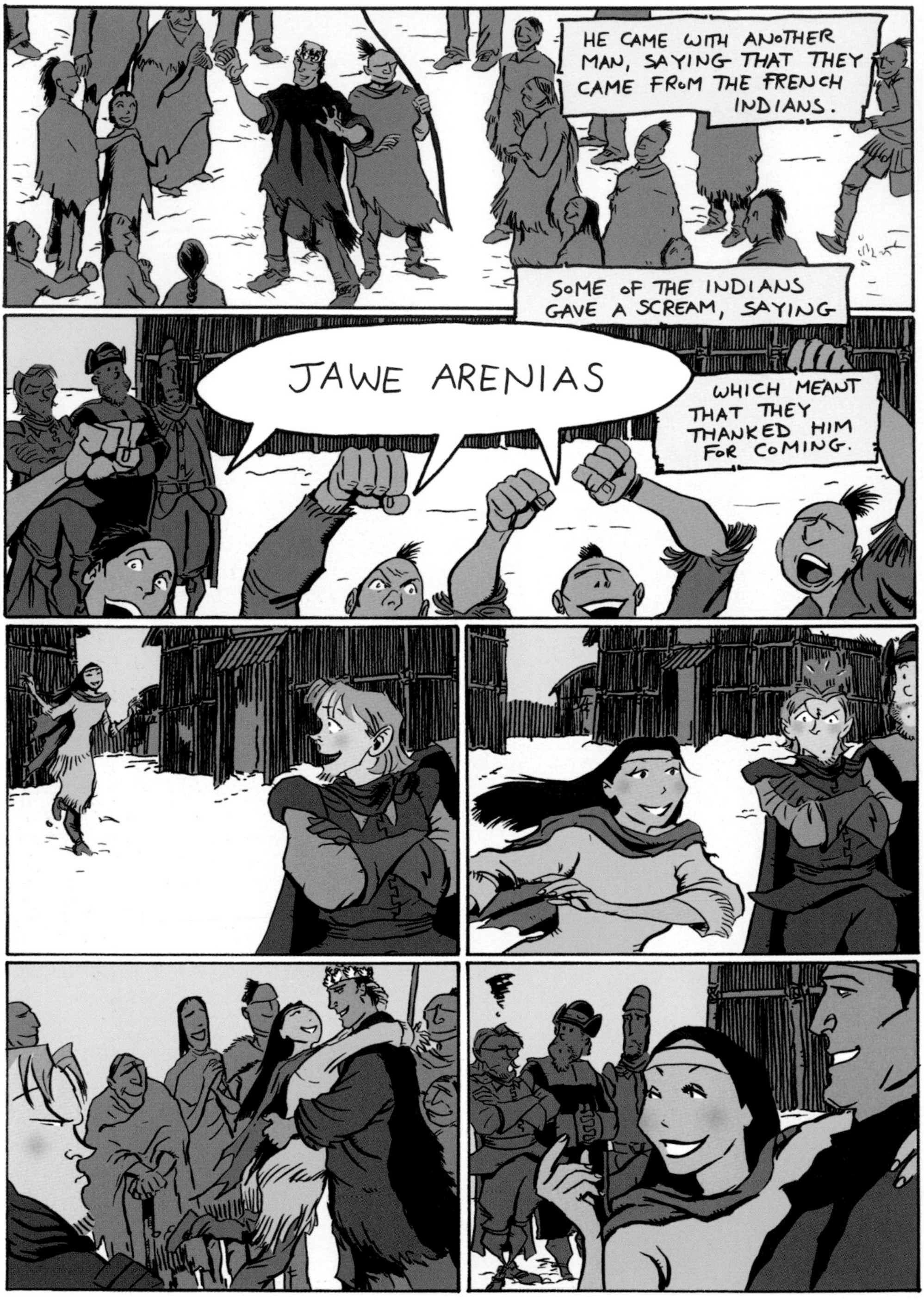
HE CAME WITH ANOTHER MAN, SAYING THAT THEY CAME FROM THE FRENCH INDIANS.
SOME OF THE INDIANS GAVE A SCREAM, SAYING
JAWE ARENIAS
WHICH MEANT THAT THEY THANKED HIM FOR COMING.

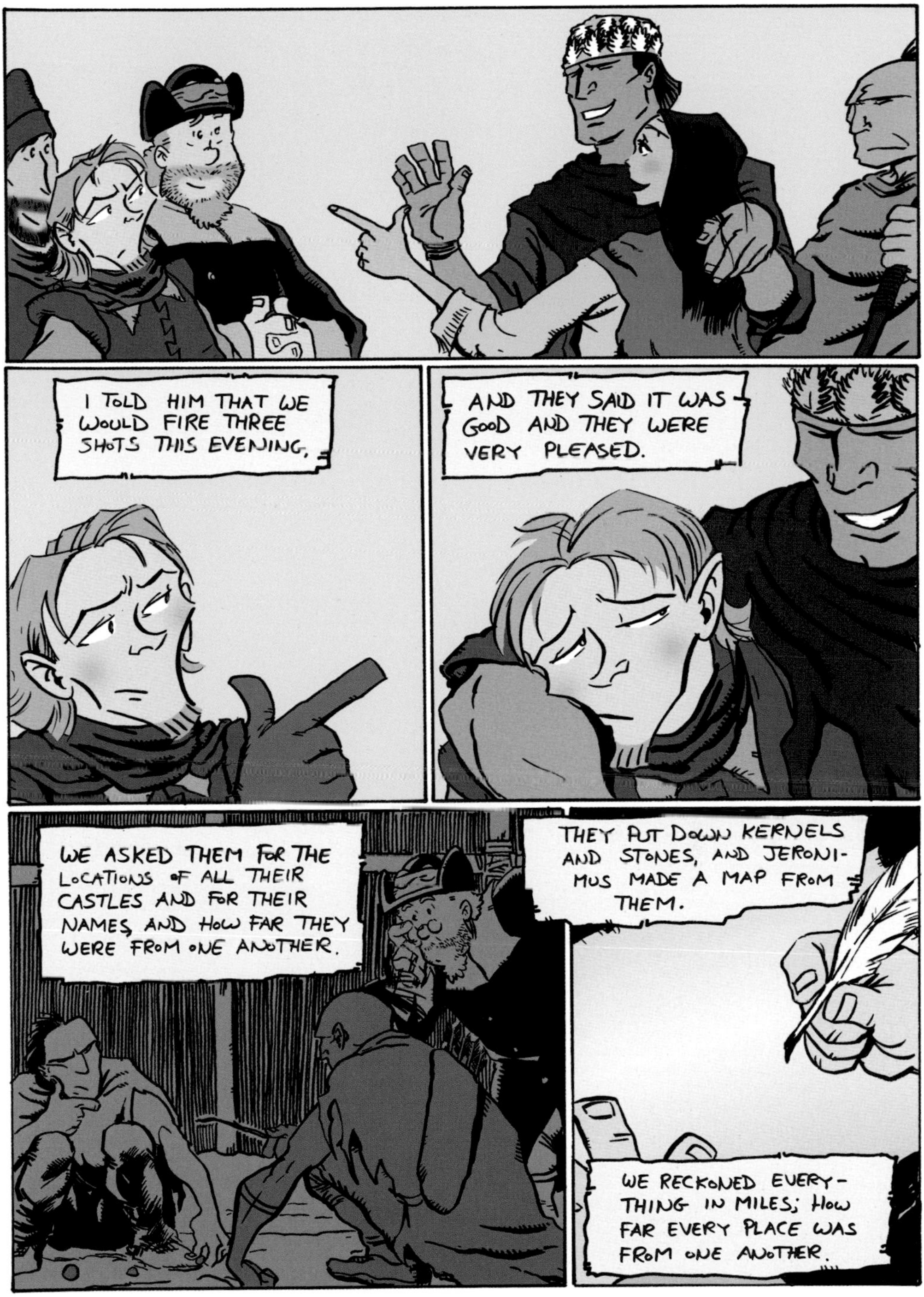
I TOLD HIM THAT WE WOULD FIRE THREE SHOTS THIS EVENING.
AND THEY SAID IT WAS GOOD AND THEY WERE VERY PLEASED.
WE ASKED THEM FOR THE LOCATIONS OF ALL THEIR CASTLES AND FOR THEIR NAMES, AND HOW FAR THEY WERE FROM ONE ANOTHER.
THEY PUT DOWN KERNELS AND STONES, AND JERONIMUS MADE A MAP FROM THEM.
WE RECKONED EVERYTHING IN MILES; HOW FAR EVERY PLACE WAS FROM ONE ANOTHER.

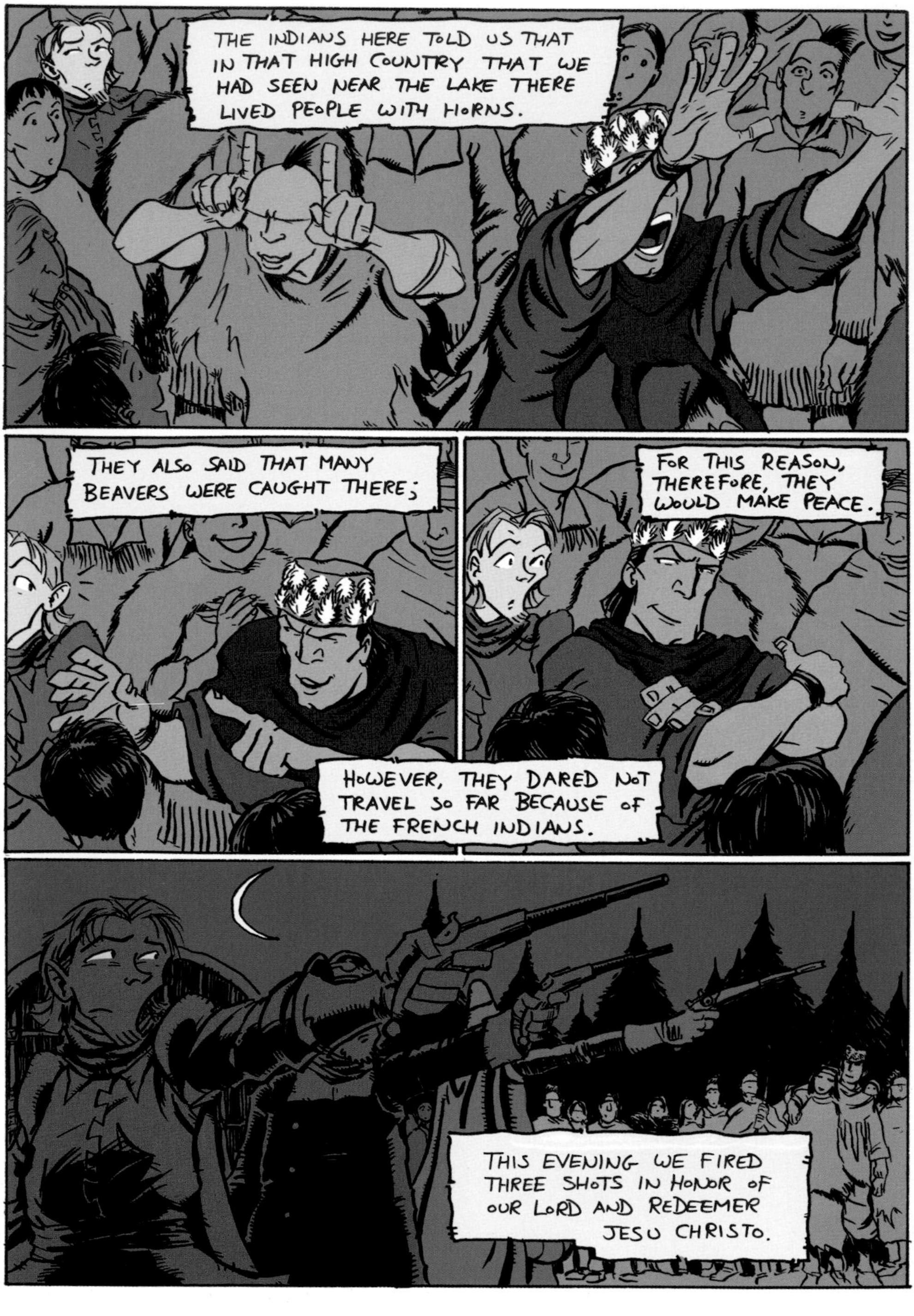
THE INDIANS HERE TOLD US THAT IN THAT HIGH COUNTRY THAT WE HAD SEEN NEAR THE LAKE THERE LIVED PEOPLE WITH HORNS.
THEY ALSO SAID THAT MANY BEAVERS WERE CAUGHT THERE;
FOR THIS REASON, THEREFORE, THEY WOULD MAKE PEACE.
HOWEVER, THEY DARED NOT TRAVEL SO FAR BECAUSE OF THE FRENCH INDIANS.
THIS EVENING WE FIRED THREE SHOTS IN HONOR OF OUR LORD AND REDEEMER JESU CHRISTO.

Praise The
LORD
Above All

In the Castle
ONNEYUTTEHAGE
or Sinnekens

1635 January

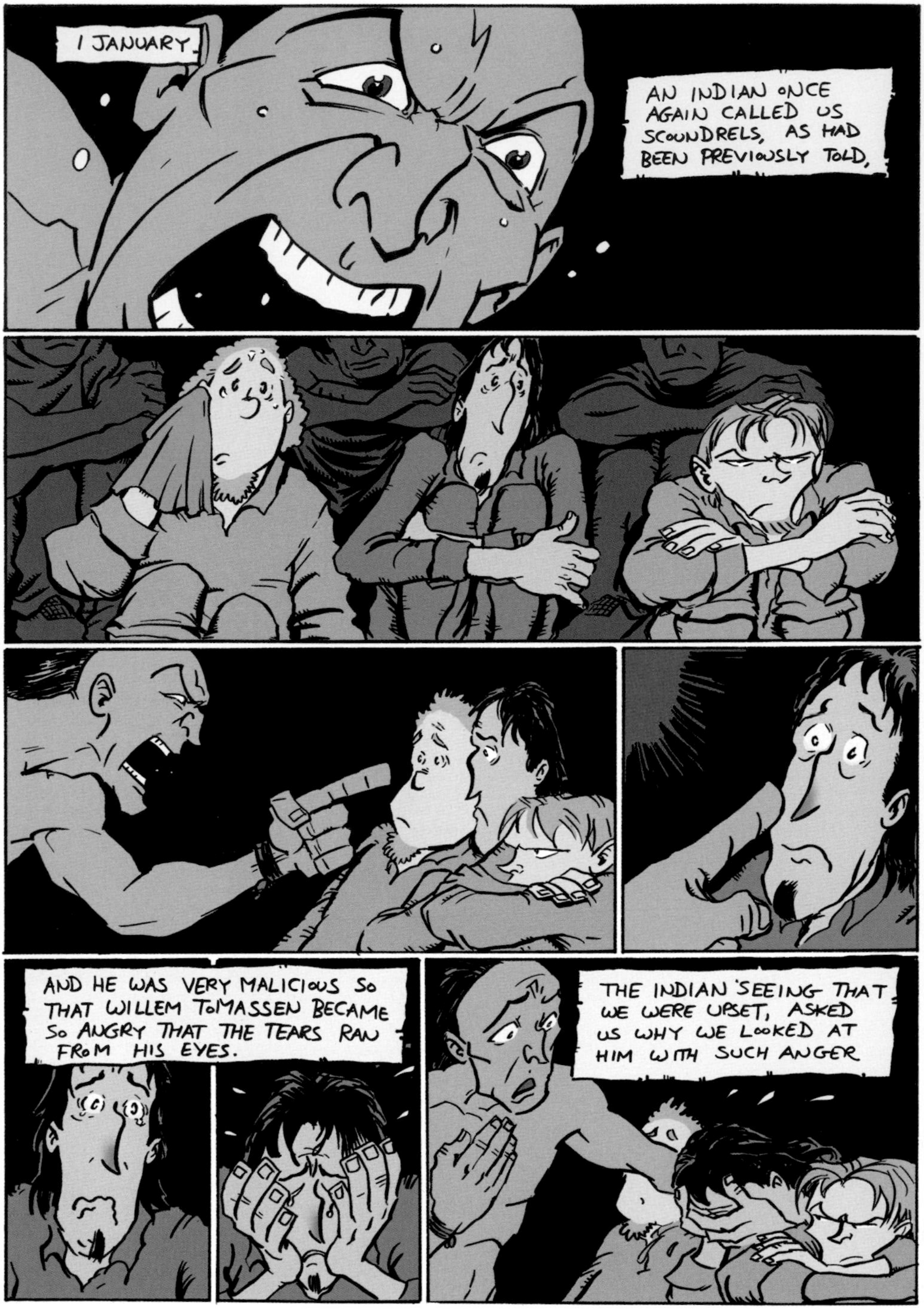
1 JANUARY
AN INDIAN ONCE AGAIN CALLED US SCOUNDRELS, AS HAD BEEN PREVIOUSLY TOLD,
AND HE WAS VERY MALICIOUS SO THAT WILLEM TOMASSEN BECAME SO ANGRY THAT THE TEARS RAN FROM HIS EYES.
THE INDIAN SEEING THAT WE WERE UPSET, ASKED US WHY WE LOOKED AT HIM WITH SUCH ANGER

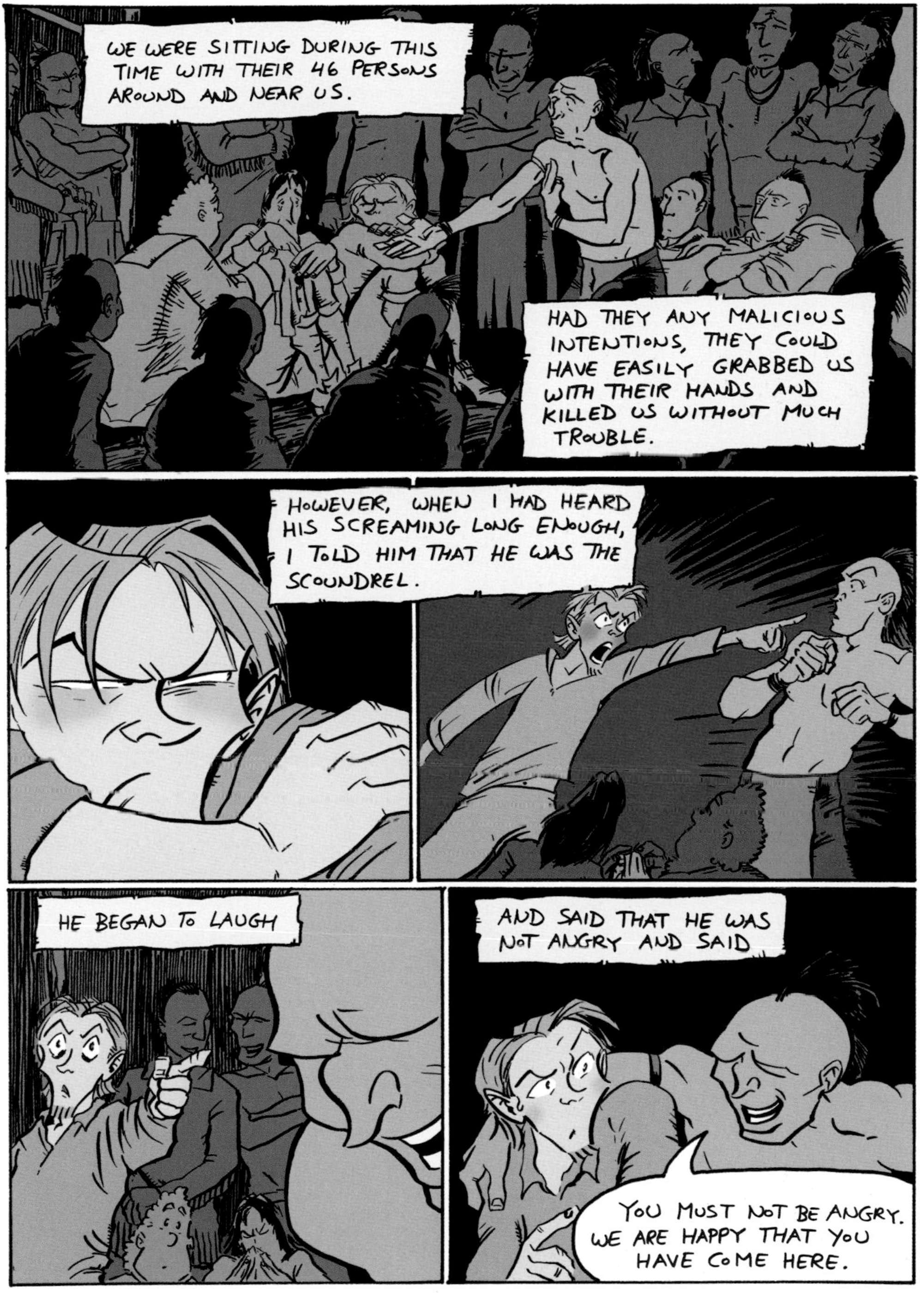
WE WERE SITTING DURING THIS TIME WITH THEIR 46 PERSONS AROUND AND NEAR US.
HAD THEY ANY MALICIOUS INTENTIONS, THEY COULD HAVE EASILY GRABBED US WITH THEIR HANDS AND KILLED US WITHOUT MUCH TROUBLE.
HOWEVER, WHEN I HAD HEARD HIS SCREAMING LONG ENOUGH, I TOLD HIM THAT HE WAS THE SCOUNDREL.
HE BEGAN TO LAUGH
AND SAID THAT HE WAS NOT ANGRY AND SAID
YOU MUST NOT BE ANGRY. WE ARE HAPPY THAT YOU HAVE COME HERE.

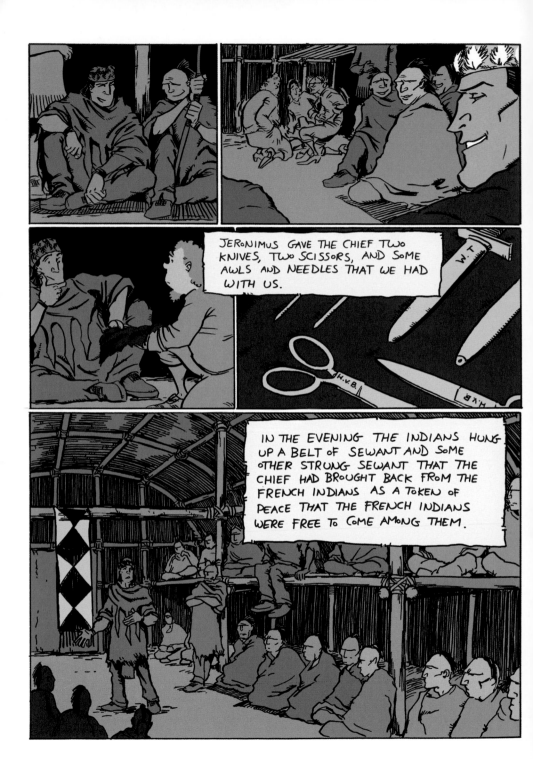

JERONIMUS GAVE THE CHIEF TWO KNIVES, TWO SCISSORS, AND SOME AWLS AND NEEDLES THAT WE HAD WITH US.

IN THE EVENING THE INDIANS HUNG UP A BELT OF SEWANT AND SOME OTHER STRUNG SEWANT THAT THE CHIEF HAD BROUGHT BACK FROM THE FRENCH INDIANS AS A TOKEN OF PEACE THAT THE FRENCH INDIANS WERE FREE TO COME AMONG THEM.

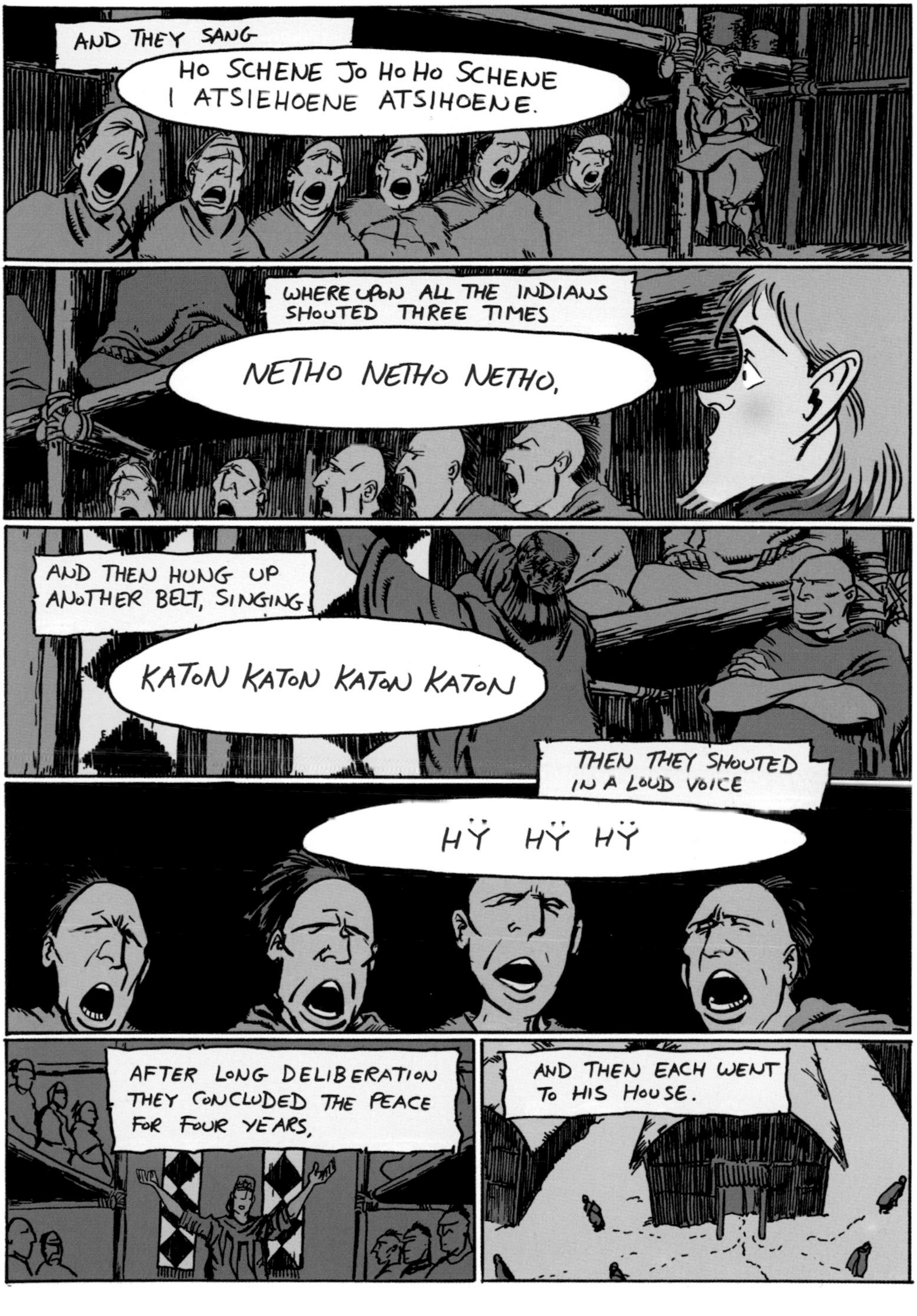
AND THEY SANG
HO SCHENE JO HO HO SCHENE I ATSIEHOENE ATSIHOENE.
WHEREUPON ALL THE INDIANS SHOUTED THREE TIMES
NETHO NETHO NETHO.
AND THEN HUNG UP ANOTHER BELT, SINGING
KATON KATON KATON KATON
THEN THEY SHOUTED IN A LOUD VOICE
HŸ HŸ HŸ
AFTER LONG DELIBERATION THEY CONCLUDED THE PEACE FOR FOUR YEARS,
AND THEN EACH WENT TO HIS HOUSE.

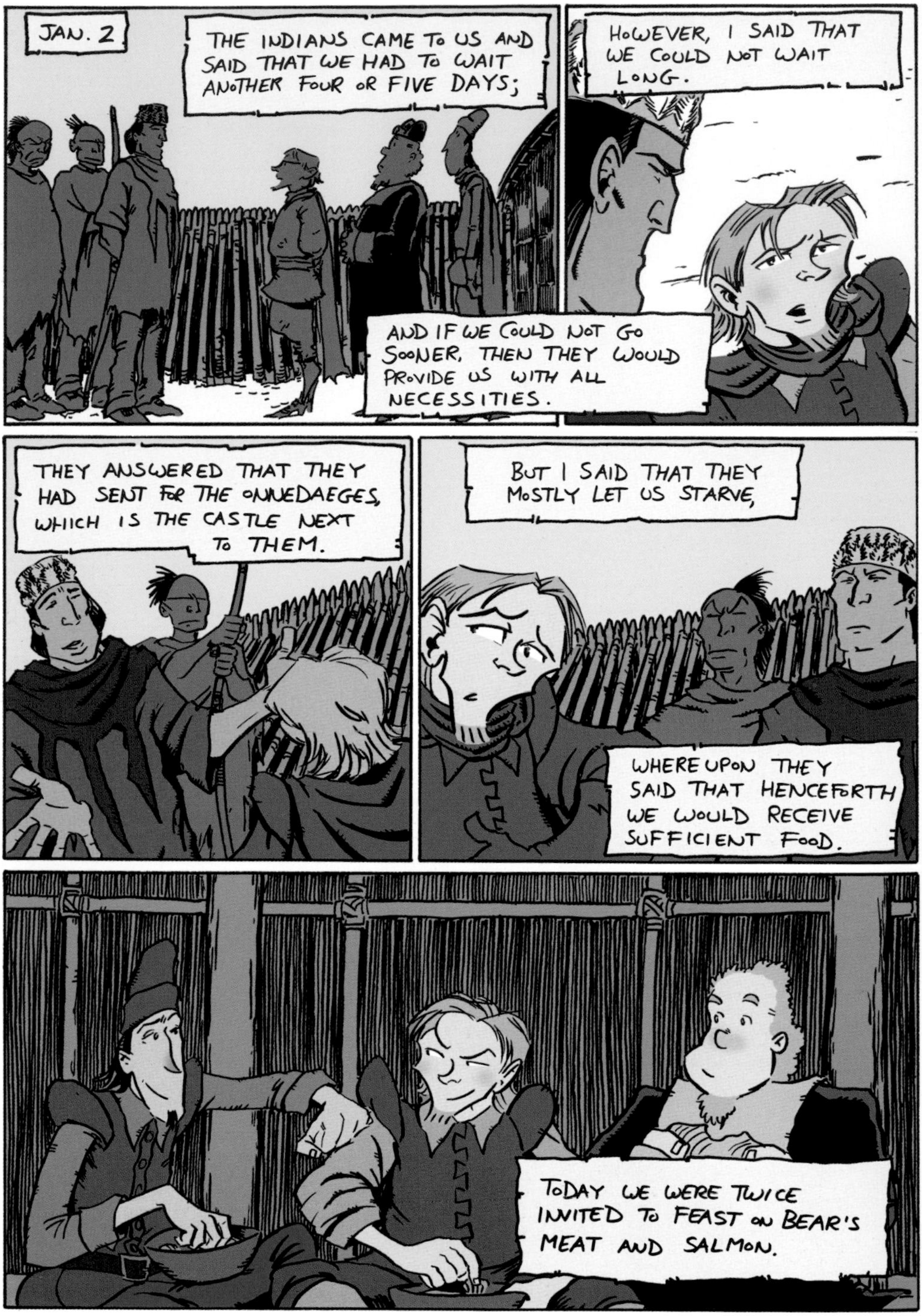
JAN. 2
THE INDIANS CAME TO US AND SAID THAT WE HAD TO WAIT ANOTHER FOUR OR FIVE DAYS;
HOWEVER, I SAID THAT WE COULD NOT WAIT LONG.
AND IF WE COULD NOT GO SOONER, THEN THEY WOULD PROVIDE US WITH ALL NECESSITIES.
THEY ANSWERED THAT THEY HAD SENT FOR THE ONNEDAEGES, WHICH IS THE CASTLE NEXT TO THEM.
BUT I SAID THAT THEY MOSTLY LET US STARVE,
WHEREUPON THEY SAID THAT HENCEFORTH WE WOULD RECEIVE SUFFICIENT FOOD.
TODAY WE WERE TWICE INVITED TO FEAST ON BEAR'S MEAT AND SALMON.

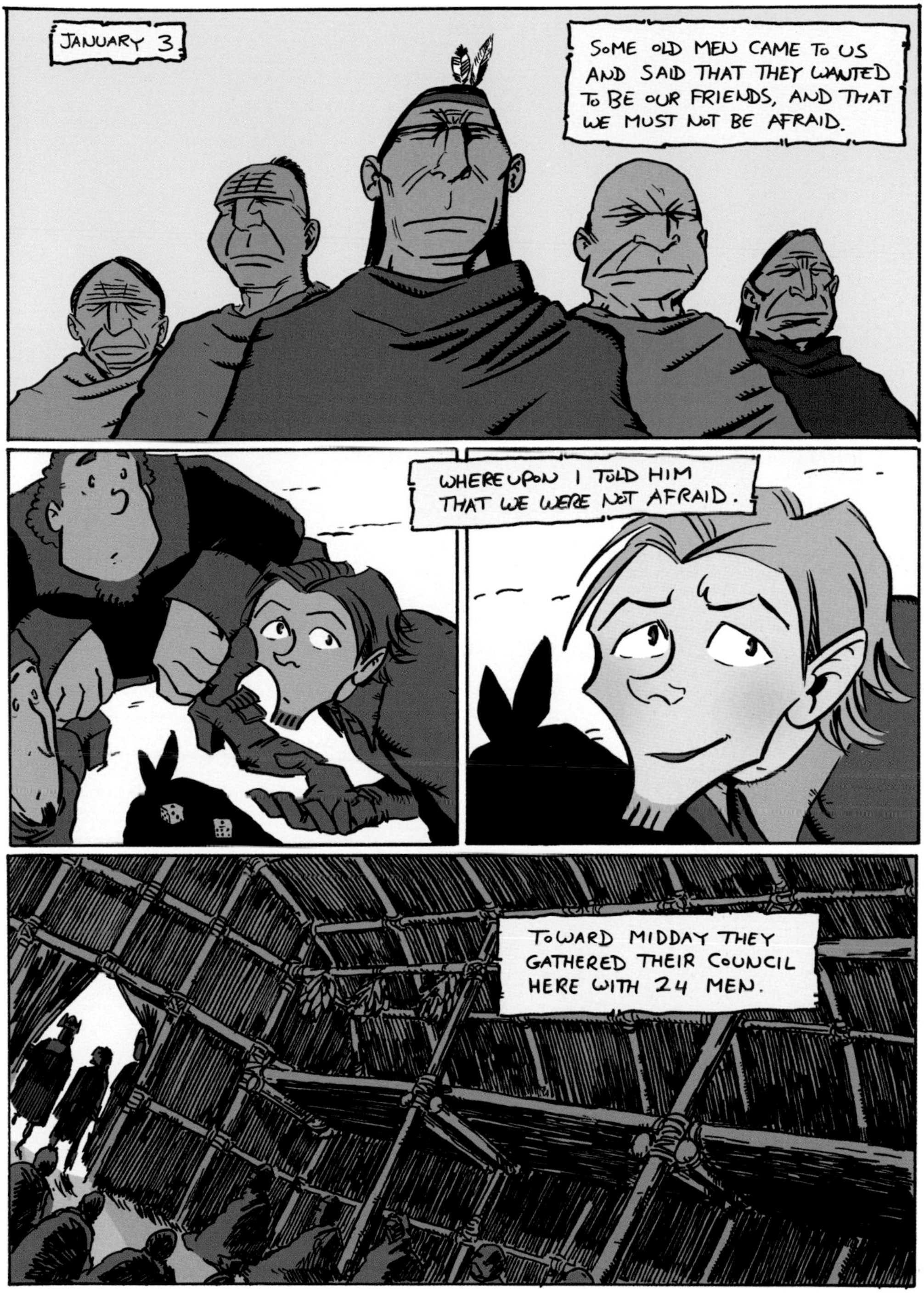
JANUARY 3
SOME OLD MEN CAME TO US AND SAID THAT THEY WANTED TO BE OUR FRIENDS, AND THAT WE MUST NOT BE AFRAID.
WHEREUPON I TOLD HIM THAT WE WERE NOT AFRAID.
TOWARD MIDDAY THEY GATHERED THEIR COUNCIL HERE WITH 24 MEN.

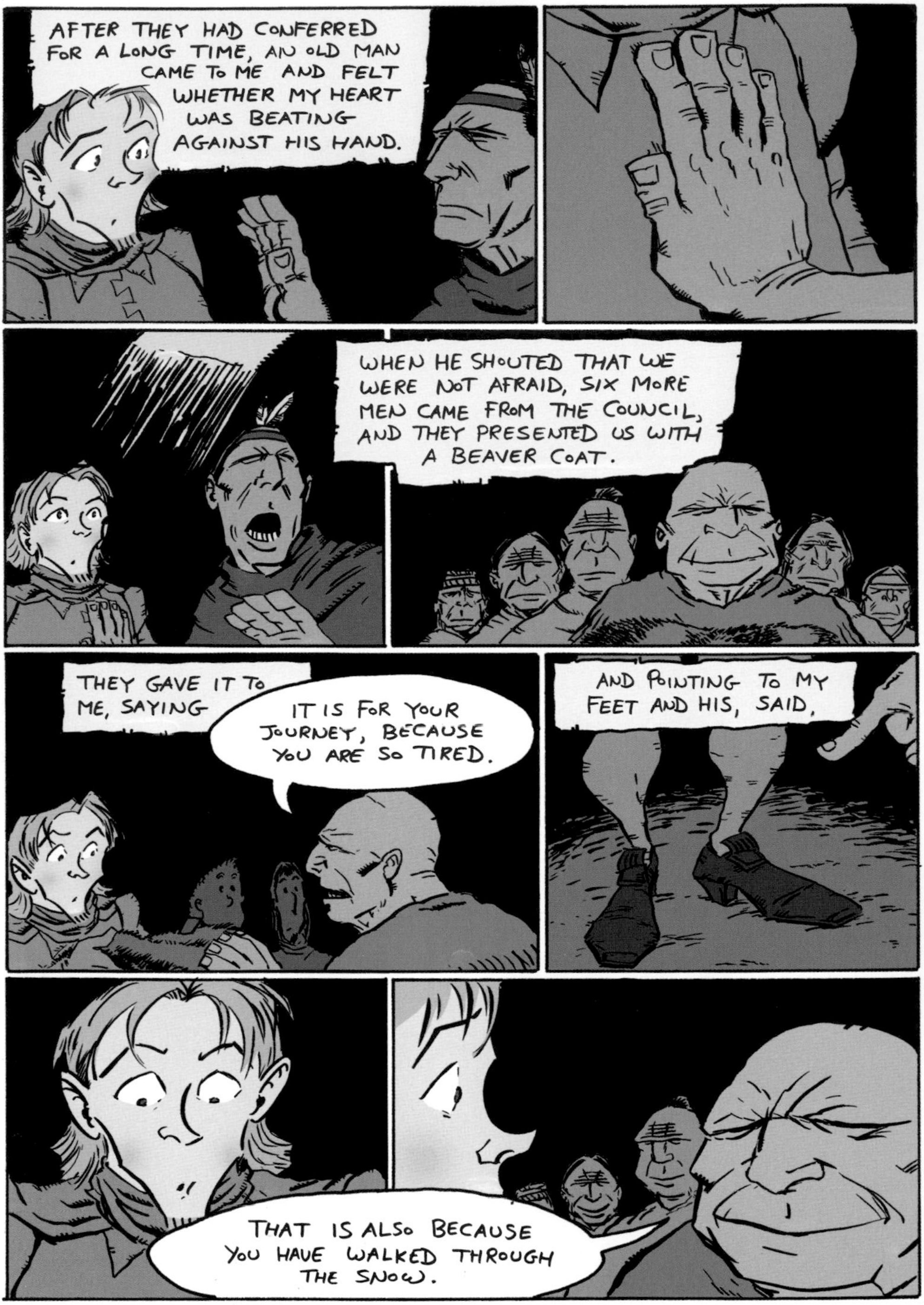
AFTER THEY HAD CONFERRED FOR A LONG TIME, AN OLD MAN CAME TO ME AND FELT WHETHER MY HEART WAS BEATING AGAINST HIS HAND.
WHEN HE SHOUTED THAT WE WERE NOT AFRAID, SIX MORE MEN CAME FROM THE COUNCIL, AND THEY PRESENTED US WITH A BEAVER COAT.
THEY GAVE IT TO ME, SAYING
IT IS FOR YOUR JOURNEY, BECAUSE YOU ARE SO TIRED.
AND POINTING TO MY FEET AND HIS, SAID,
THAT IS ALSO BECAUSE YOU HAVE WALKED THROUGH THE SNOW.

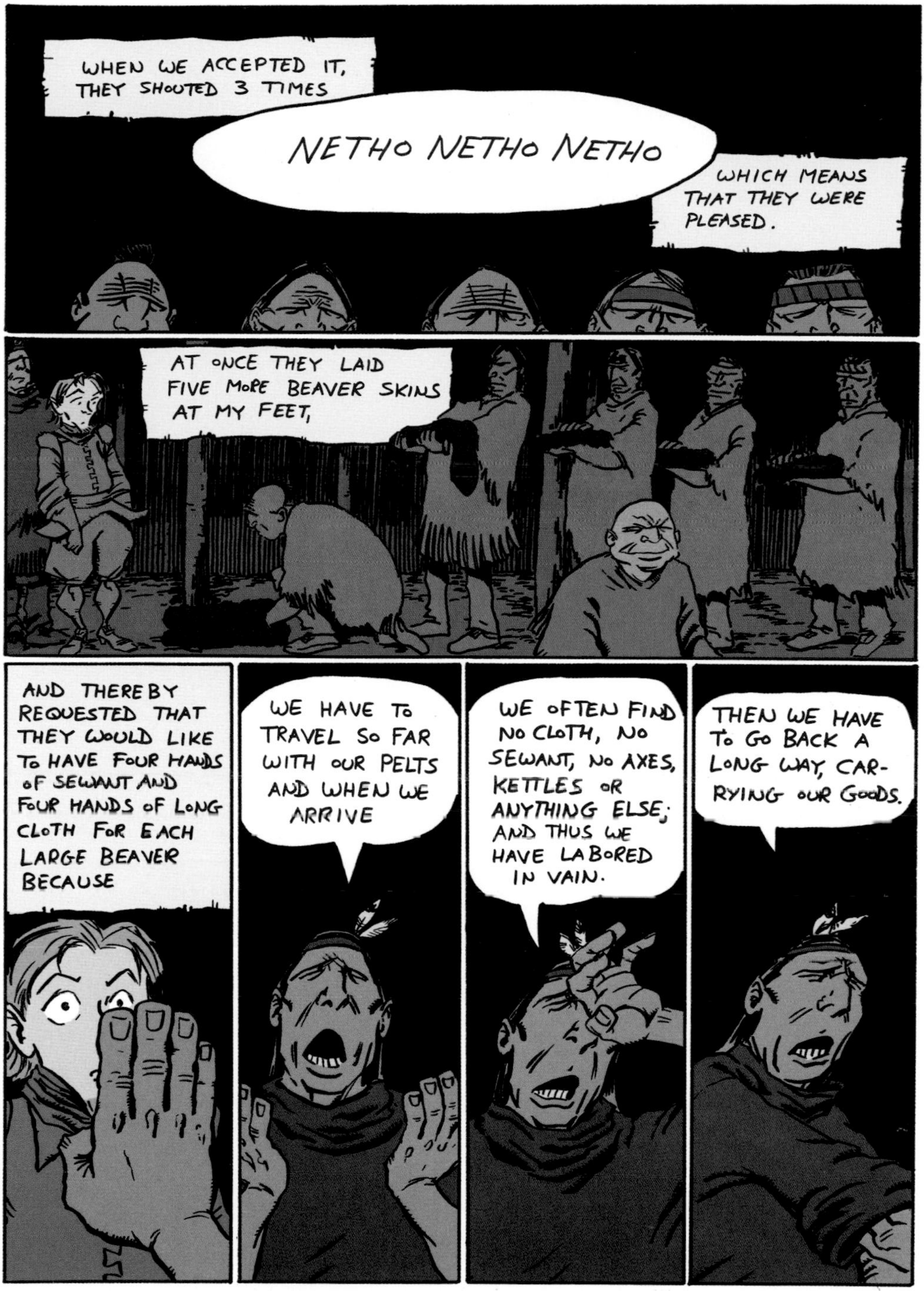

WHEN WE ACCEPTED IT, THEY SHOUTED 3 TIMES
NETHO NETHO NETHO
WHICH MEANS THAT THEY WERE PLEASED.
AT ONCE THEY LAID FIVE MORE BEAVER SKINS AT MY FEET,
AND THEREBY REQUESTED THAT THEY WOULD LIKE TO HAVE FOUR HANDS OF SEWANT AND FOUR HANDS OF LONG CLOTH FOR EACH LARGE BEAVER BECAUSE
WE HAVE TO TRAVEL SO FAR WITH OUR PELTS AND WHEN WE ARRIVE
WE OFTEN FIND NO CLOTH, NO SEWANT, NO AXES, KETTLES OR ANYTHING ELSE; AND THUS WE HAVE LABORED IN VAIN.
THEN WE HAVE TO GO BACK A LONG WAY, CARRYING OUR GOODS.

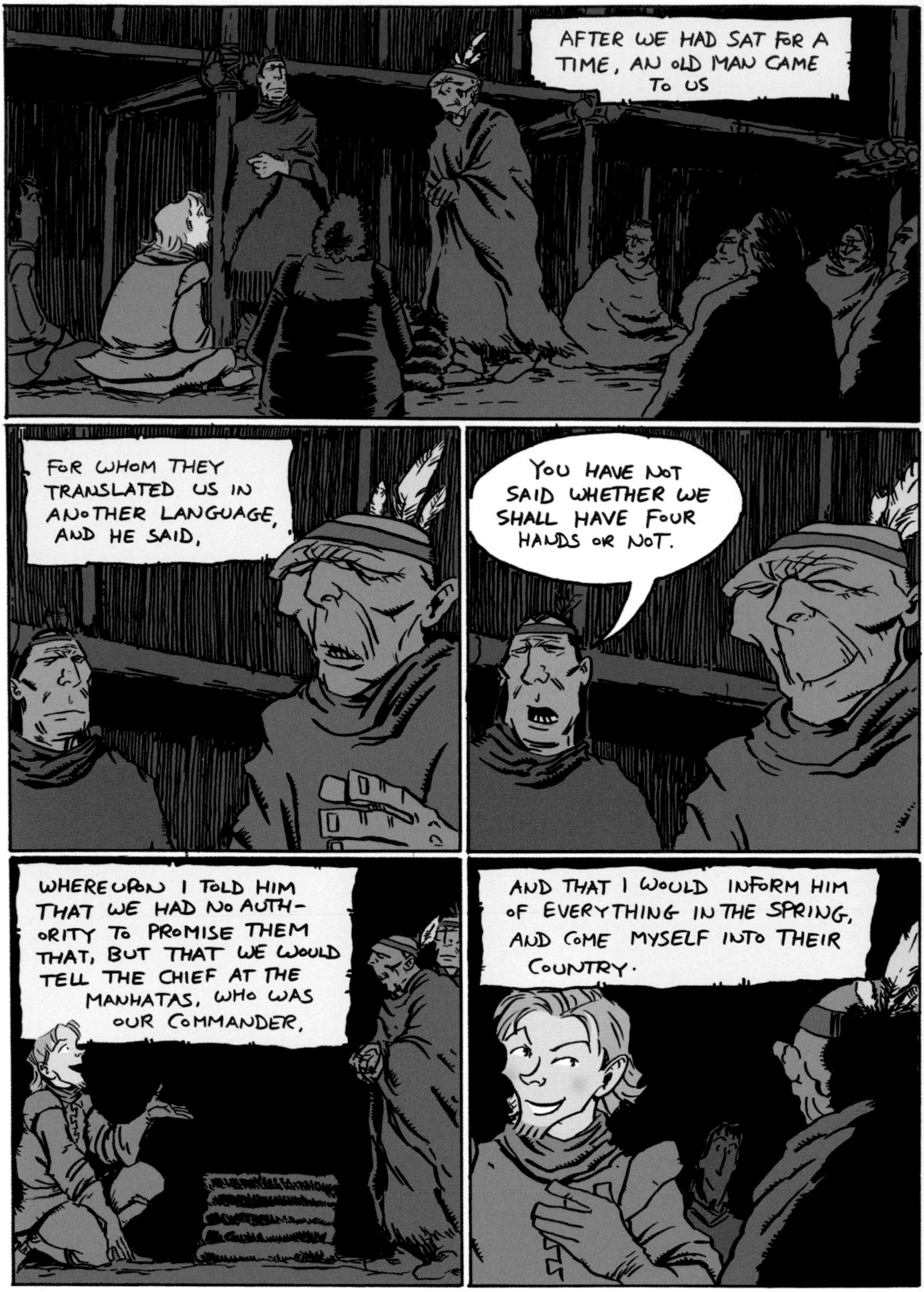
AFTER WE HAD SAT FOR A TIME, AN OLD MAN CAME TO US
FOR WHOM THEY TRANSLATED US IN ANOTHER LANGUAGE, AND HE SAID,
YOU HAVE NOT SAID WHETHER WE SHALL HAVE FOUR HANDS OR NOT.
WHEREUPON I TOLD HIM THAT WE HAD NO AUTHORITY TO PROMISE THEM THAT, BUT THAT WE WOULD TELL THE CHIEF AT THE MANHATAS, WHO WAS OUR COMMANDER,
AND THAT I WOULD INFORM HIM OF EVERYTHING IN THE SPRING, AND COME MYSELF INTO THEIR COUNTRY.

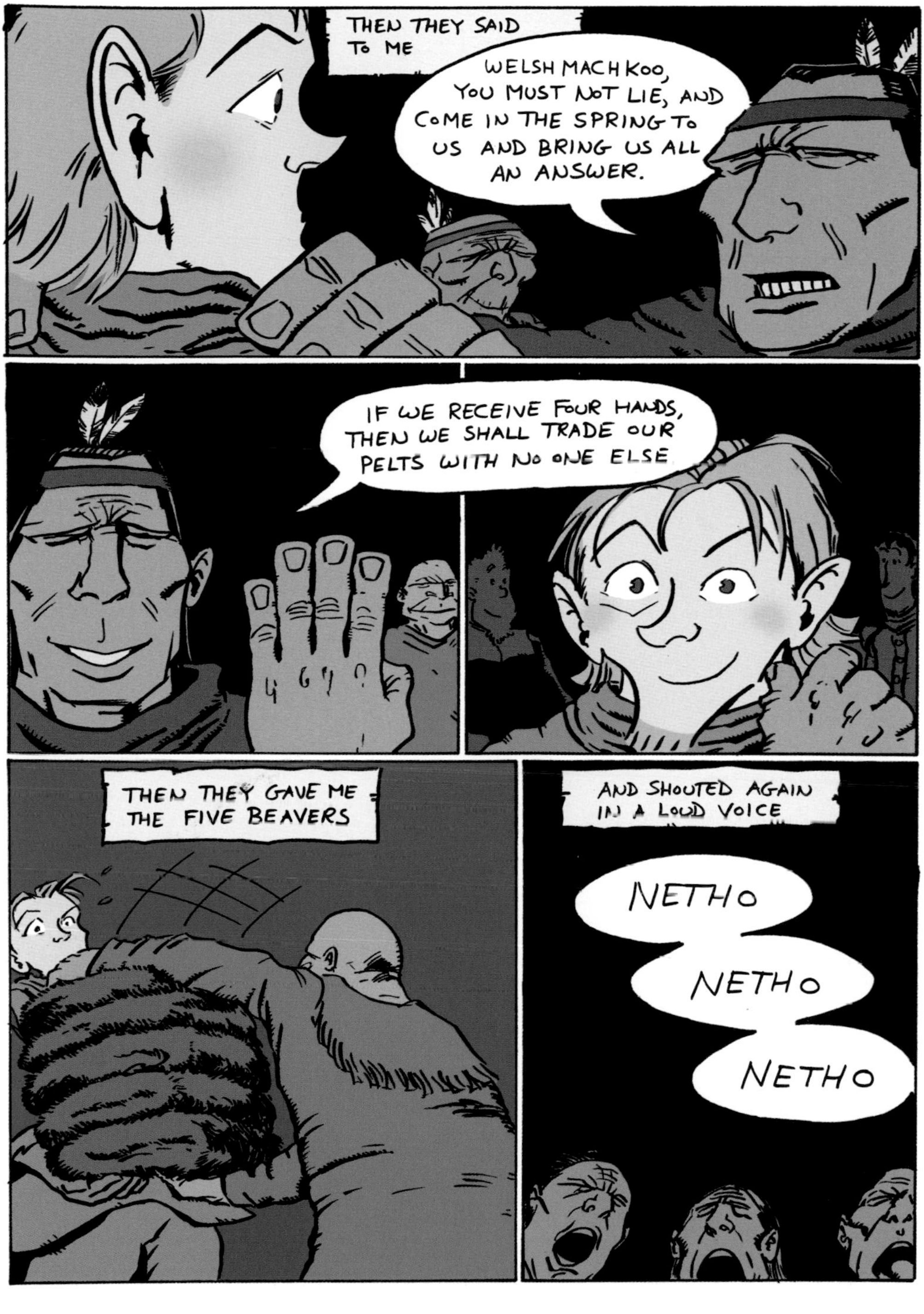
THEN THEY SAID TO ME
WELSH MACHKOO, YOU MUST NOT LIE, AND COME IN THE SPRING TO US AND BRING US ALL AN ANSWER.
IF WE RECEIVE FOUR HANDS, THEN WE SHALL TRADE OUR PELTS WITH NO ONE ELSE.
THEN THEY GAVE ME THE FIVE BEAVERS
AND SHOUTED AGAIN IN A LOUD VOICE
NETHO
NETHO
NETHO

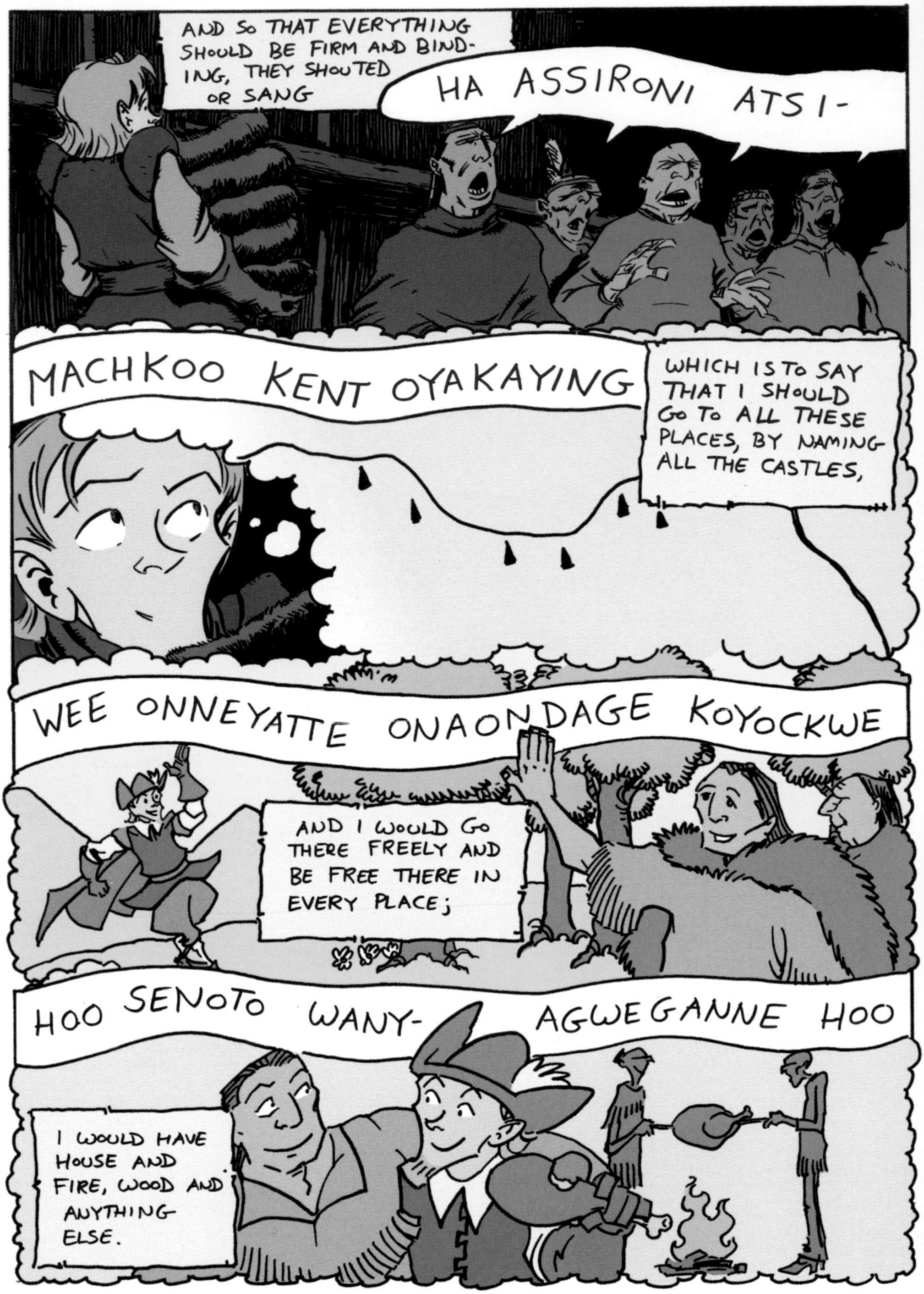
AND SO THAT EVERYTHING SHOULD BE FIRM AND BINDING, THEY SHOUTED OR SANG
HA ASSIRONI ATSI-
MACHKOO KENT OYAKAYING
WHICH IS TO SAY THAT I SHOULD GO TO ALL THESE PLACES, BY NAMING ALL THE CASTLES,
WEE ONNEYATTE ONAONDAGE KOYOCKWE
AND I WOULD GO THERE FREELY AND BE FREE THERE IN EVERY PLACE;
HOO SENOTO WANY- AGWEGANNE HOO
I WOULD HAVE HOUSE AND FIRE, WOOD AND ANYTHING ELSE.

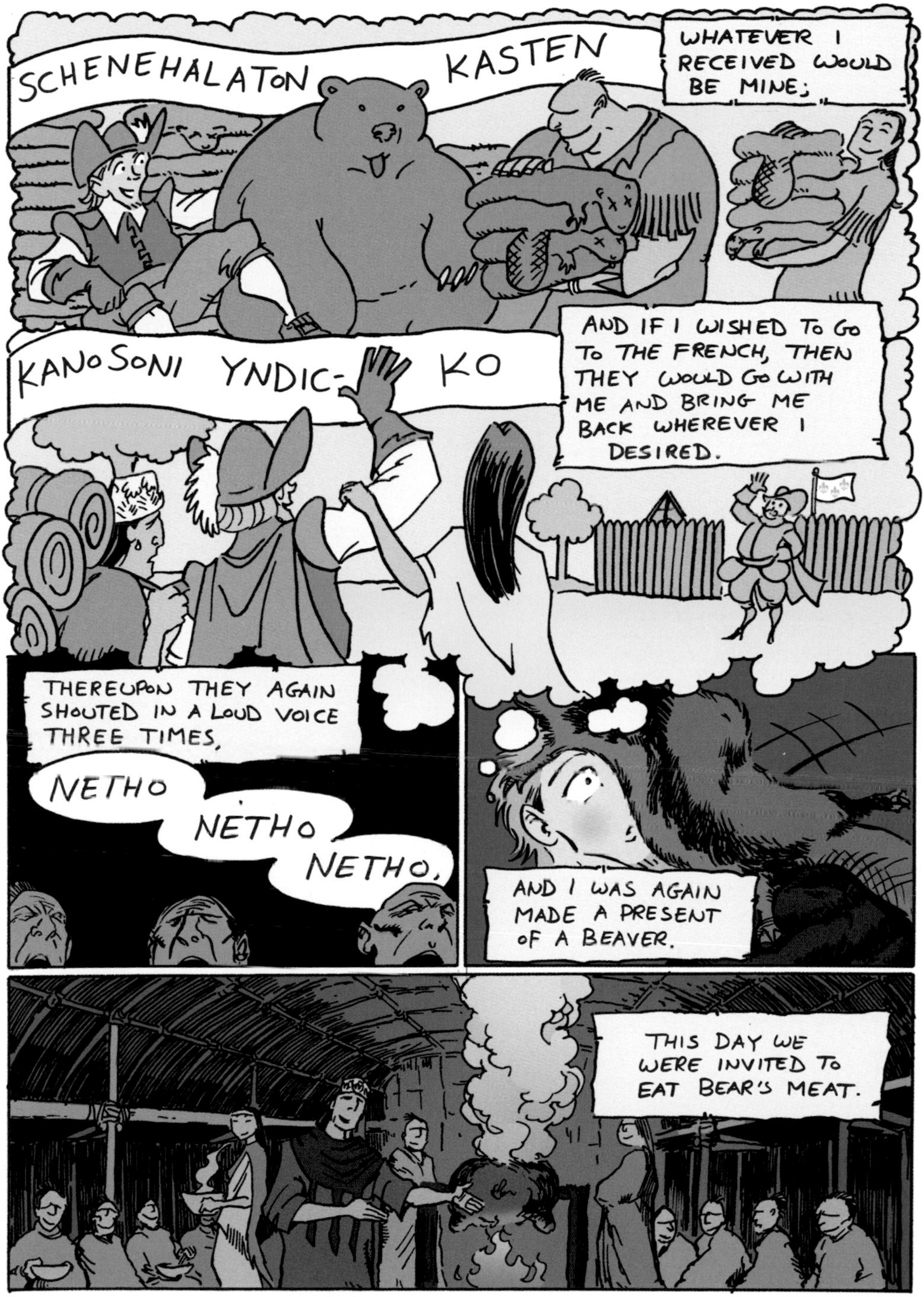
SCHENEHALATON KASTEN
WHATEVER I RECEIVED WOULD BE MINE;
KANOSONI YNDIC-KO
AND IF I WISHED TO GO TO THE FRENCH, THEN THEY WOULD GO WITH ME AND BRING ME BACK WHEREVER I DESIRED.
THEREUPON THEY AGAIN SHOUTED IN A LOUD VOICE THREE TIMES,
NETHO
NETHO
NETHO.
AND I WAS AGAIN MADE A PRESENT OF A BEAVER.
THIS DAY WE WERE INVITED TO EAT BEAR'S MEAT.

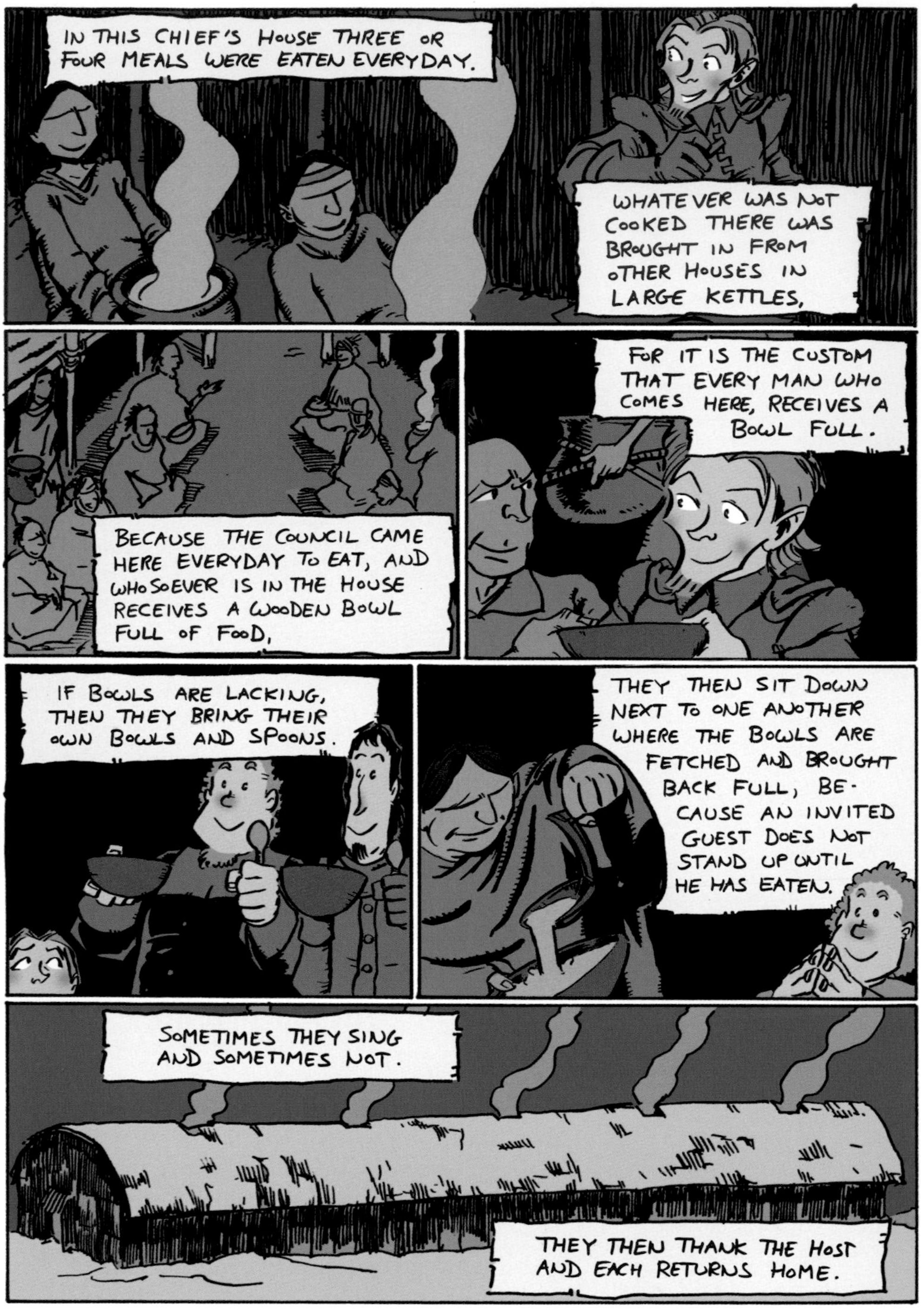
IN THIS CHIEF'S HOUSE THREE OR FOUR MEALS WERE EATEN EVERYDAY.
WHATEVER WAS NOT COOKED THERE WAS BROUGHT IN FROM OTHER HOUSES IN LARGE KETTLES,
BECAUSE THE COUNCIL CAME HERE EVERYDAY TO EAT, AND WHOSOEVER IS IN THE HOUSE RECEIVES A WOODEN BOWL FULL OF FOOD,
FOR IT IS THE CUSTOM THAT EVERY MAN WHO COMES HERE, RECEIVES A BOWL FULL.
IF BOWLS ARE LACKING, THEN THEY BRING THEIR OWN BOWLS AND SPOONS.
THEY THEN SIT DOWN NEXT TO ONE ANOTHER WHERE THE BOWLS ARE FETCHED AND BROUGHT BACK FULL, BE-CAUSE AN INVITED GUEST DOES NOT STAND UP UNTIL HE HAS EATEN.
SOMETIMES THEY SING AND SOMETIMES NOT.
THEY THEN THANK THE HOST AND EACH RETURNS HOME.

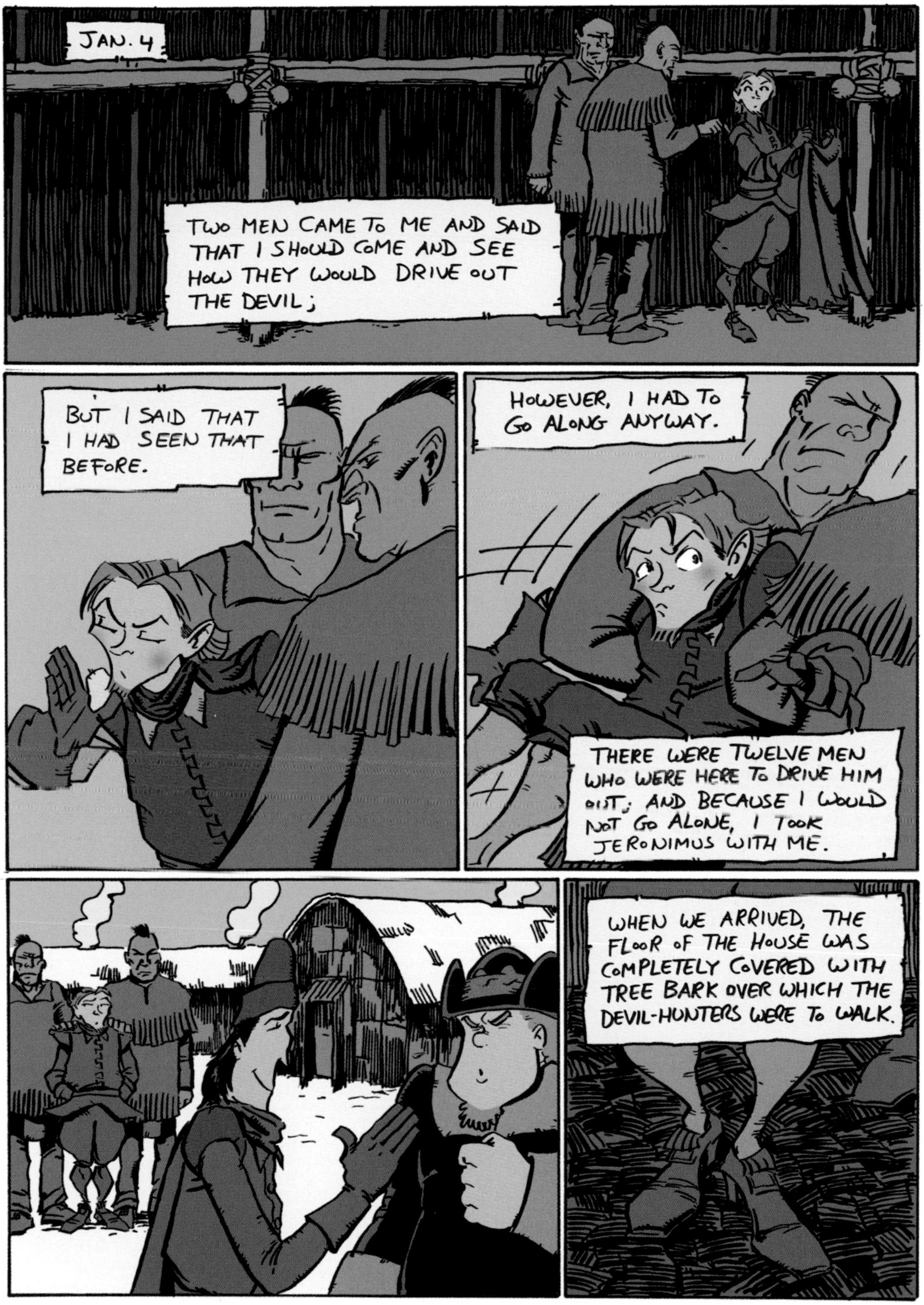
JAN. 4
TWO MEN CAME TO ME AND SAID THAT I SHOULD COME AND SEE HOW THEY WOULD DRIVE OUT THE DEVIL;
BUT I SAID THAT I HAD SEEN THAT BEFORE.
HOWEVER, I HAD TO GO ALONG ANYWAY.
THERE WERE TWELVE MEN WHO WERE HERE TO DRIVE HIM OUT; AND BECAUSE I WOULD NOT GO ALONE, I TOOK JERONIMUS WITH ME.
WHEN WE ARRIVED, THE FLOOR OF THE HOUSE WAS COMPLETELY COVERED WITH TREE BARK OVER WHICH THE DEVIL-HUNTERS WERE TO WALK.

THEY WERE MOSTLY OLD MEN WHO WERE ALL COLORED OR PAINTED WITH RED PAINT ON THEIR FACES

BECAUSE THEY WERE TO PERFORM SOME-THING STRANGE.

THREE OF THEM HAD GARLANDS AROUND THEIR HEADS UPON WHICH WERE FIVE WHITE CROSSES.

THESE GARLANDS WERE MADE OF DEER'S HAIR WHICH THEY DYED WITH THE ROOTS OF HERBS.

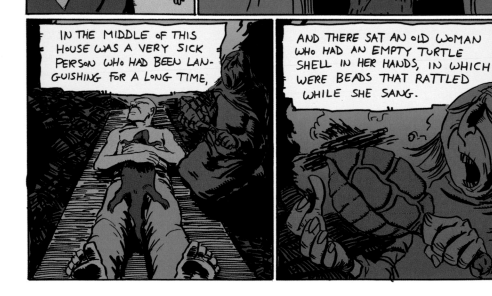

IN THE MIDDLE OF THIS HOUSE WAS A VERY SICK PERSON WHO HAD BEEN LAN-GUISHING FOR A LONG TIME,

AND THERE SAT AN OLD WOMAN WHO HAD AN EMPTY TURTLE SHELL IN HER HANDS, IN WHICH WERE BEADS THAT RATTLED WHILE SHE SANG.

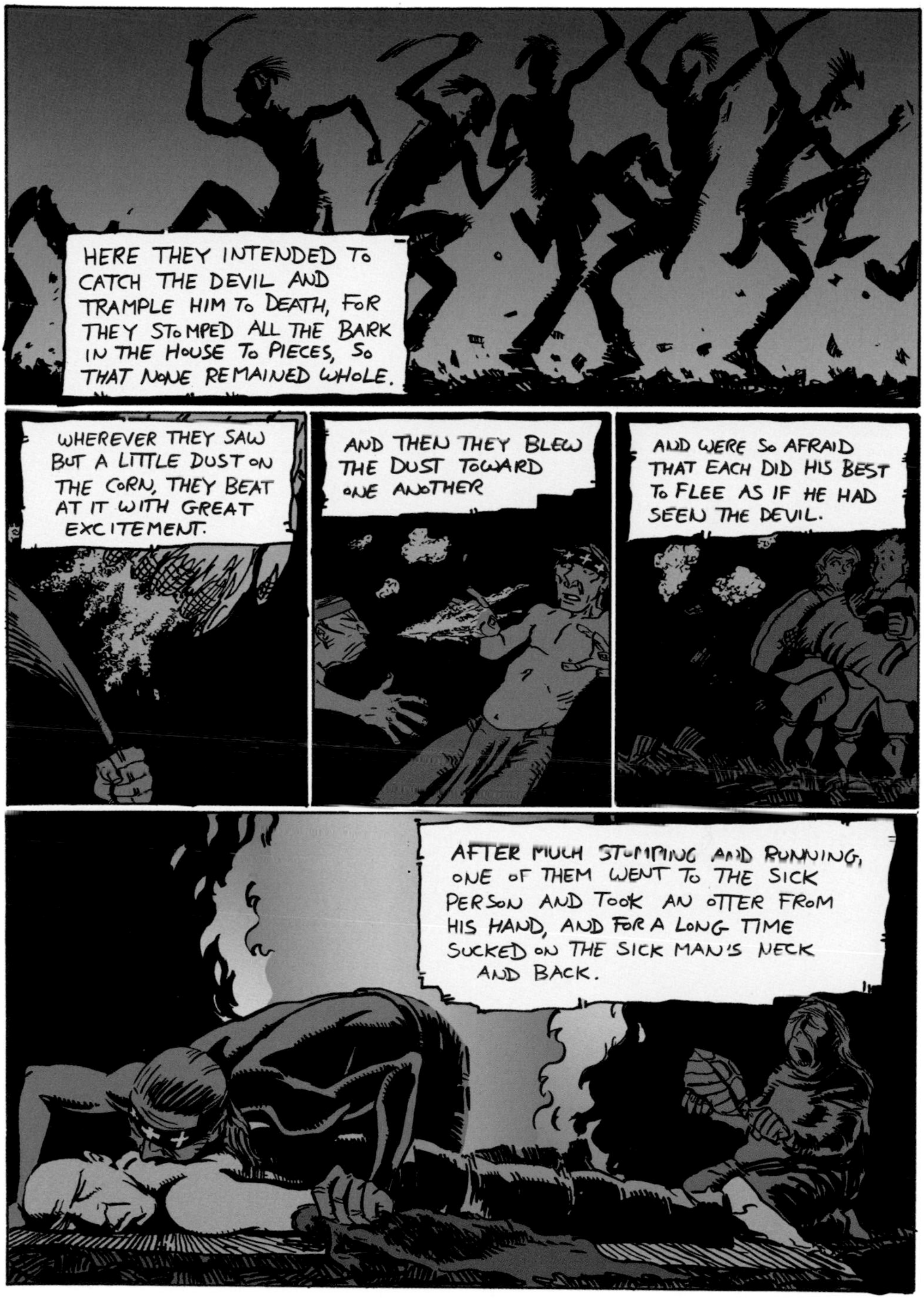
HERE THEY INTENDED TO CATCH THE DEVIL AND TRAMPLE HIM TO DEATH, FOR THEY STOMPED ALL THE BARK IN THE HOUSE TO PIECES, SO THAT NONE REMAINED WHOLE.
WHEREVER THEY SAW BUT A LITTLE DUST ON THE CORN, THEY BEAT AT IT WITH GREAT EXCITEMENT.
AND THEN THEY BLEW THE DUST TOWARD ONE ANOTHER
AND WERE SO AFRAID THAT EACH DID HIS BEST TO FLEE AS IF HE HAD SEEN THE DEVIL.
AFTER MUCH STOMPING AND RUNNING, ONE OF THEM WENT TO THE SICK PERSON AND TOOK AN OTTER FROM HIS HAND, AND FOR A LONG TIME SUCKED ON THE SICK MAN'S NECK AND BACK.

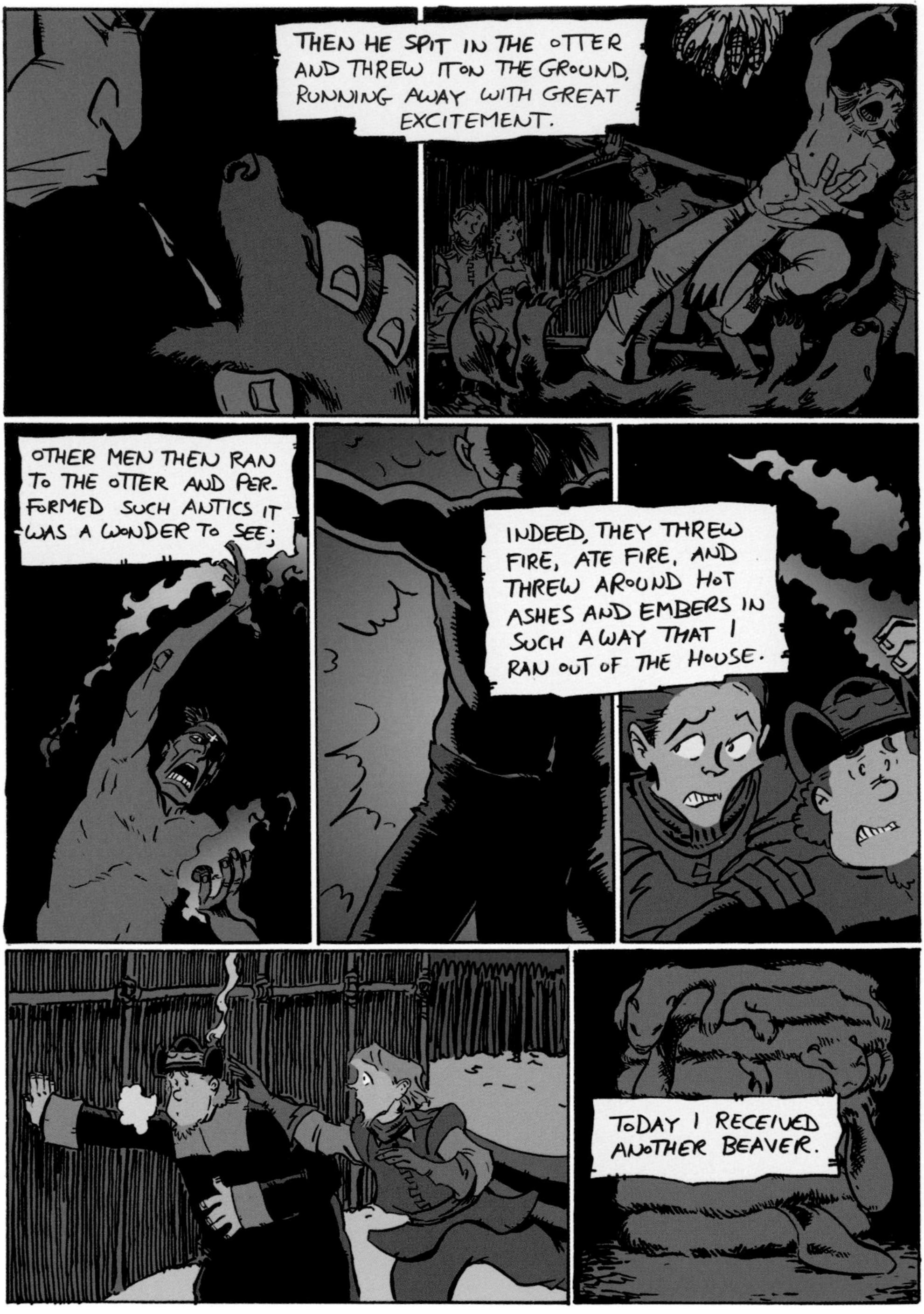
THEN HE SPIT IN THE OTTER AND THREW IT ON THE GROUND, RUNNING AWAY WITH GREAT EXCITEMENT.
OTHER MEN THEN RAN TO THE OTTER AND PERFORMED SUCH ANTICS IT WAS A WONDER TO SEE;
INDEED, THEY THREW FIRE, ATE FIRE, AND THREW AROUND HOT ASHES AND EMBERS IN SUCH A WAY THAT I RAN OUT OF THE HOUSE.
TODAY I RECEIVED ANOTHER BEAVER.

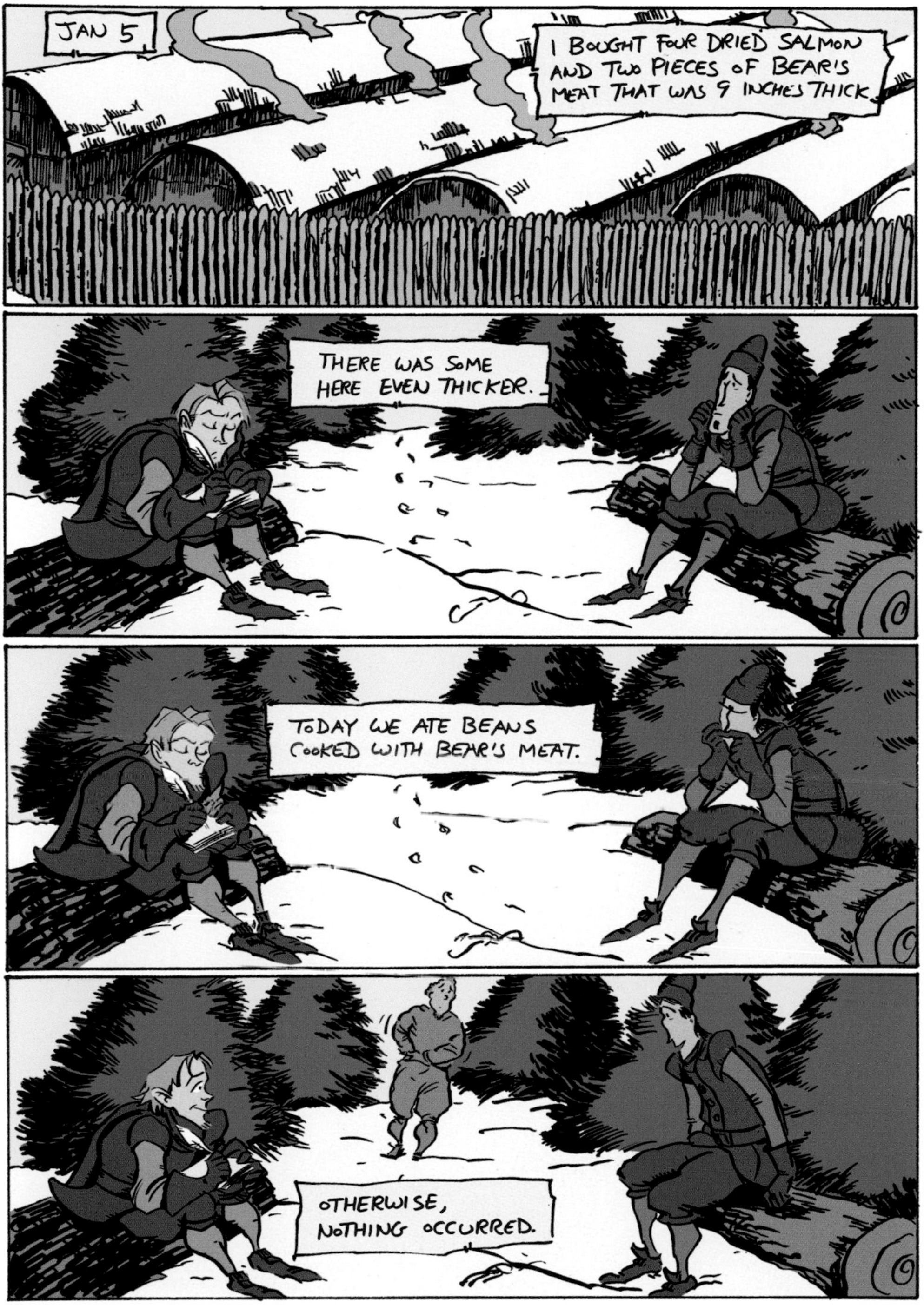
JAN 5
I BOUGHT FOUR DRIED SALMON AND TWO PIECES OF BEAR'S MEAT THAT WAS 9 INCHES THICK.
THERE WAS SOME HERE EVEN THICKER.
TODAY WE ATE BEANS COOKED WITH BEAR'S MEAT.
OTHERWISE, NOTHING OCCURRED.

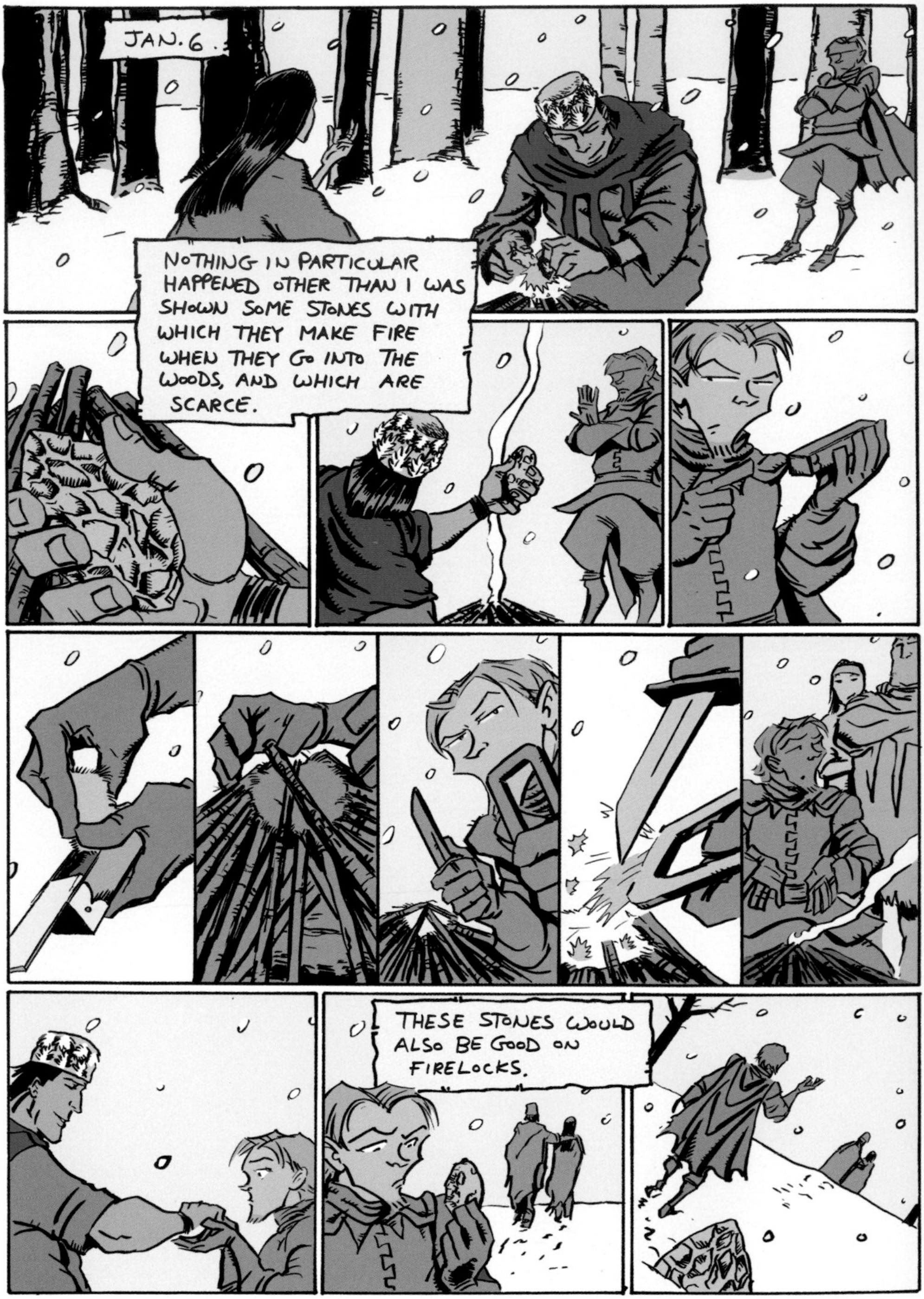
JAN. 6.
NOTHING IN PARTICULAR HAPPENED OTHER THAN I WAS SHOWN SOME STONES WITH WHICH THEY MAKE FIRE WHEN THEY GO INTO THE WOODS, AND WHICH ARE SCARCE.
THESE STONES WOULD ALSO BE GOOD ON FIRELOCKS.

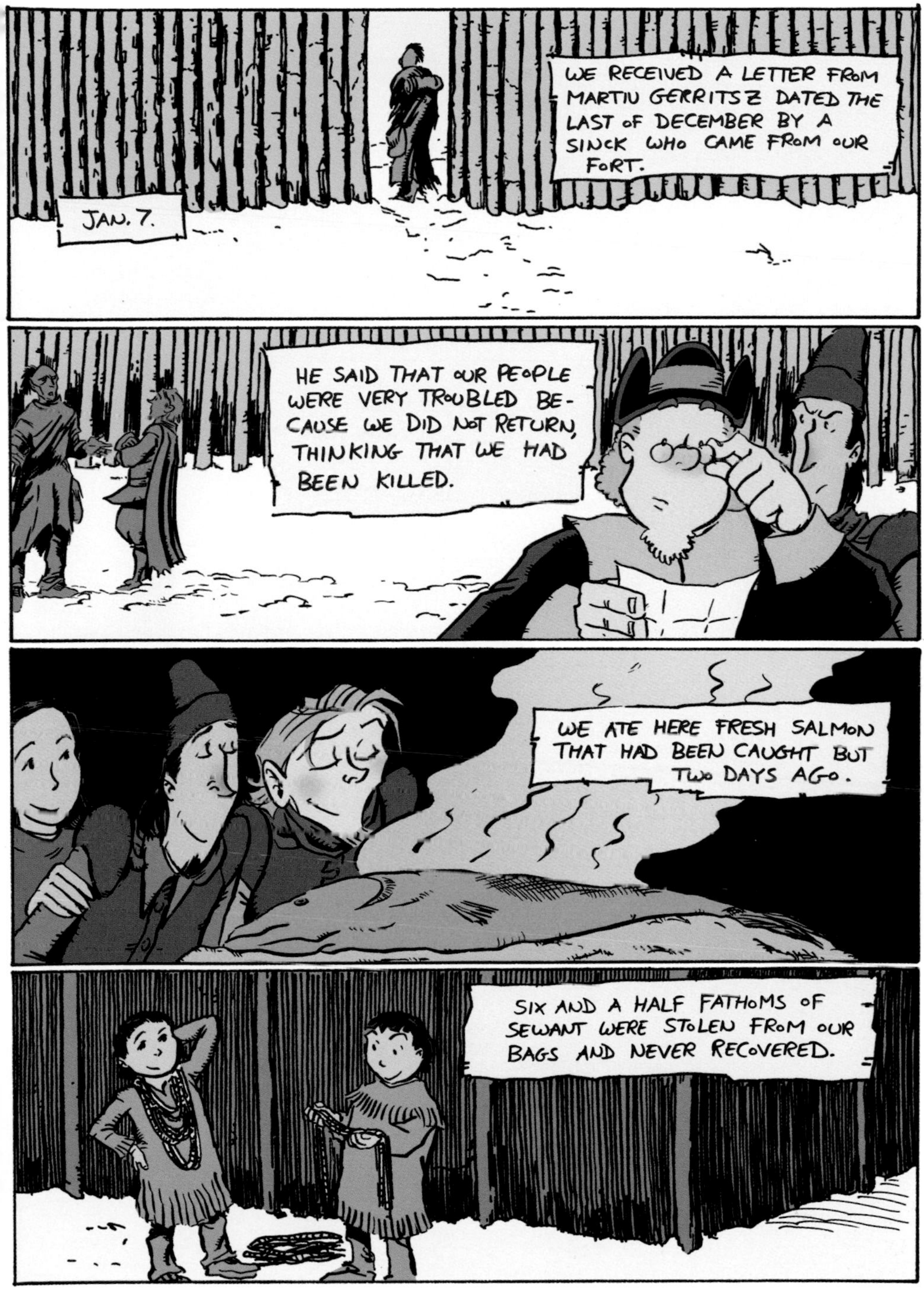
JAN. 7.
WE RECEIVED A LETTER FROM MARTIU GERRITSZ DATED THE LAST OF DECEMBER BY A SINCK WHO CAME FROM OUR FORT.
HE SAID THAT OUR PEOPLE WERE VERY TROUBLED BECAUSE WE DID NOT RETURN, THINKING THAT WE HAD BEEN KILLED.
WE ATE HERE FRESH SALMON THAT HAD BEEN CAUGHT BUT TWO DAYS AGO.
SIX AND A HALF FATHOMS OF SEWANT WERE STOLEN FROM OUR BAGS AND NEVER RECOVERED.

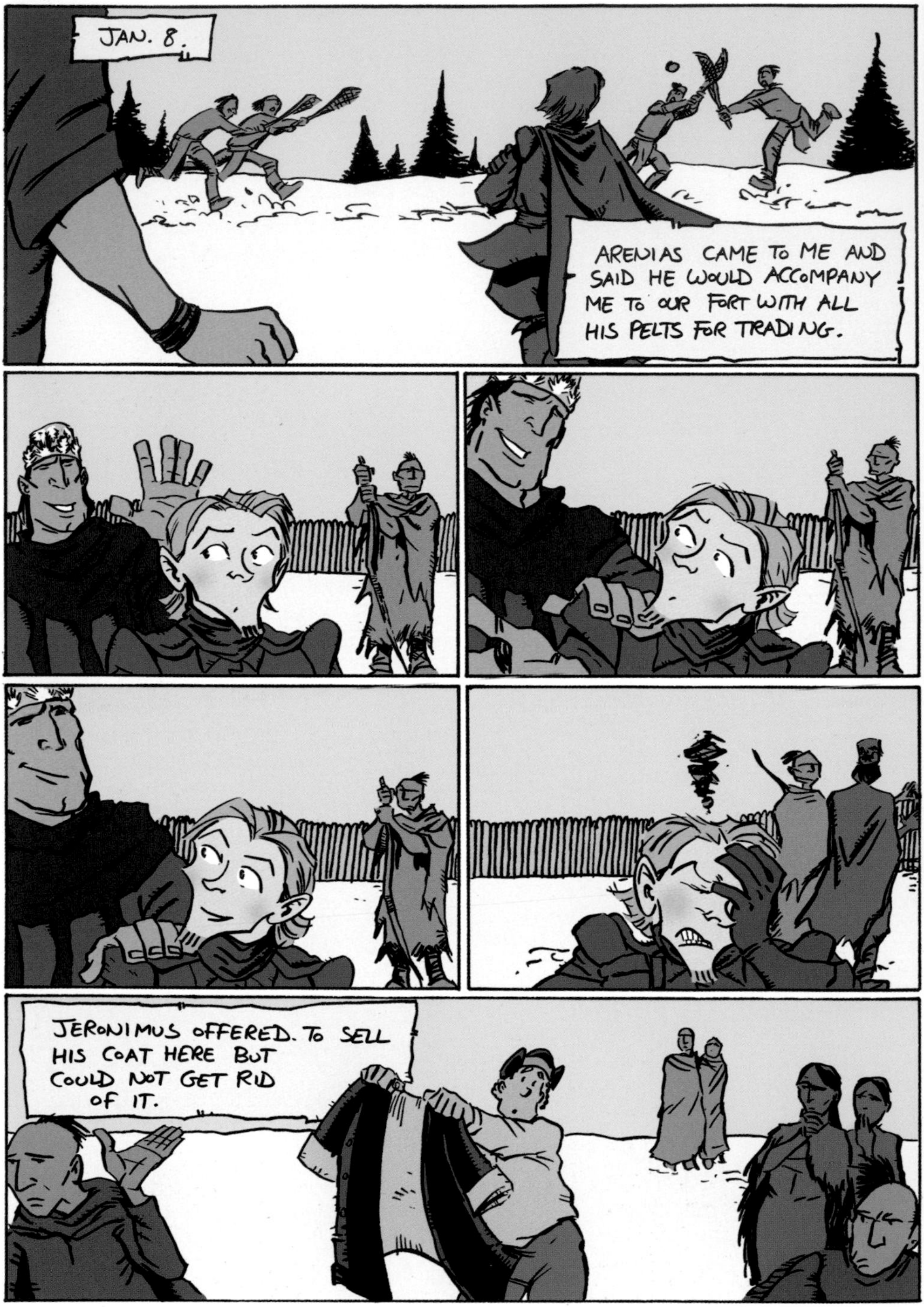
JAN. 8.
ARENIAS CAME TO ME AND SAID HE WOULD ACCOMPANY ME TO OUR FORT WITH ALL HIS PELTS FOR TRADING.
JERONIMUS OFFERED TO SELL HIS COAT HERE BUT COULD NOT GET RID OF IT.

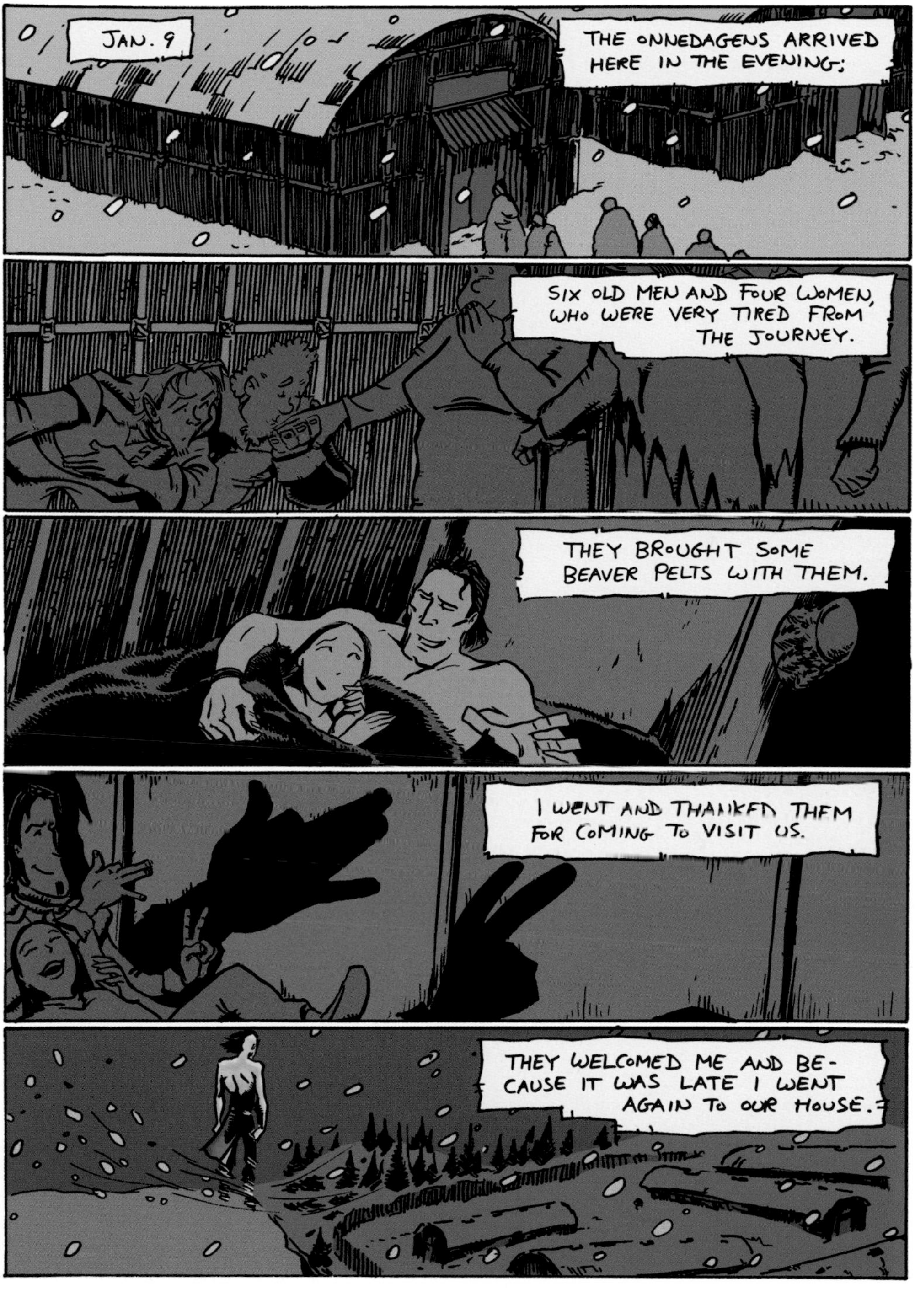
JAN. 9
THE ONNEDAGENS ARRIVED HERE IN THE EVENING;
SIX OLD MEN AND FOUR WOMEN, WHO WERE VERY TIRED FROM THE JOURNEY.
THEY BROUGHT SOME BEAVER PELTS WITH THEM.
I WENT AND THANKED THEM FOR COMING TO VISIT US.
THEY WELCOMED ME AND BE-CAUSE IT WAS LATE I WENT AGAIN TO OUR HOUSE.

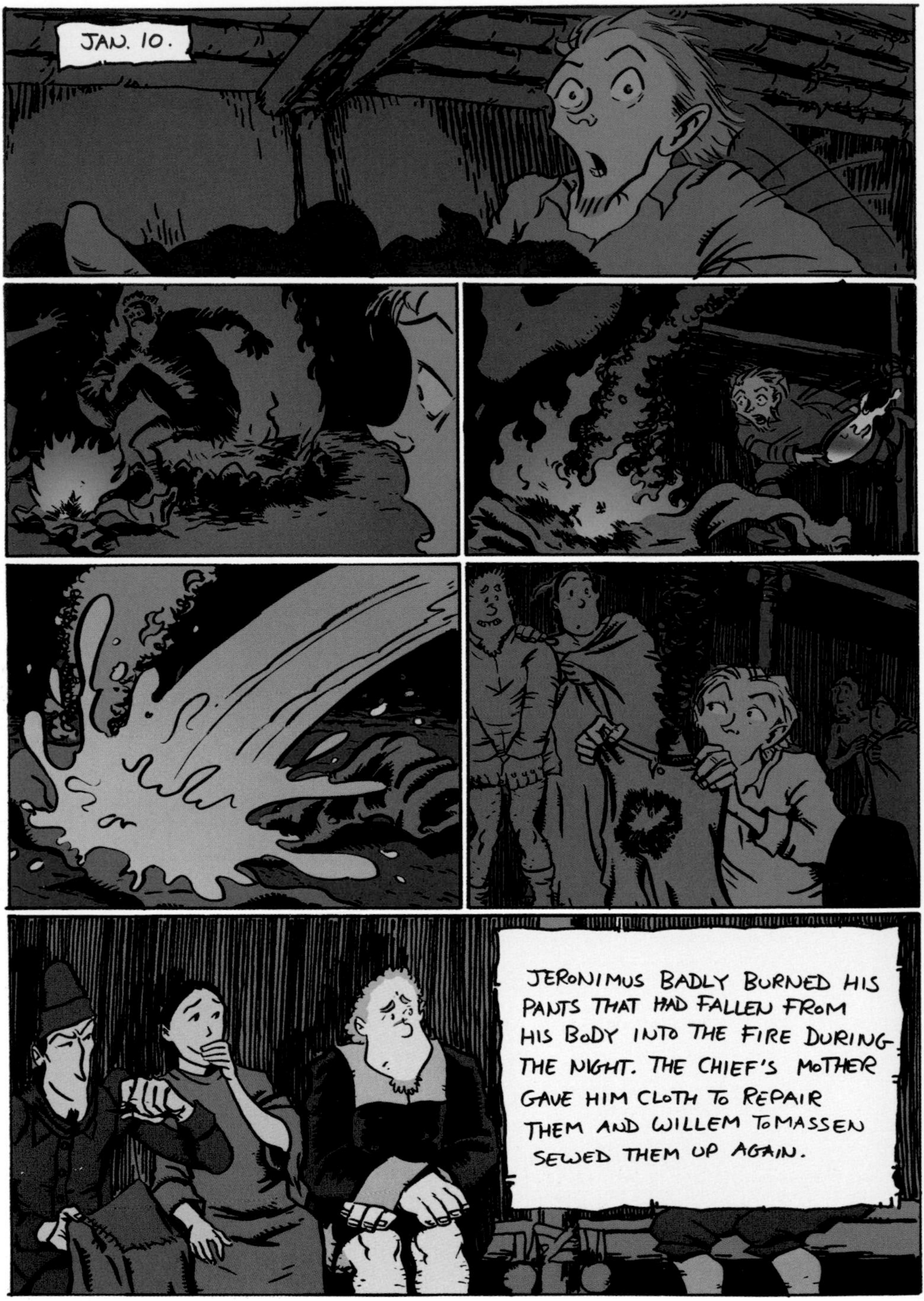
JAN. 10.
JERONIMUS BADLY BURNED HIS PANTS THAT HAD FALLEN FROM HIS BODY INTO THE FIRE DURING THE NIGHT. THE CHIEF'S MOTHER GAVE HIM CLOTH TO REPAIR THEM AND WILLEM TOMASSEN SEWED THEM UP AGAIN.

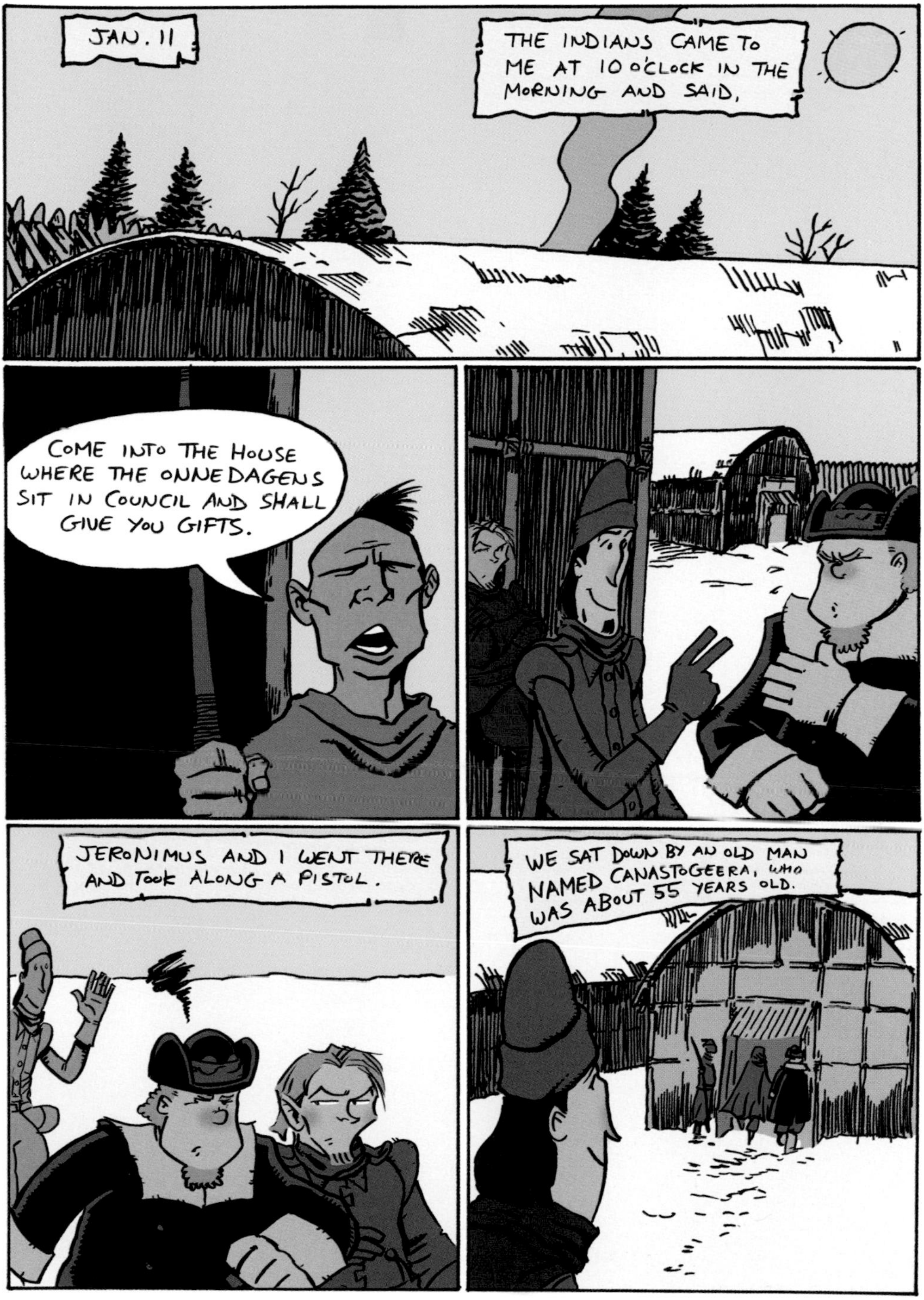
JAN. 11
THE INDIANS CAME TO ME AT 10 O'CLOCK IN THE MORNING AND SAID,
COME INTO THE HOUSE WHERE THE ONNEDAGENS SIT IN COUNCIL AND SHALL GIVE YOU GIFTS.
JERONIMUS AND I WENT THERE AND TOOK ALONG A PISTOL.
WE SAT DOWN BY AN OLD MAN NAMED CANASTOGEERA, WHO WAS ABOUT 55 YEARS OLD.

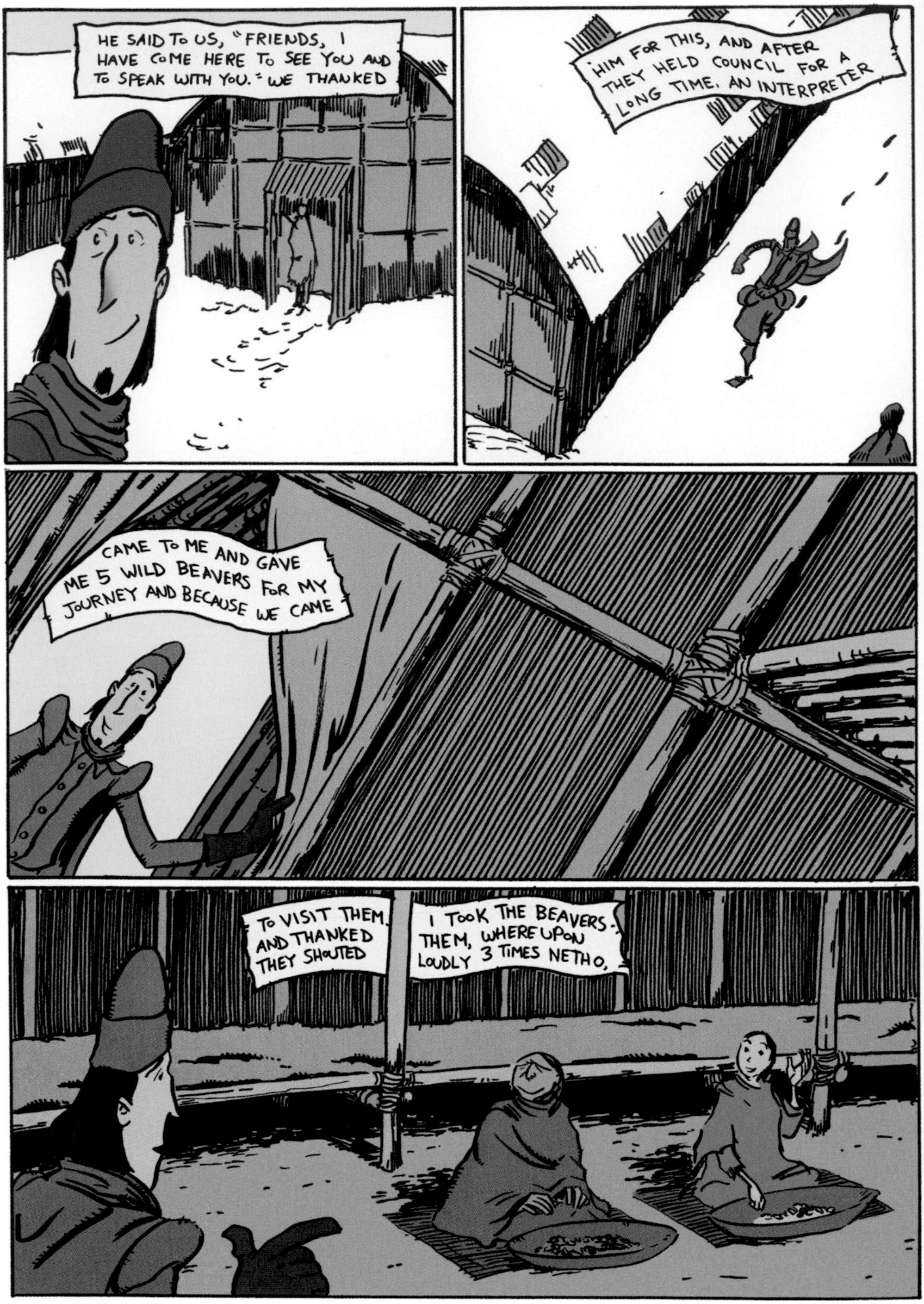
HE SAID TO US, "FRIENDS, I HAVE COME HERE TO SEE YOU AND TO SPEAK WITH YOU." WE THANKED
HIM FOR THIS, AND AFTER THEY HELD COUNCIL FOR A LONG TIME, AN INTERPRETER
CAME TO ME AND GAVE ME 5 WILD BEAVERS FOR MY JOURNEY AND BECAUSE WE CAME
TO VISIT THEM. AND THANKED THEY SHOUTED
I TOOK THE BEAVERS. THEM, WHEREUPON LOUDLY 3 TIMES NETHO,

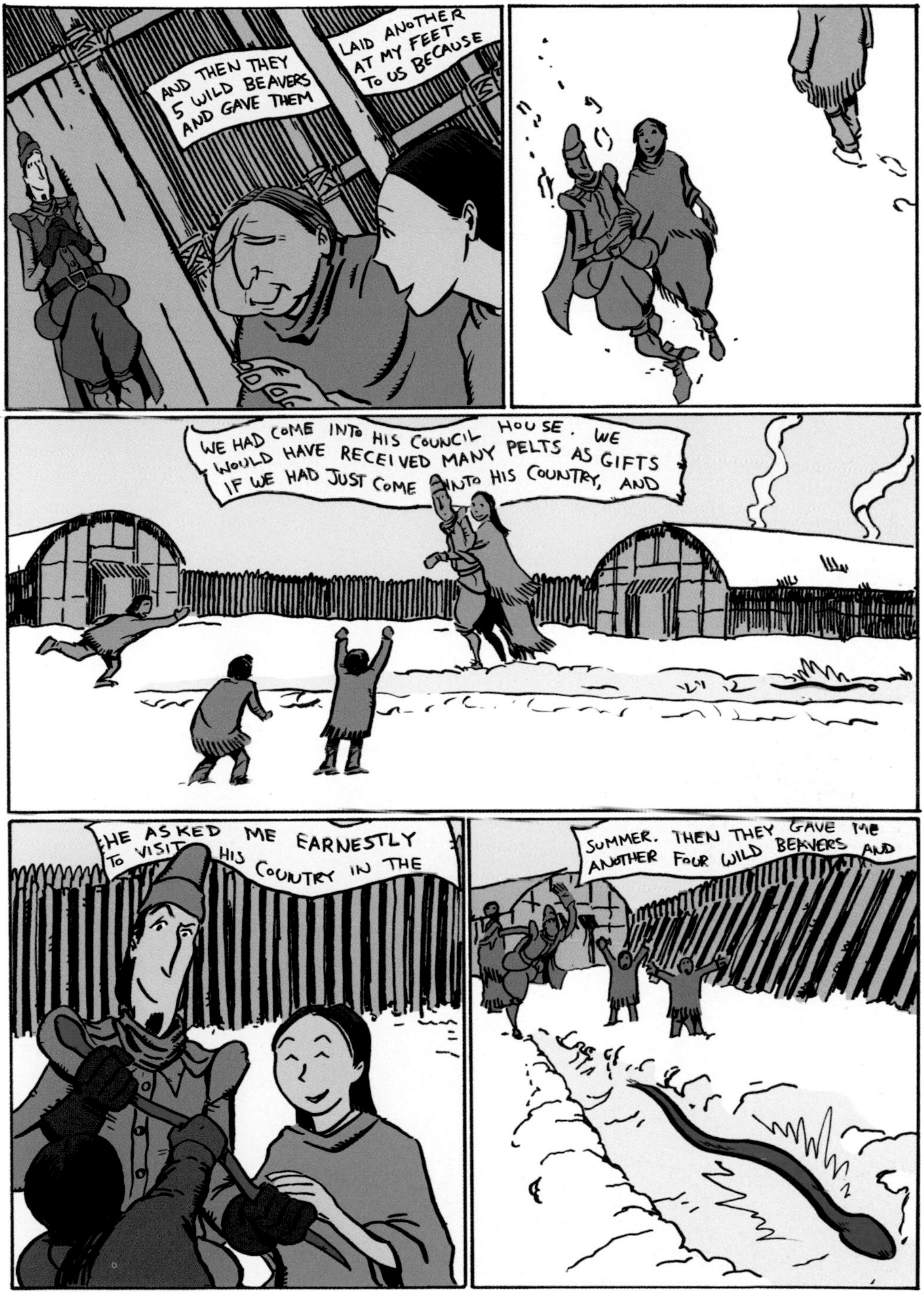
AND THEN THEY 5 WILD BEAVERS AND GAVE THEM
LAID ANOTHER AT MY FEET TO US BECAUSE
WE HAD COME INTO HIS COUNCIL HOUSE. WE WOULD HAVE RECEIVED MANY PELTS AS GIFTS IF WE HAD JUST COME INTO HIS COUNTRY, AND
HE ASKED ME EARNESTLY TO VISIT HIS COUNTRY IN THE
SUMMER. THEN THEY GAVE ME ANOTHER FOUR WILD BEAVERS AND

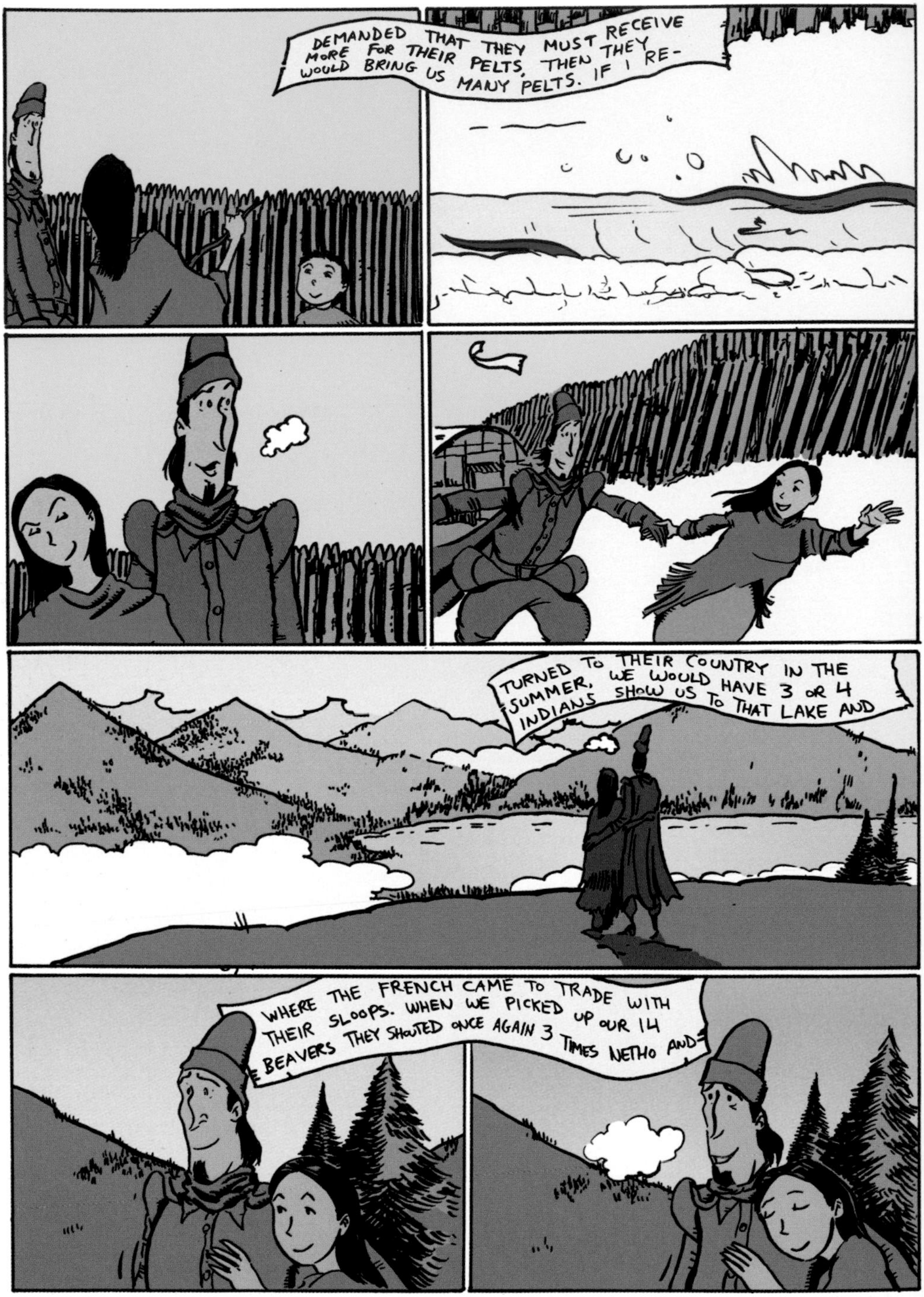
DEMANDED THAT THEY MUST RECEIVE MORE FOR THEIR PELTS, THEN THEY WOULD BRING US MANY PELTS. IF I RE-
TURNED TO THEIR COUNTRY IN THE SUMMER, WE WOULD HAVE 3 OR 4 INDIANS SHOW US TO THAT LAKE AND
WHERE THE FRENCH CAME TO TRADE WITH THEIR SLOOPS. WHEN WE PICKED UP OUR 14 BEAVERS THEY SHOUTED ONCE AGAIN 3 TIMES NETHO AND

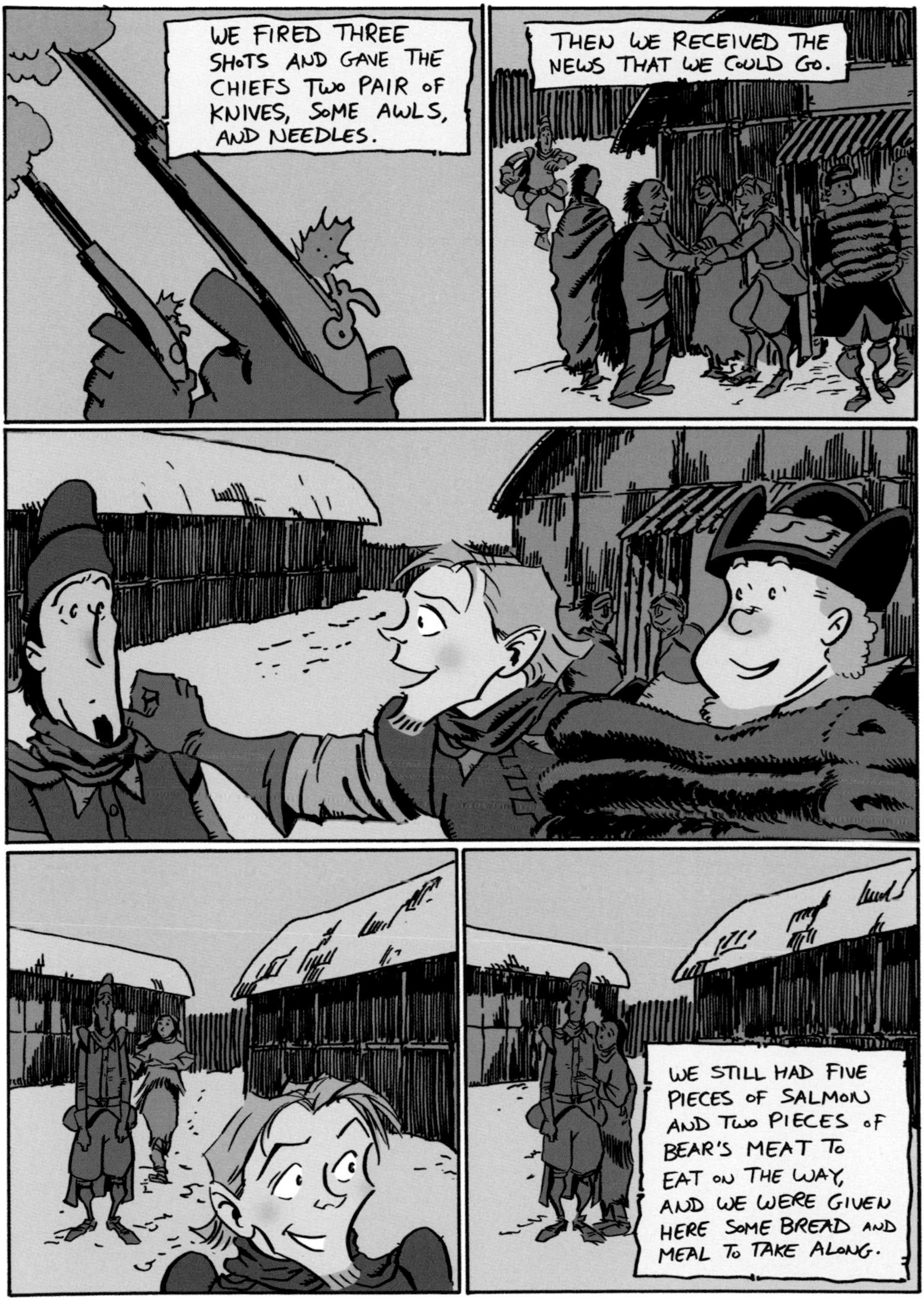
WE FIRED THREE SHOTS AND GAVE THE CHIEFS TWO PAIR OF KNIVES, SOME AWLS, AND NEEDLES.
THEN WE RECEIVED THE NEWS THAT WE COULD GO.
WE STILL HAD FIVE PIECES OF SALMON AND TWO PIECES OF BEAR'S MEAT TO EAT ON THE WAY, AND WE WERE GIVEN HERE SOME BREAD AND MEAL TO TAKE ALONG.

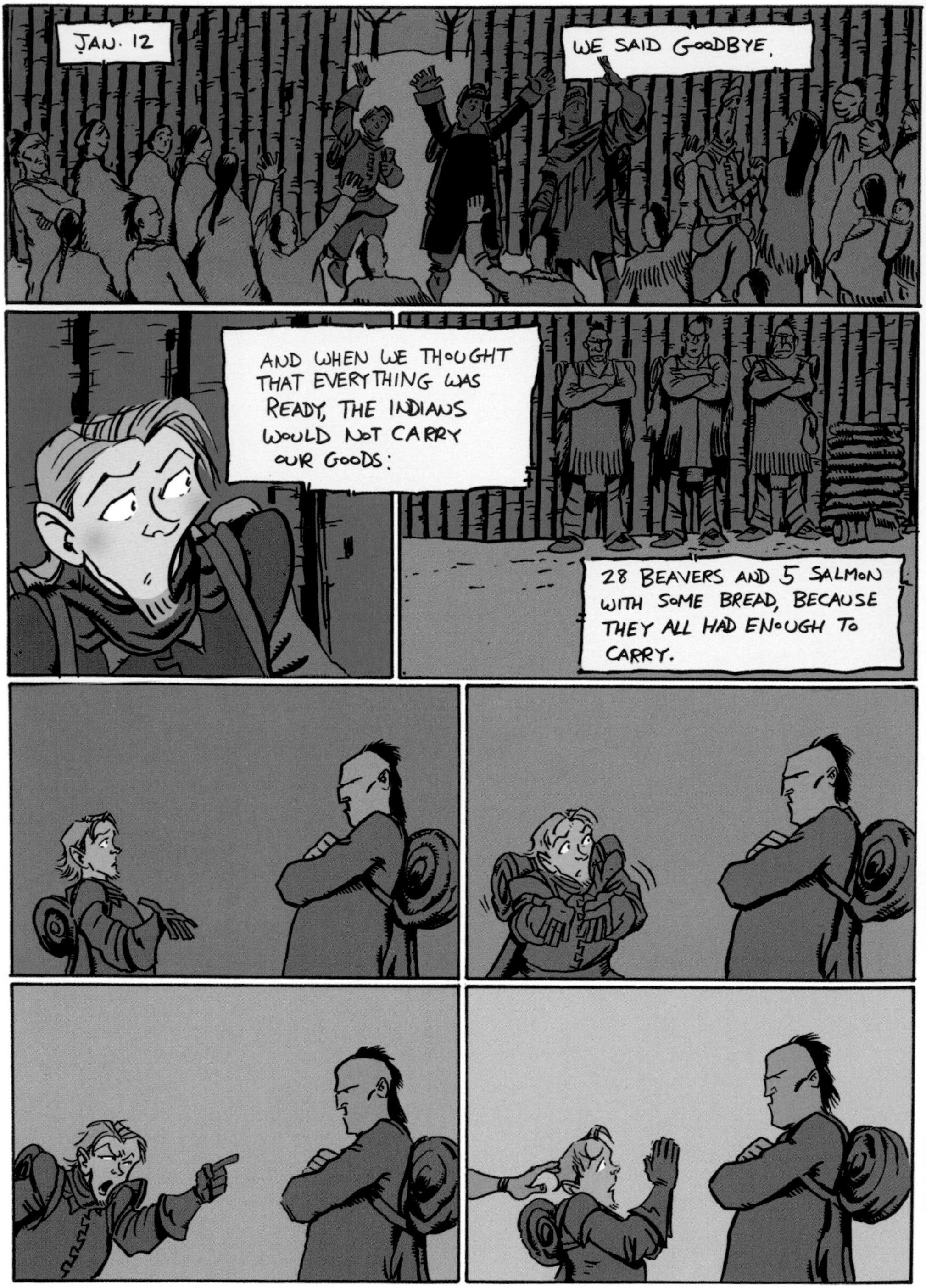
JAN. 12
WE SAID GOODBYE.
AND WHEN WE THOUGHT THAT EVERYTHING WAS READY, THE INDIANS WOULD NOT CARRY OUR GOODS:
28 BEAVERS AND 5 SALMON WITH SOME BREAD, BECAUSE THEY ALL HAD ENOUGH TO CARRY.

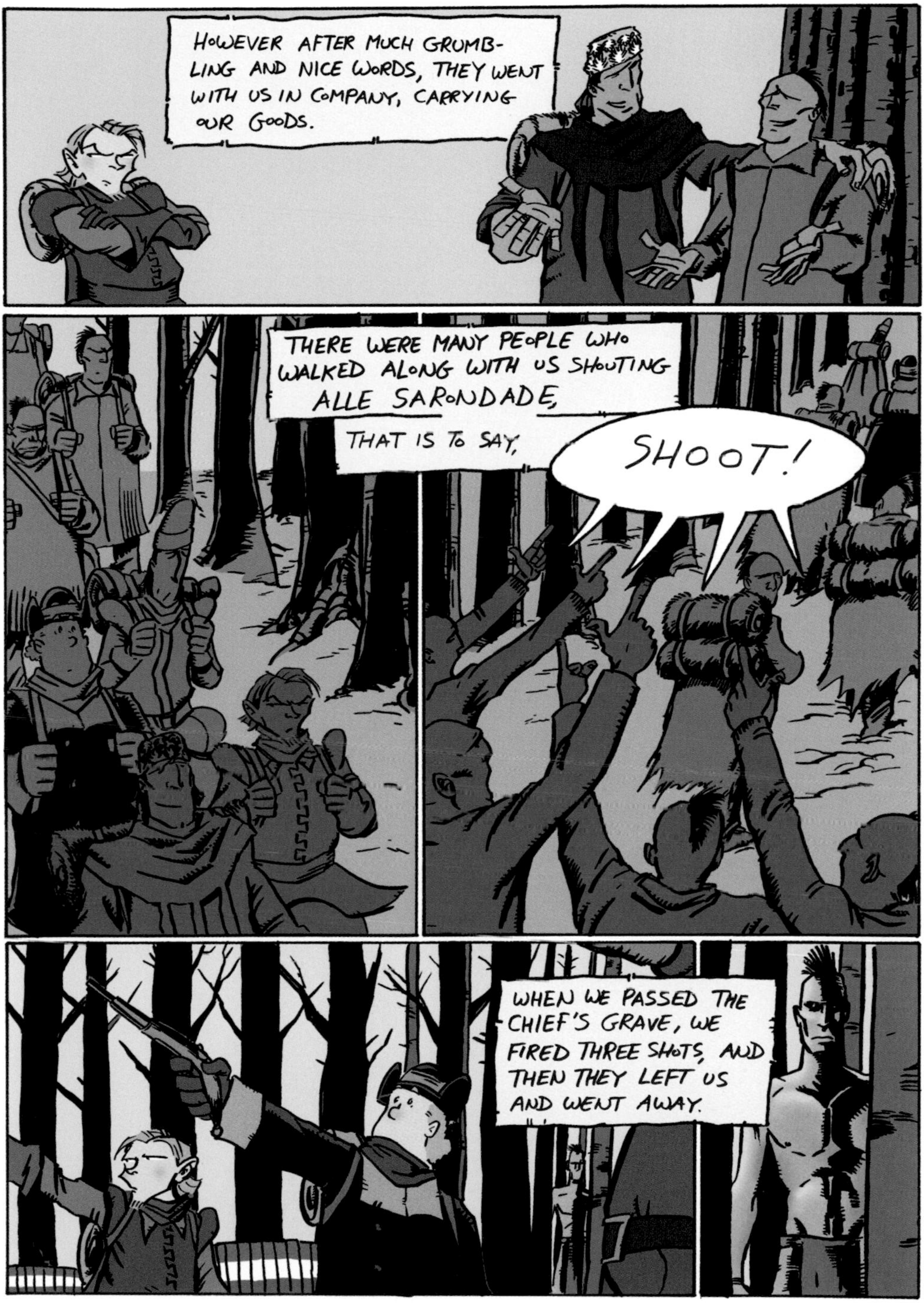
HOWEVER AFTER MUCH GRUMBLING AND NICE WORDS, THEY WENT WITH US IN COMPANY, CARRYING OUR GOODS.
THERE WERE MANY PEOPLE WHO WALKED ALONG WITH US SHOUTING ALLE SARONDADE,
THAT IS TO SAY,
SHOOT!
WHEN WE PASSED THE CHIEF'S GRAVE, WE FIRED THREE SHOTS, AND THEN THEY LEFT US AND WENT AWAY.

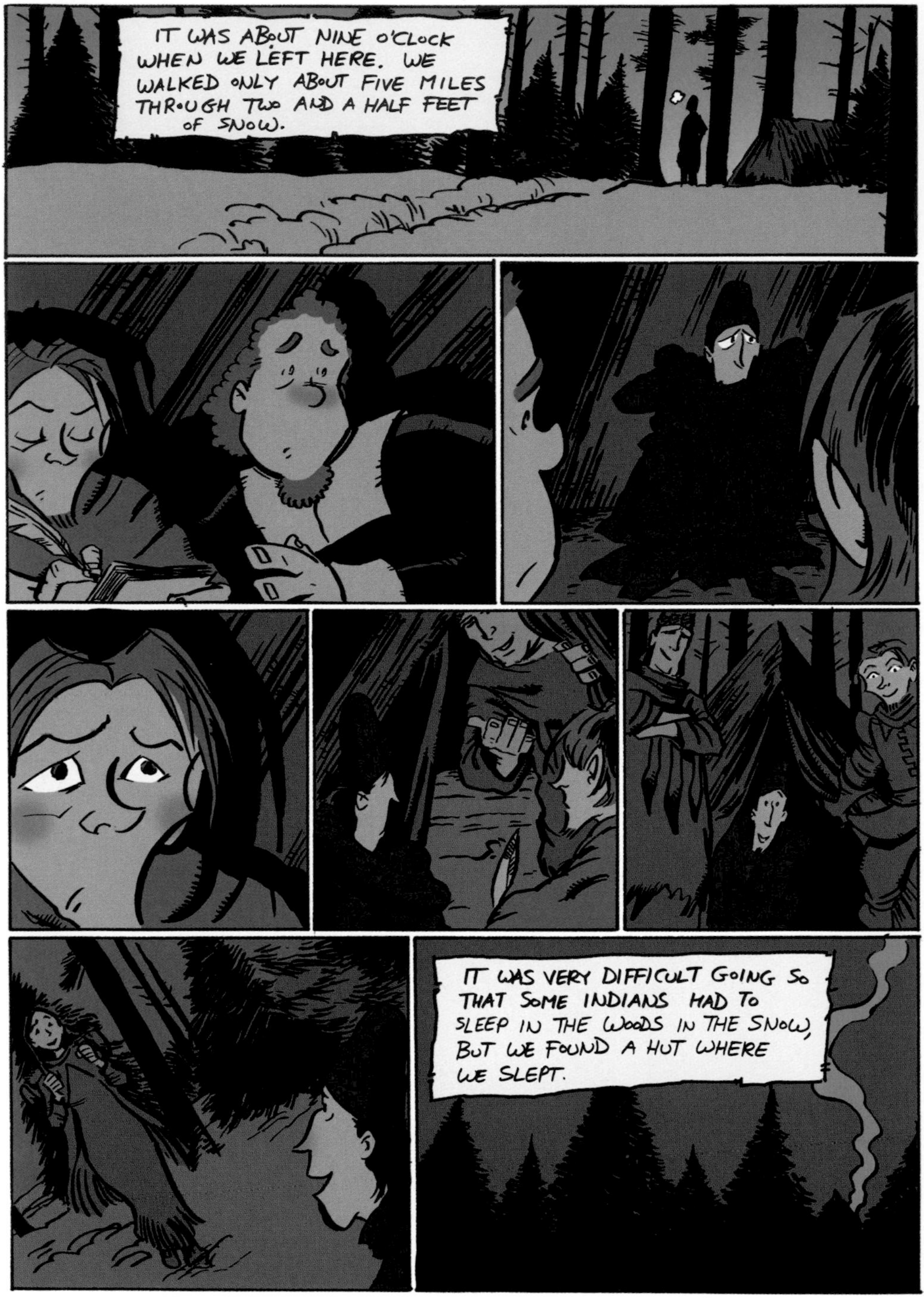
IT WAS ABOUT NINE O'CLOCK WHEN WE LEFT HERE. WE WALKED ONLY ABOUT FIVE MILES THROUGH TWO AND A HALF FEET OF SNOW.
IT WAS VERY DIFFICULT GOING SO THAT SOME INDIANS HAD TO SLEEP IN THE WOODS IN THE SNOW, BUT WE FOUND A HUT WHERE WE SLEPT.

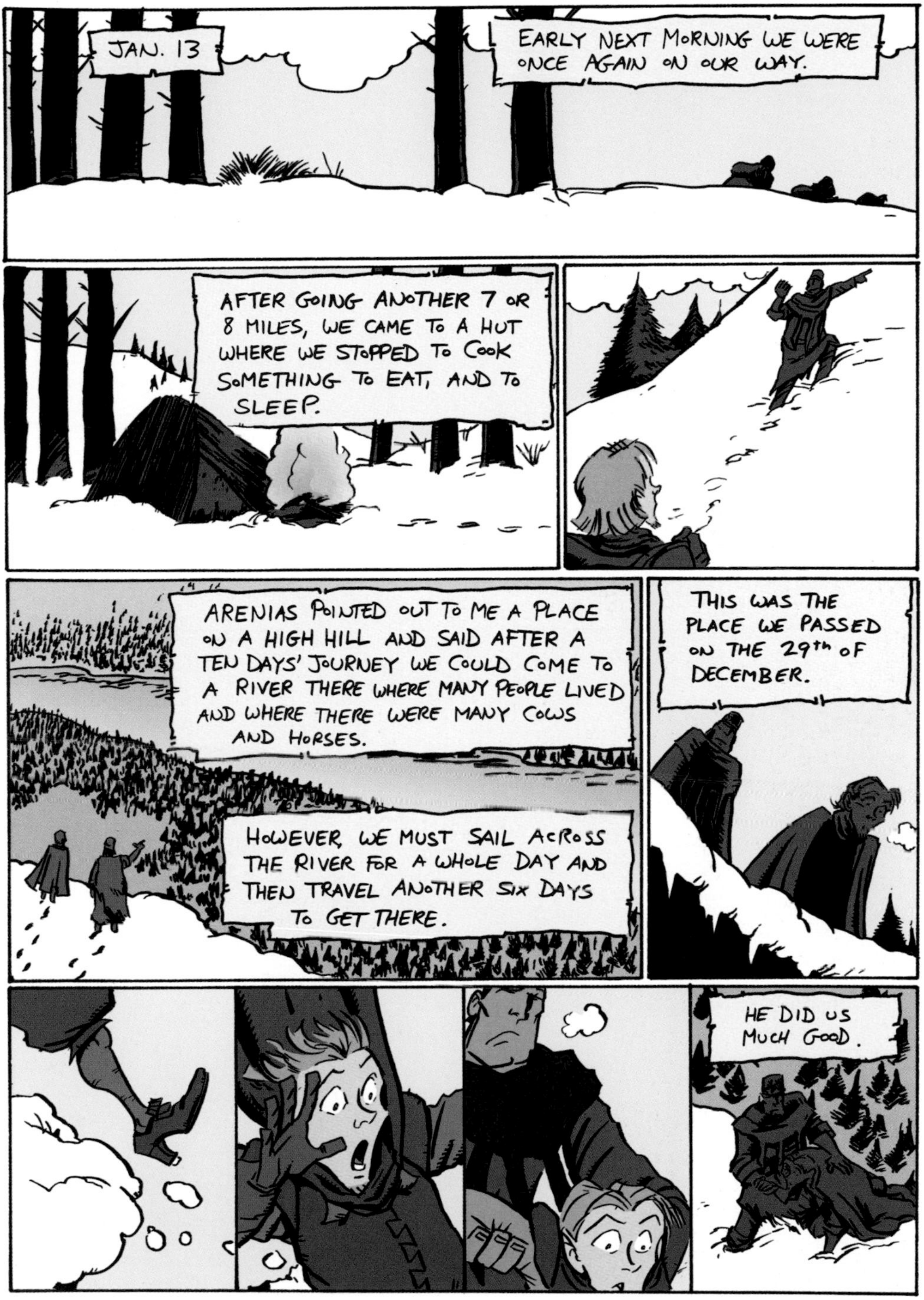
JAN. 13
EARLY NEXT MORNING WE WERE ONCE AGAIN ON OUR WAY.
AFTER GOING ANOTHER 7 OR 8 MILES, WE CAME TO A HUT WHERE WE STOPPED TO COOK SOMETHING TO EAT, AND TO SLEEP.
ARENIAS POINTED OUT TO ME A PLACE ON A HIGH HILL AND SAID AFTER A TEN DAYS' JOURNEY WE COULD COME TO A RIVER THERE WHERE MANY PEOPLE LIVED AND WHERE THERE WERE MANY COWS AND HORSES.
HOWEVER, WE MUST SAIL ACROSS THE RIVER FOR A WHOLE DAY AND THEN TRAVEL ANOTHER SIX DAYS TO GET THERE.
THIS WAS THE PLACE WE PASSED ON THE 29th OF DECEMBER.
HE DID US MUCH GOOD.

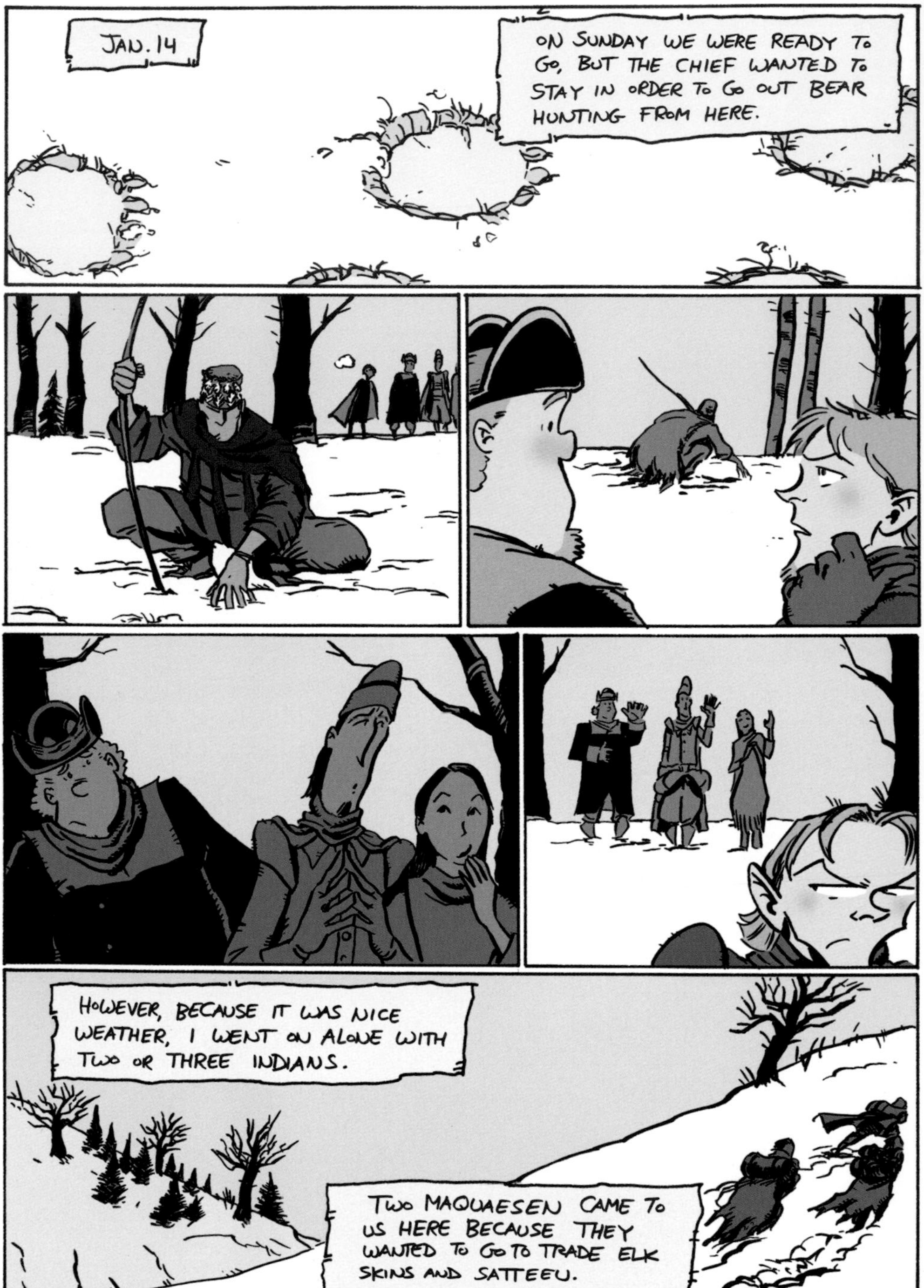
JAN. 14
ON SUNDAY WE WERE READY TO GO, BUT THE CHIEF WANTED TO STAY IN ORDER TO GO OUT BEAR HUNTING FROM HERE.
HOWEVER, BECAUSE IT WAS NICE WEATHER, I WENT ON ALONE WITH TWO OR THREE INDIANS.
TWO MAQUAESEN CAME TO US HERE BECAUSE THEY WANTED TO GO TO TRADE ELK SKINS AND SATTEEU.

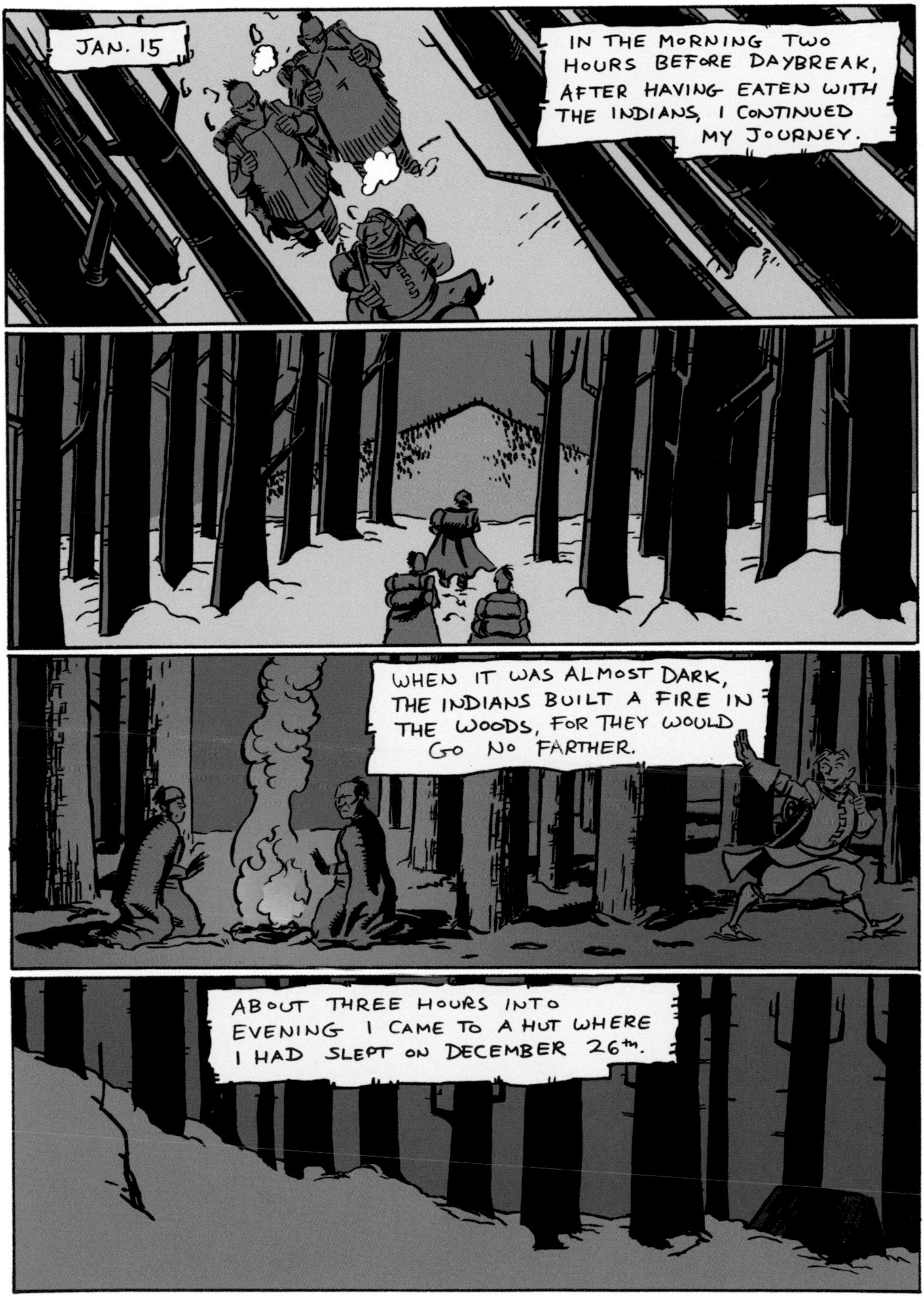
JAN. 15
IN THE MORNING TWO HOURS BEFORE DAYBREAK, AFTER HAVING EATEN WITH THE INDIANS, I CONTINUED MY JOURNEY.
WHEN IT WAS ALMOST DARK, THE INDIANS BUILT A FIRE IN THE WOODS, FOR THEY WOULD GO NO FARTHER.
ABOUT THREE HOURS INTO EVENING I CAME TO A HUT WHERE I HAD SLEPT ON DECEMBER 26th.

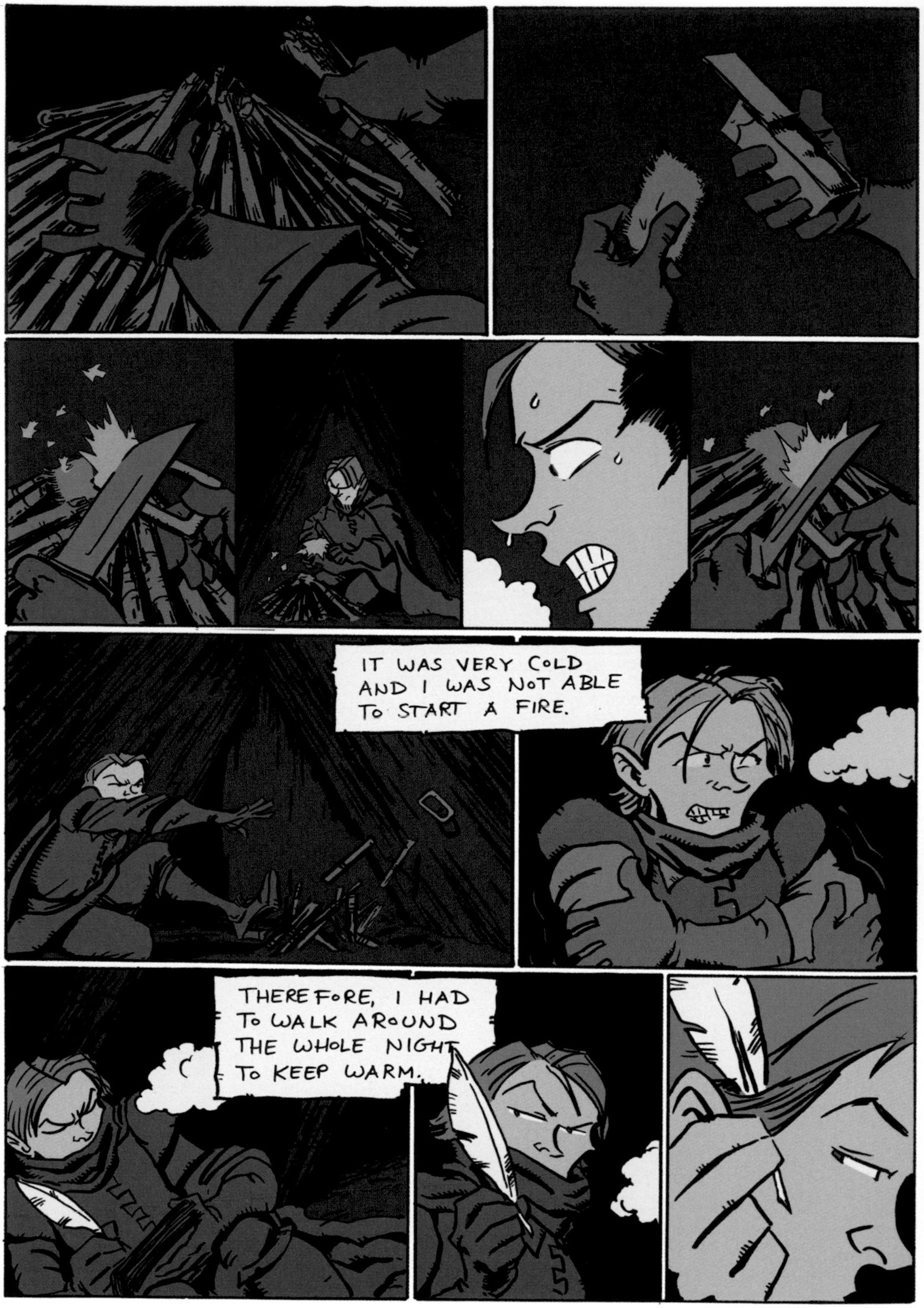
IT WAS VERY COLD AND I WAS NOT ABLE TO START A FIRE.
THEREFORE, I HAD TO WALK AROUND THE WHOLE NIGHT TO KEEP WARM.

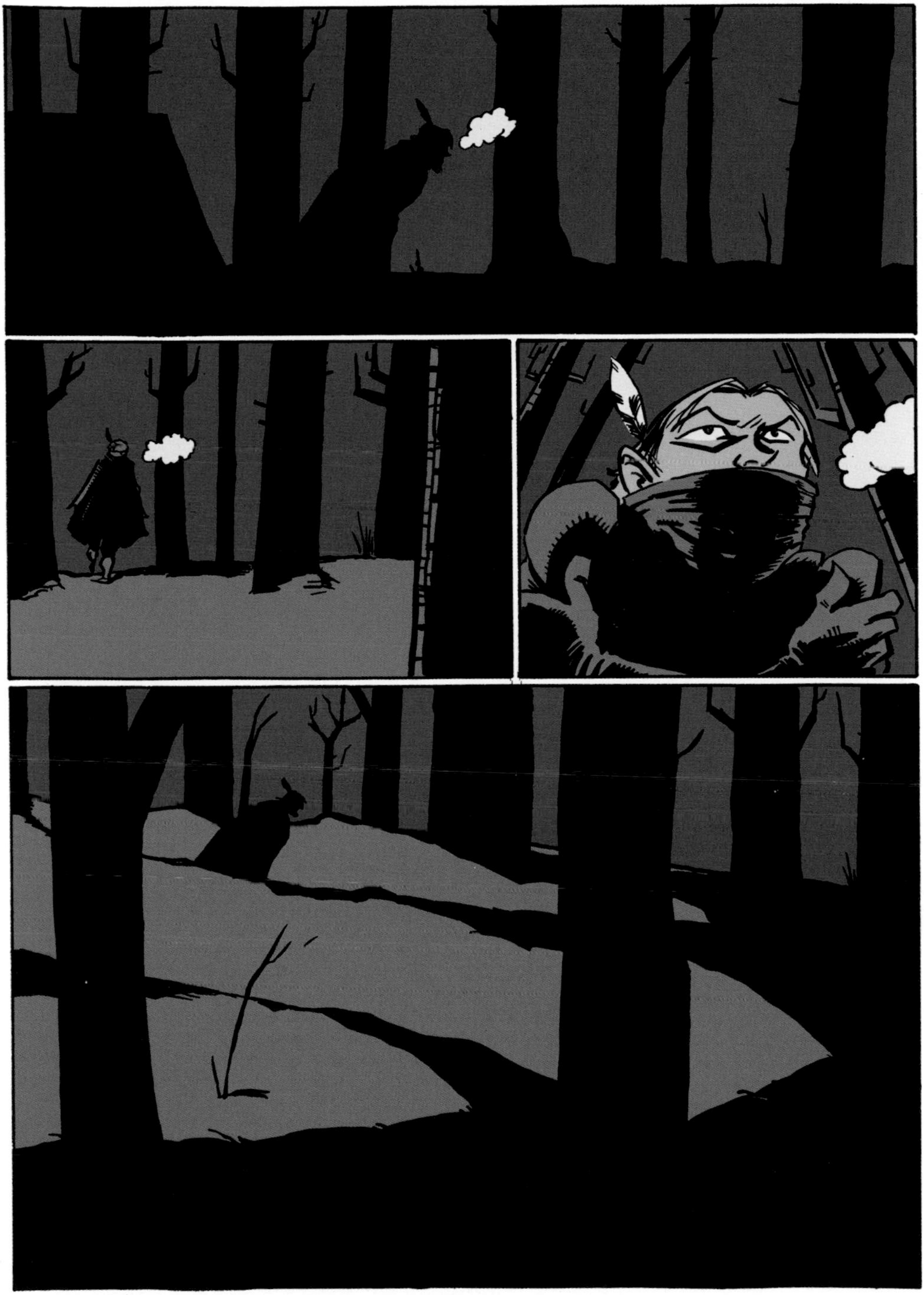

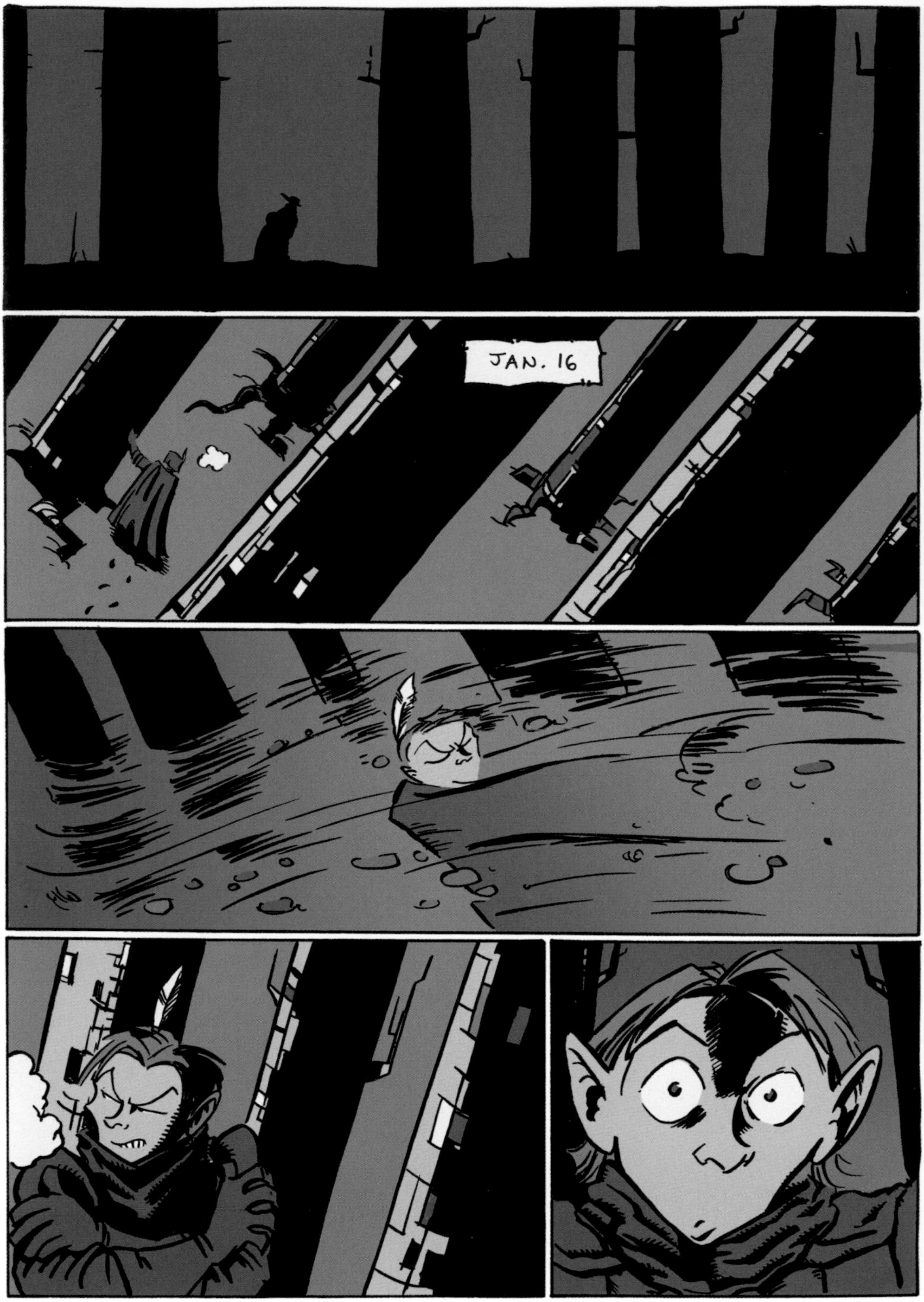
JAN. 16

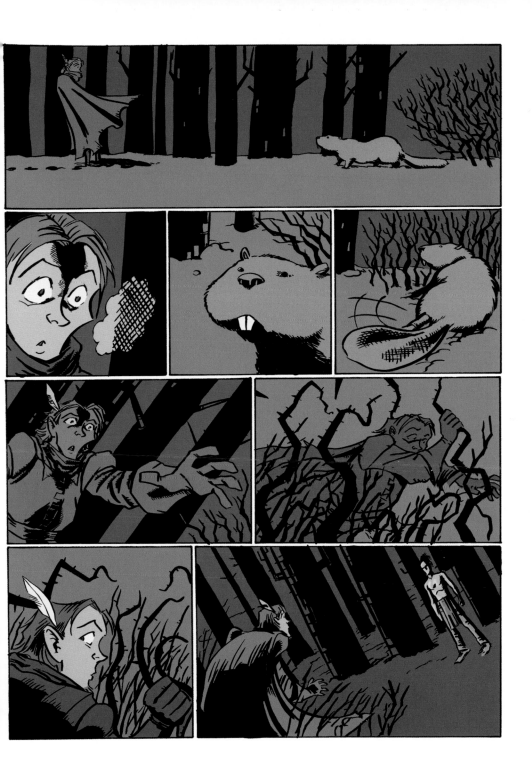

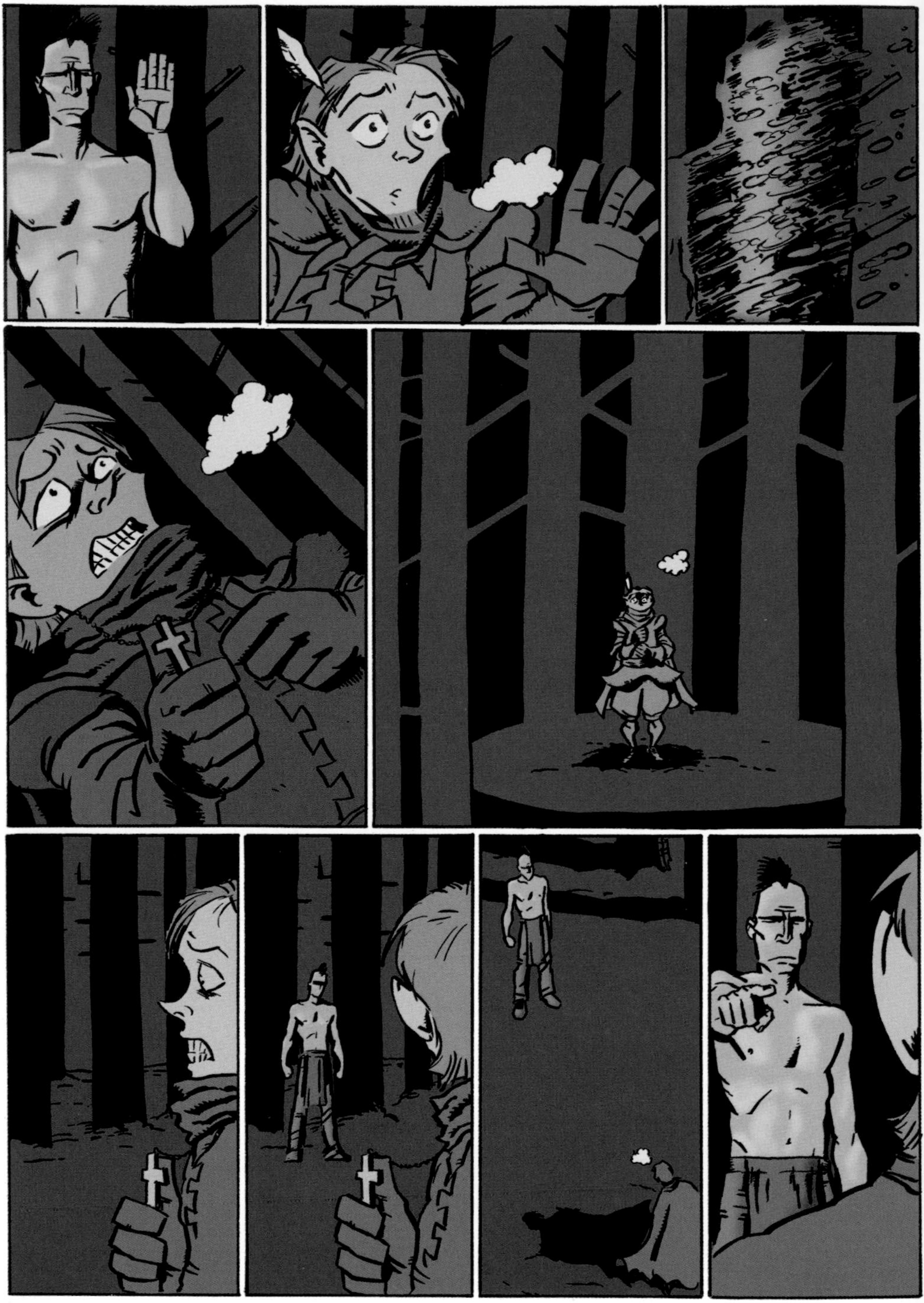

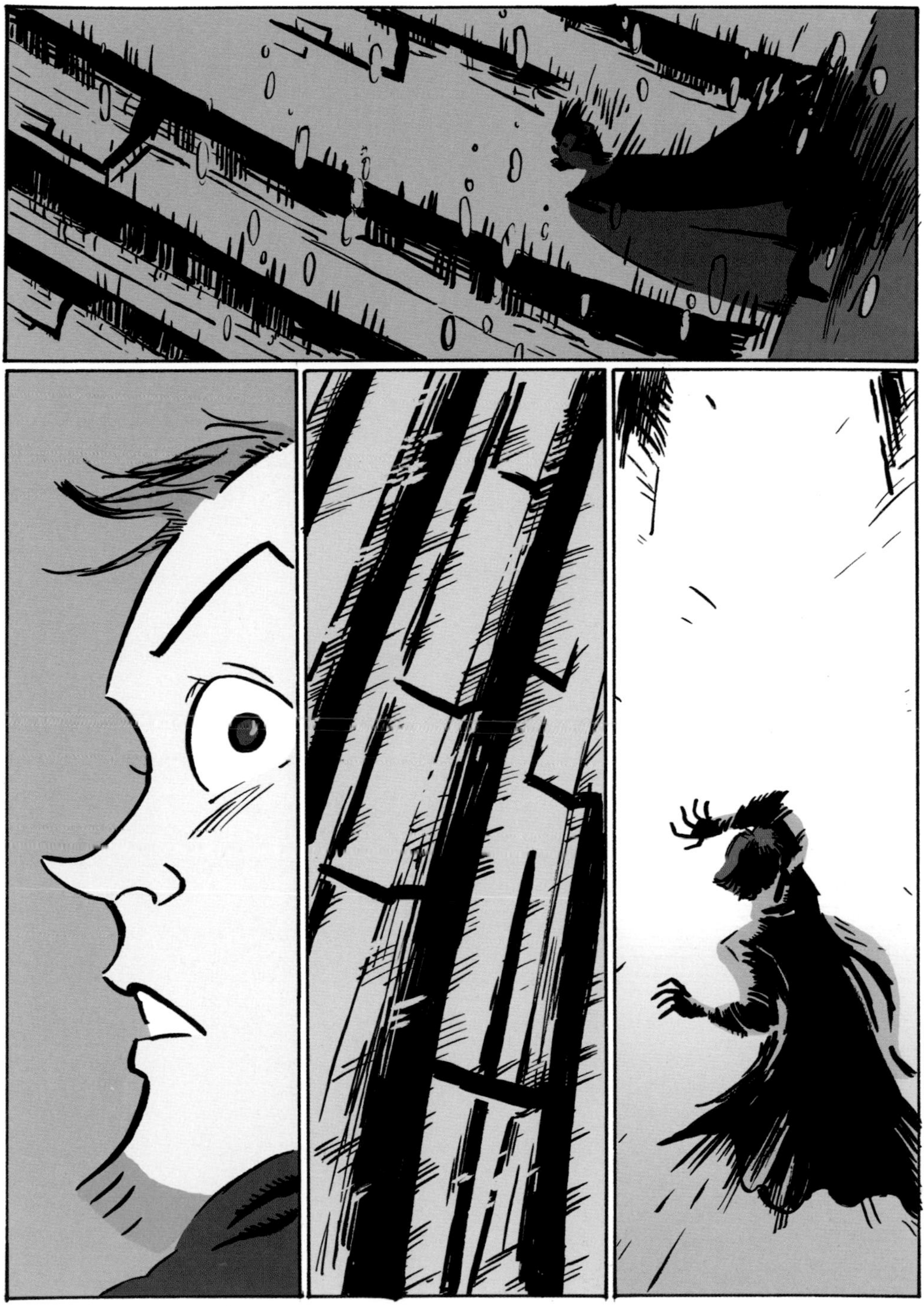

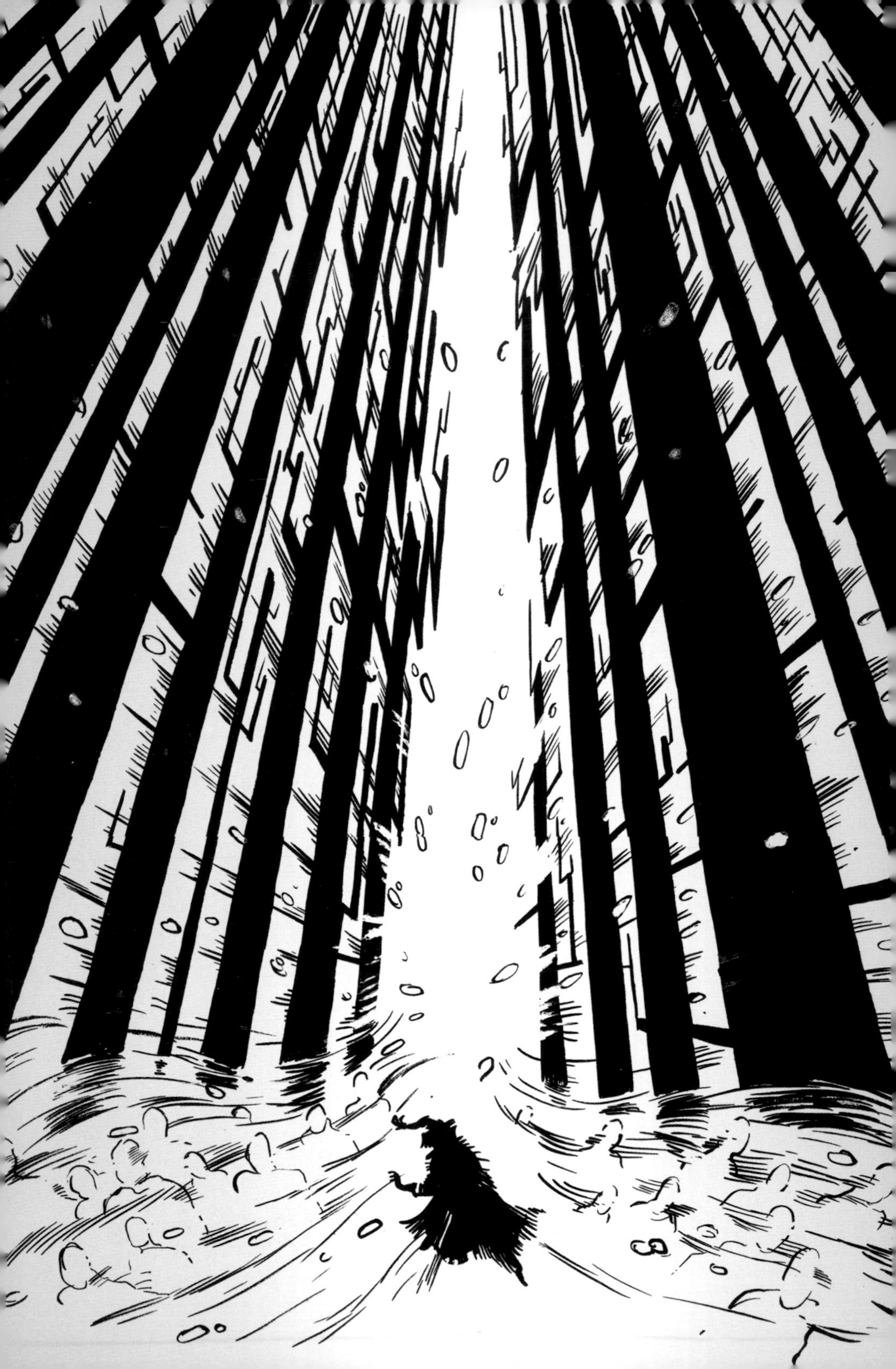

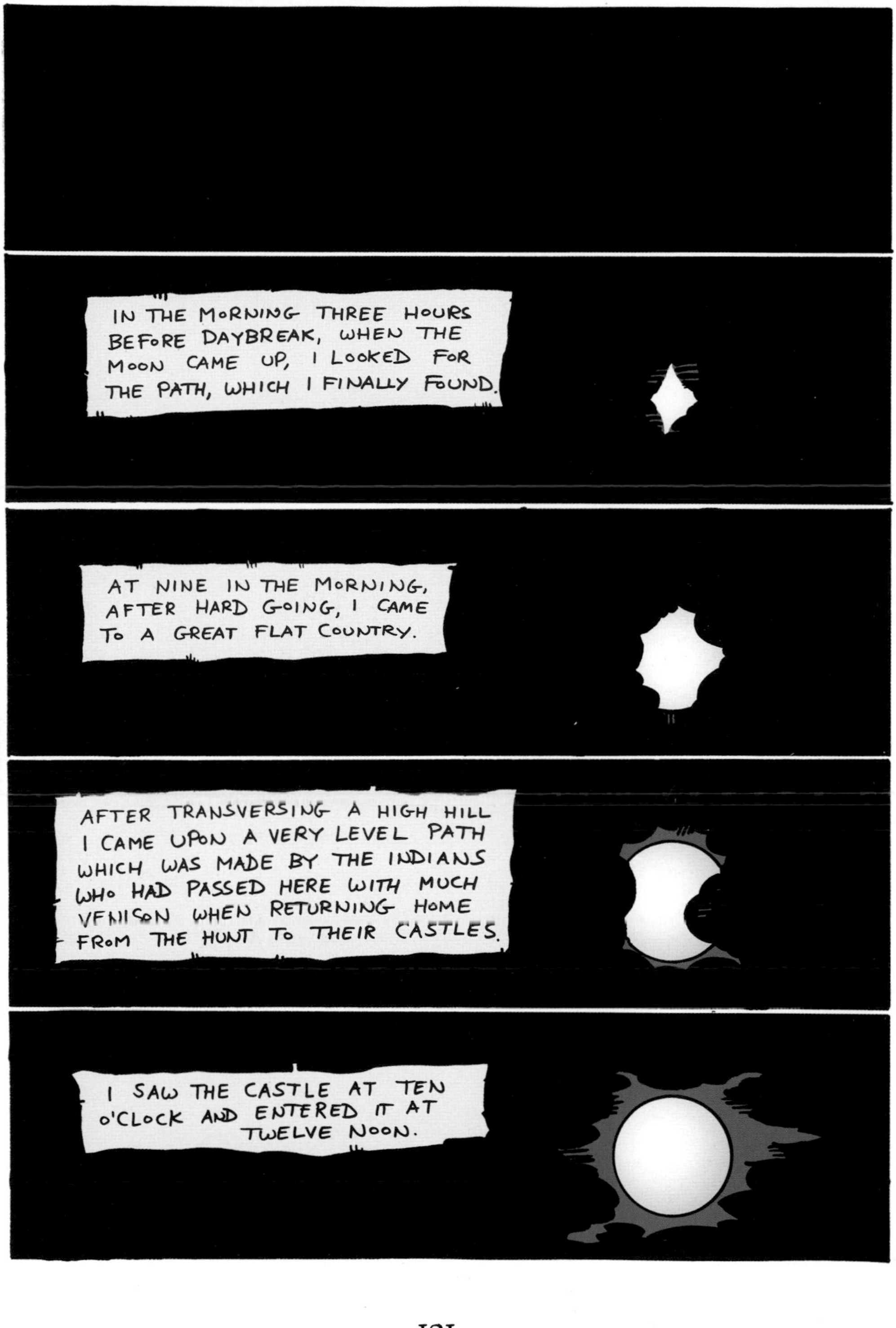
IN THE MORNING THREE HOURS BEFORE DAYBREAK, WHEN THE MOON CAME UP, I LOOKED FOR THE PATH, WHICH I FINALLY FOUND.
AT NINE IN THE MORNING, AFTER HARD GOING, I CAME TO A GREAT FLAT COUNTRY.
AFTER TRANSVERSING A HIGH HILL I CAME UPON A VERY LEVEL PATH WHICH WAS MADE BY THE INDIANS WHO HAD PASSED HERE WITH MUCH VENISON WHEN RETURNING HOME FROM THE HUNT TO THEIR CASTLES.
I SAW THE CASTLE AT TEN o'CLOCK AND ENTERED IT AT TWELVE NOON.

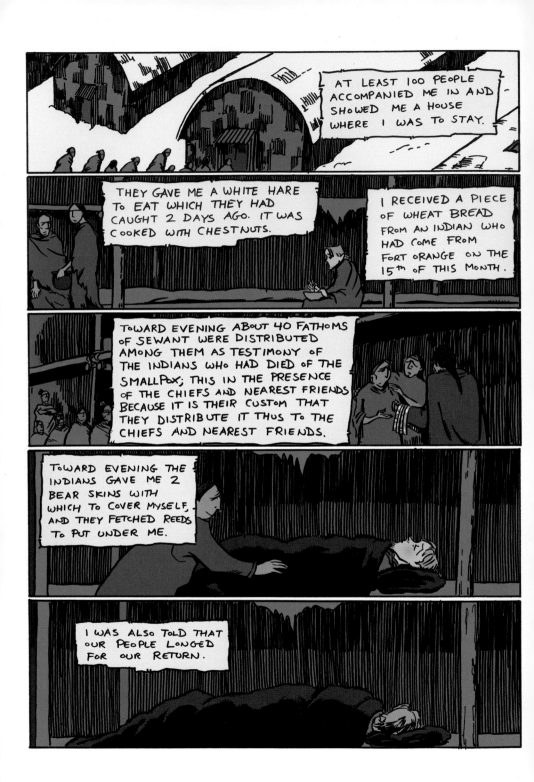

AT LEAST 100 PEOPLE ACCOMPANIED ME IN AND SHOWED ME A HOUSE WHERE I WAS TO STAY.

THEY GAVE ME A WHITE HARE TO EAT WHICH THEY HAD CAUGHT 2 DAYS AGO. IT WAS COOKED WITH CHESTNUTS.

I RECEIVED A PIECE OF WHEAT BREAD FROM AN INDIAN WHO HAD COME FROM FORT ORANGE ON THE 15th OF THIS MONTH.

TOWARD EVENING ABOUT 40 FATHOMS OF SEWANT WERE DISTRIBUTED AMONG THEM AS TESTIMONY OF THE INDIANS WHO HAD DIED OF THE SMALLPOX; THIS IN THE PRESENCE OF THE CHIEFS AND NEAREST FRIENDS BECAUSE IT IS THEIR CUSTOM THAT THEY DISTRIBUTE IT THUS TO THE CHIEFS AND NEAREST FRIENDS.

TOWARD EVENING THE INDIANS GAVE ME 2 BEAR SKINS WITH WHICH TO COVER MYSELF, AND THEY FETCHED REEDS TO PUT UNDER ME.

I WAS ALSO TOLD THAT OUR PEOPLE LONGED FOR OUR RETURN.

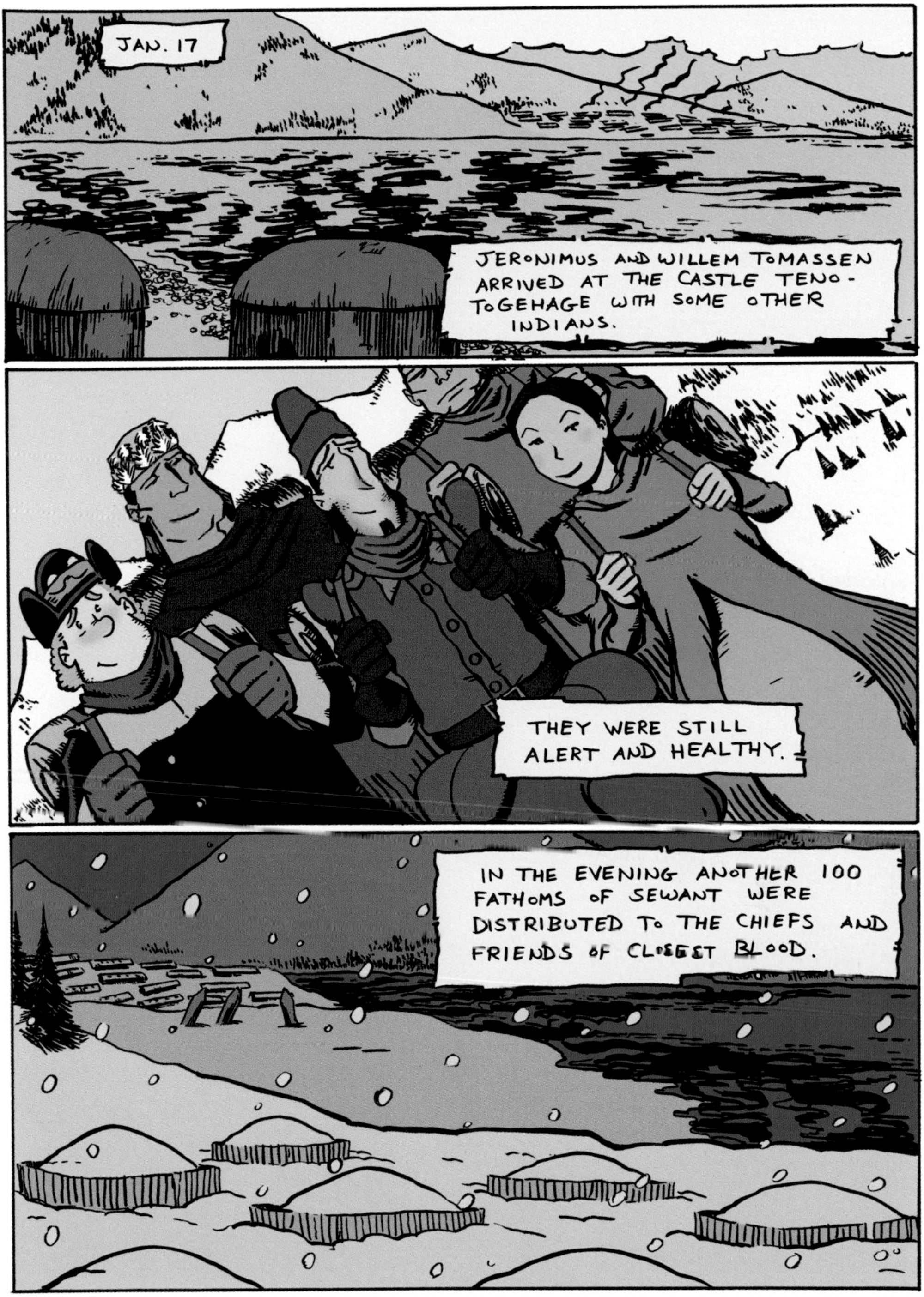
JAN. 17
JERONIMUS AND WILLEM TOMASSEN ARRIVED AT THE CASTLE TENO-TOGEHAGE WITH SOME OTHER INDIANS.
THEY WERE STILL ALERT AND HEALTHY.
IN THE EVENING ANOTHER 100 FATHOMS OF SEWANT WERE DISTRIBUTED TO THE CHIEFS AND FRIENDS OF CLOSEST BLOOD.

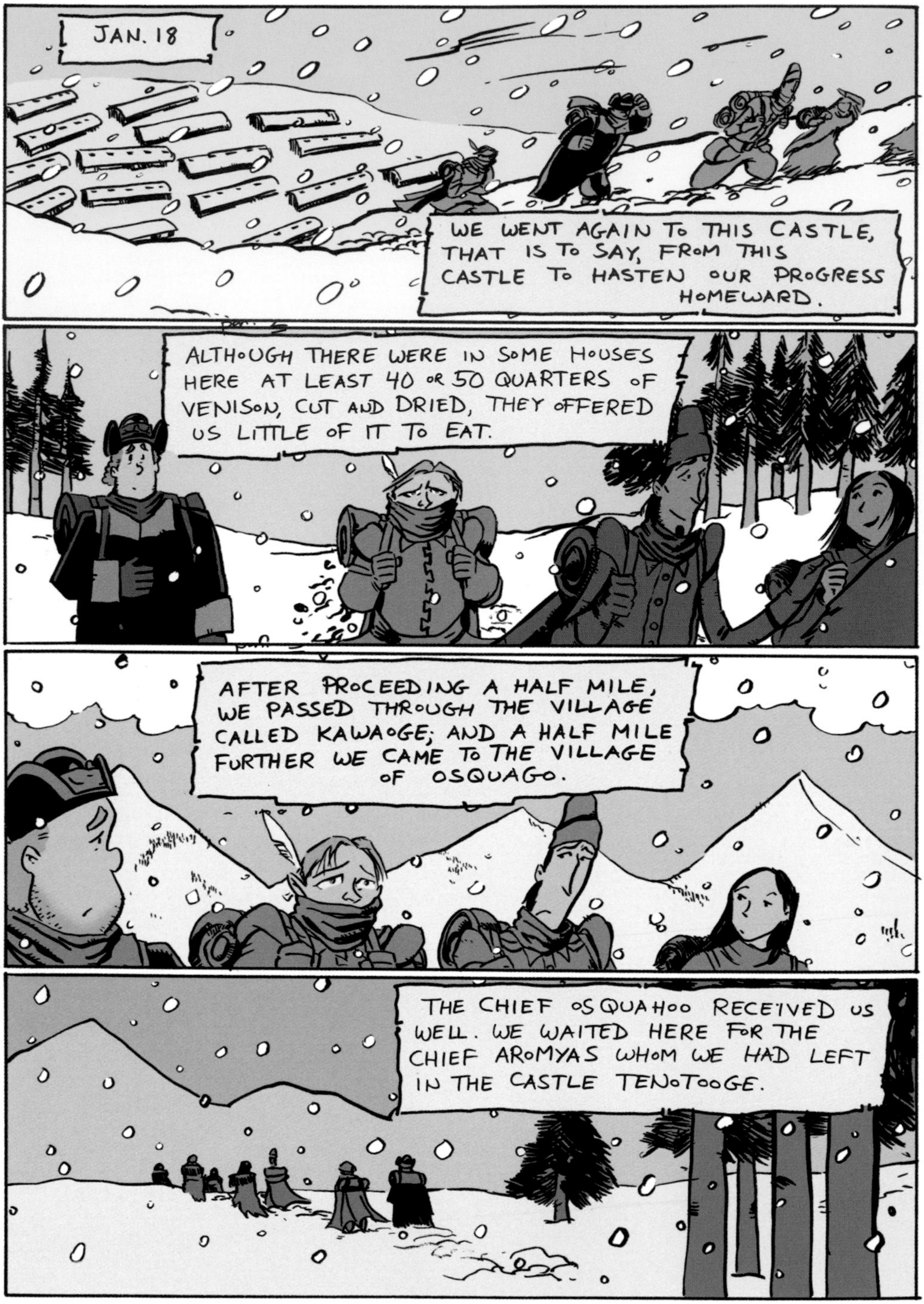
JAN. 18
WE WENT AGAIN TO THIS CASTLE, THAT IS TO SAY, FROM THIS CASTLE TO HASTEN OUR PROGRESS HOMEWARD.
ALTHOUGH THERE WERE IN SOME HOUSES HERE AT LEAST 40 OR 50 QUARTERS OF VENISON, CUT AND DRIED, THEY OFFERED US LITTLE OF IT TO EAT.
AFTER PROCEEDING A HALF MILE, WE PASSED THROUGH THE VILLAGE CALLED KAWAOGE; AND A HALF MILE FURTHER WE CAME TO THE VILLAGE OF OSQUAGO.
THE CHIEF OSQUAHOO RECEIVED US WELL. WE WAITED HERE FOR THE CHIEF AROMYAS WHOM WE HAD LEFT IN THE CASTLE TENOTOOGE.

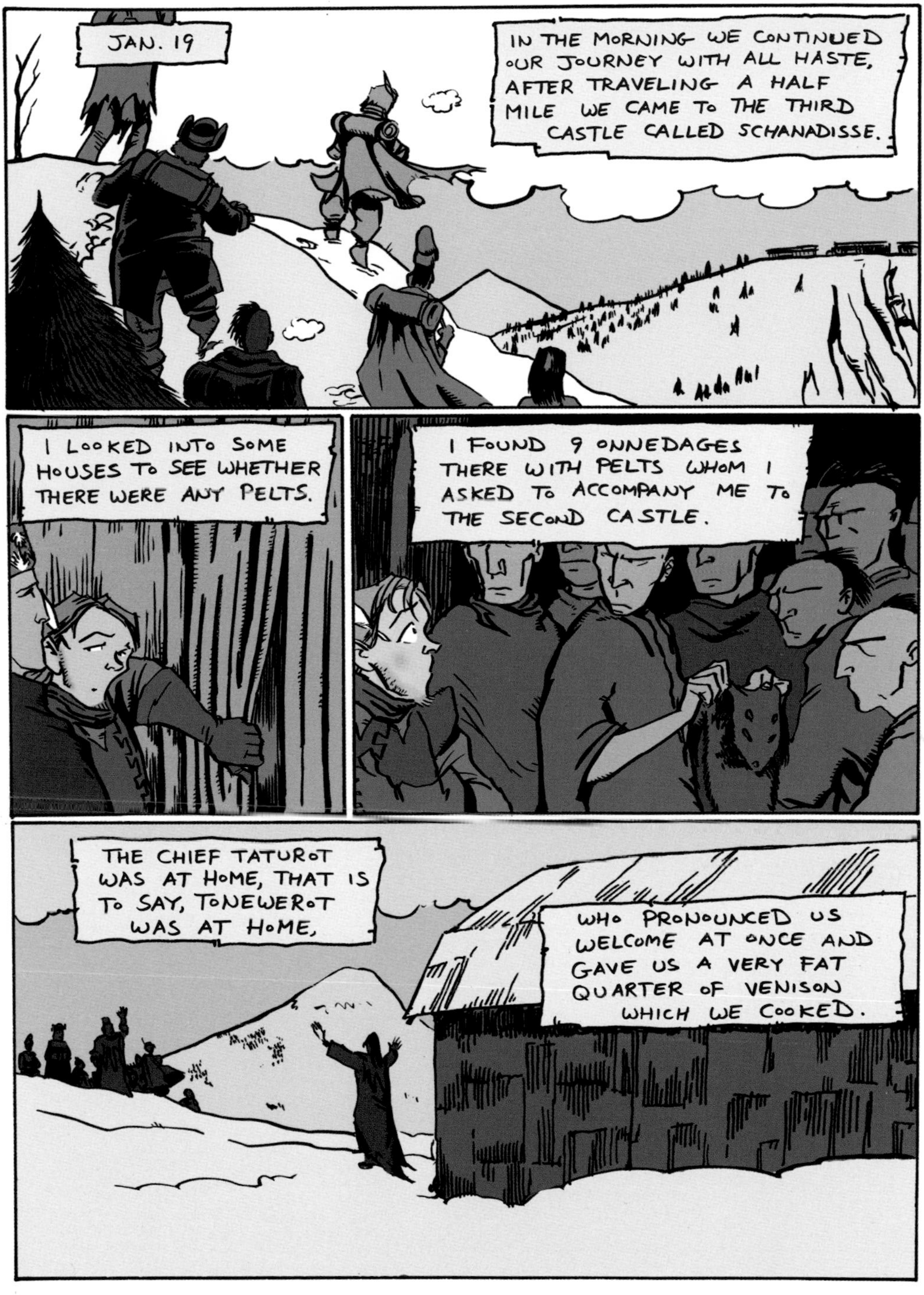
JAN. 19
IN THE MORNING WE CONTINUED OUR JOURNEY WITH ALL HASTE, AFTER TRAVELING A HALF MILE WE CAME TO THE THIRD CASTLE CALLED SCHANADISSE.
I LOOKED INTO SOME HOUSES TO SEE WHETHER THERE WERE ANY PELTS.
I FOUND 9 ONNEDAGES THERE WITH PELTS WHOM I ASKED TO ACCOMPANY ME TO THE SECOND CASTLE.
THE CHIEF TATUROT WAS AT HOME, THAT IS TO SAY, TONEWEROT WAS AT HOME,
WHO PRONOUNCED US WELCOME AT ONCE AND GAVE US A VERY FAT QUARTER OF VENISON WHICH WE COOKED.

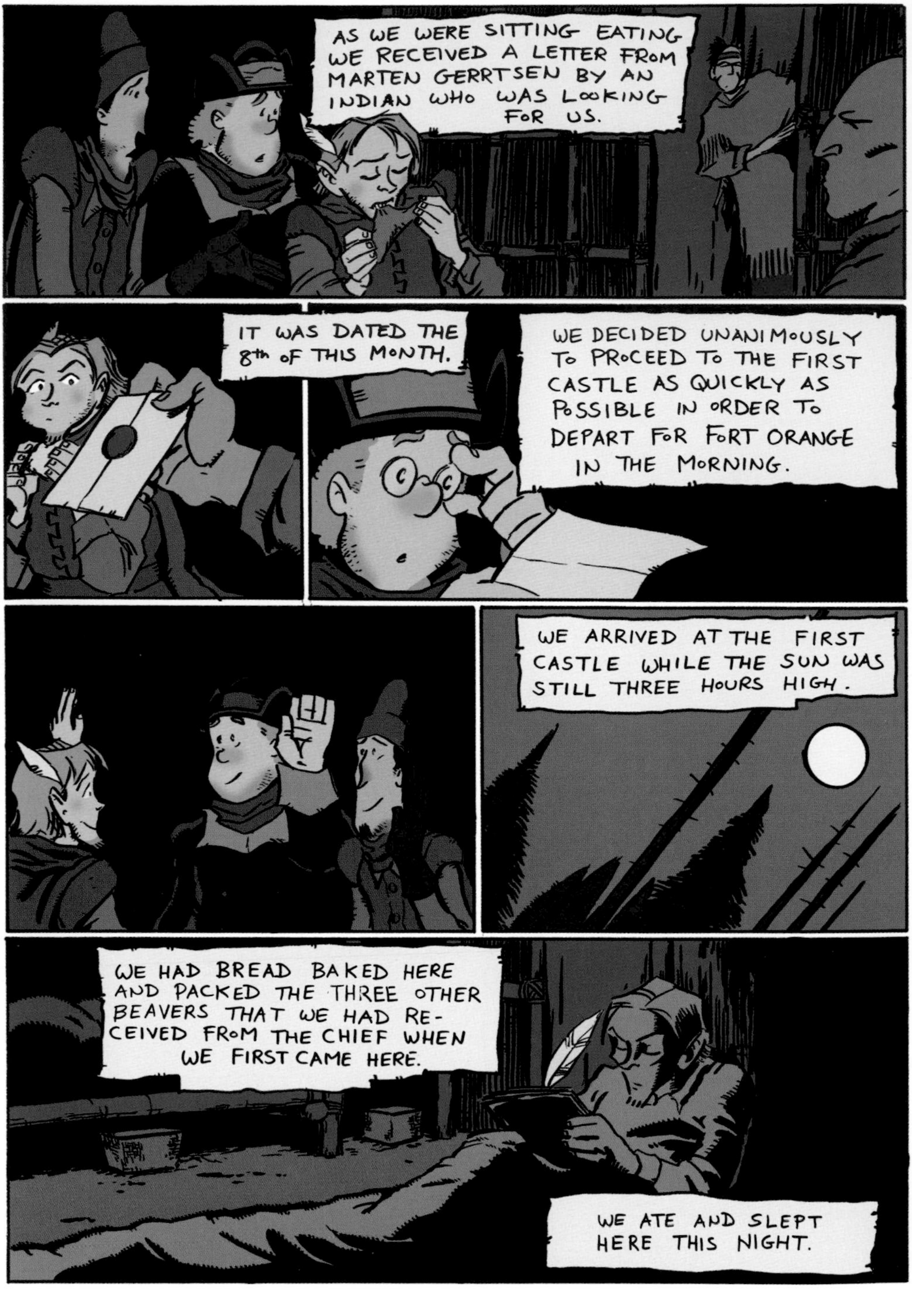

AS WE WERE SITTING EATING WE RECEIVED A LETTER FROM MARTEN GERRTSEN BY AN INDIAN WHO WAS LOOKING FOR US.
IT WAS DATED THE 8th OF THIS MONTH.
WE DECIDED UNANIMOUSLY TO PROCEED TO THE FIRST CASTLE AS QUICKLY AS POSSIBLE IN ORDER TO DEPART FOR FORT ORANGE IN THE MORNING.
WE ARRIVED AT THE FIRST CASTLE WHILE THE SUN WAS STILL THREE HOURS HIGH.
WE HAD BREAD BAKED HERE AND PACKED THE THREE OTHER BEAVERS THAT WE HAD RE-CEIVED FROM THE CHIEF WHEN WE FIRST CAME HERE.
WE ATE AND SLEPT HERE THIS NIGHT.

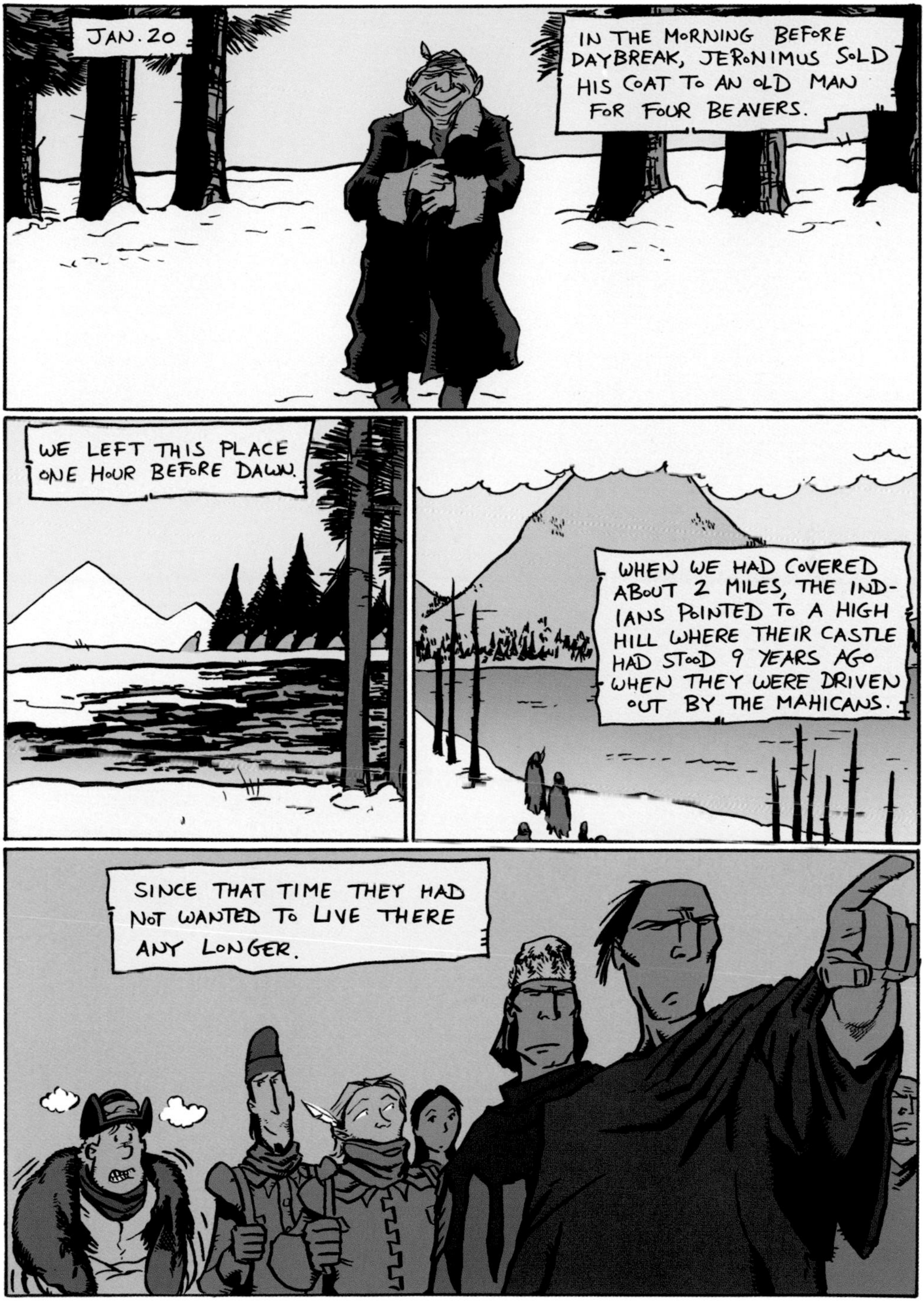
JAN. 20
IN THE MORNING BEFORE DAYBREAK, JERONIMUS SOLD HIS COAT TO AN OLD MAN FOR FOUR BEAVERS.
WE LEFT THIS PLACE ONE HOUR BEFORE DAWN.
WHEN WE HAD COVERED ABOUT 2 MILES, THE INDIANS POINTED TO A HIGH HILL WHERE THEIR CASTLE HAD STOOD 9 YEARS AGO WHEN THEY WERE DRIVEN OUT BY THE MAHICANS.
SINCE THAT TIME THEY HAD NOT WANTED TO LIVE THERE ANY LONGER.

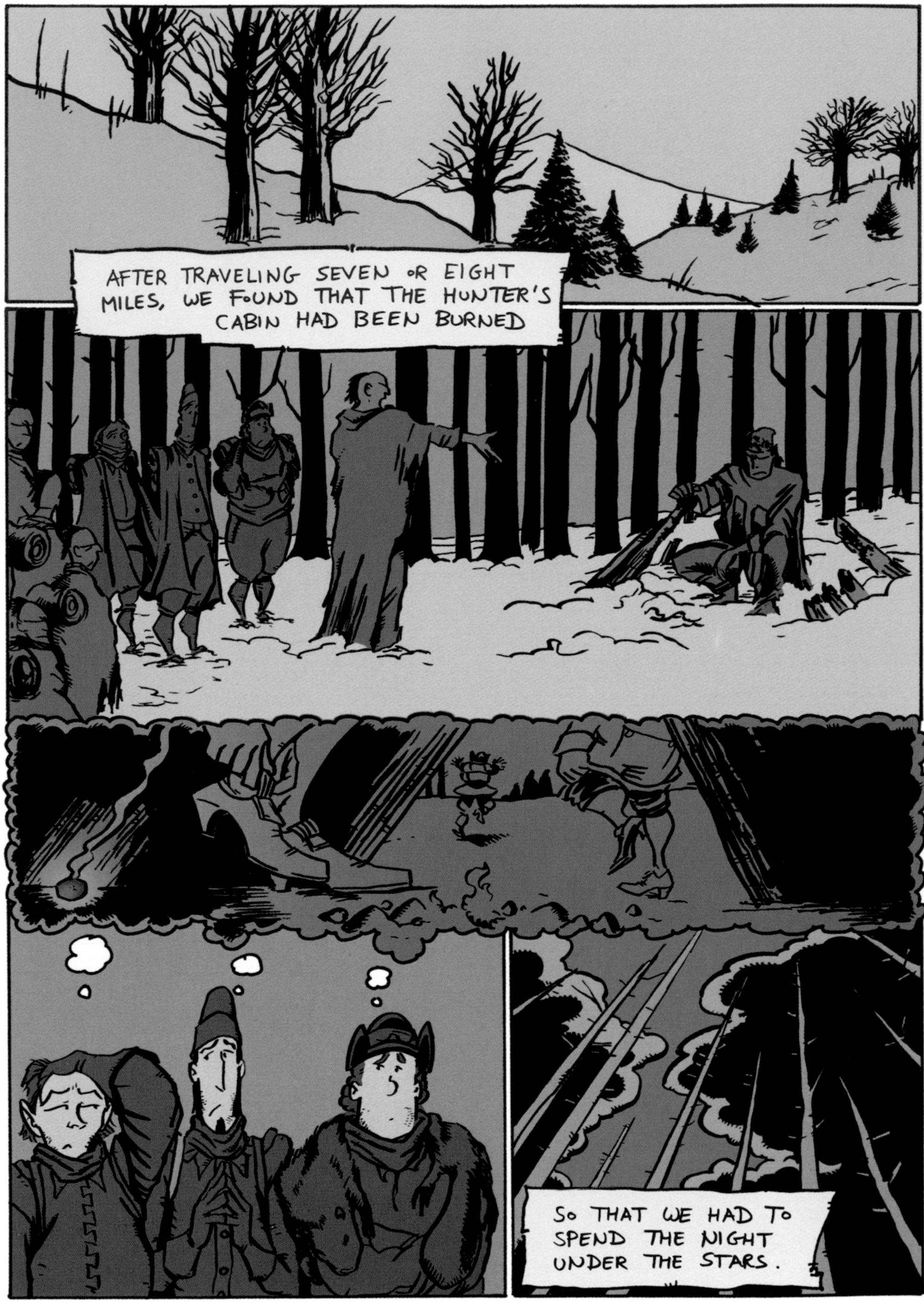
AFTER TRAVELING SEVEN OR EIGHT MILES, WE FOUND THAT THE HUNTER'S CABIN HAD BEEN BURNED
SO THAT WE HAD TO SPEND THE NIGHT UNDER THE STARS.

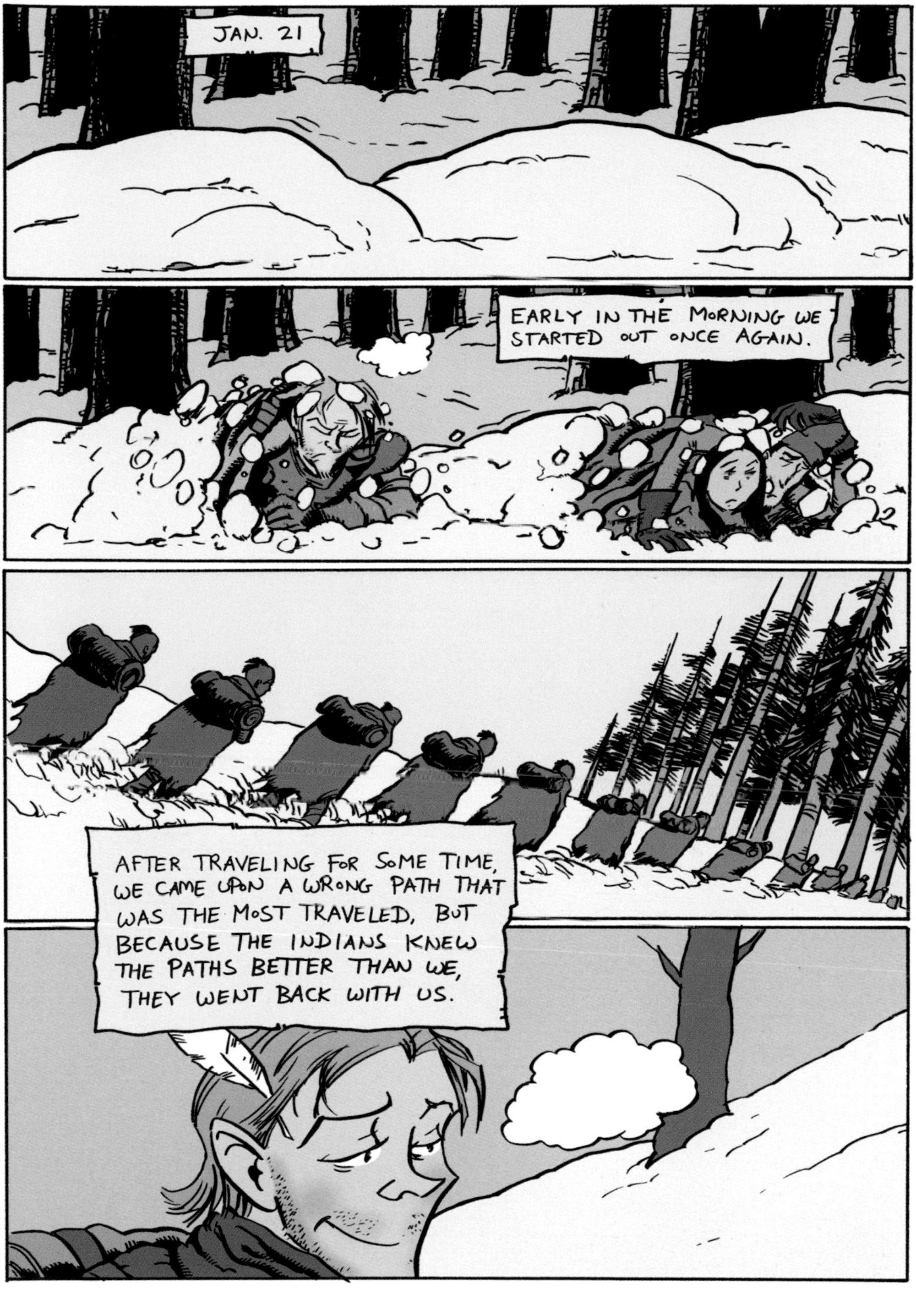
JAN. 21
EARLY IN THE MORNING WE STARTED OUT ONCE AGAIN.
AFTER TRAVELING FOR SOME TIME, WE CAME UPON A WRONG PATH THAT WAS THE MOST TRAVELED, BUT BECAUSE THE INDIANS KNEW THE PATHS BETTER THAN WE, THEY WENT BACK WITH US.

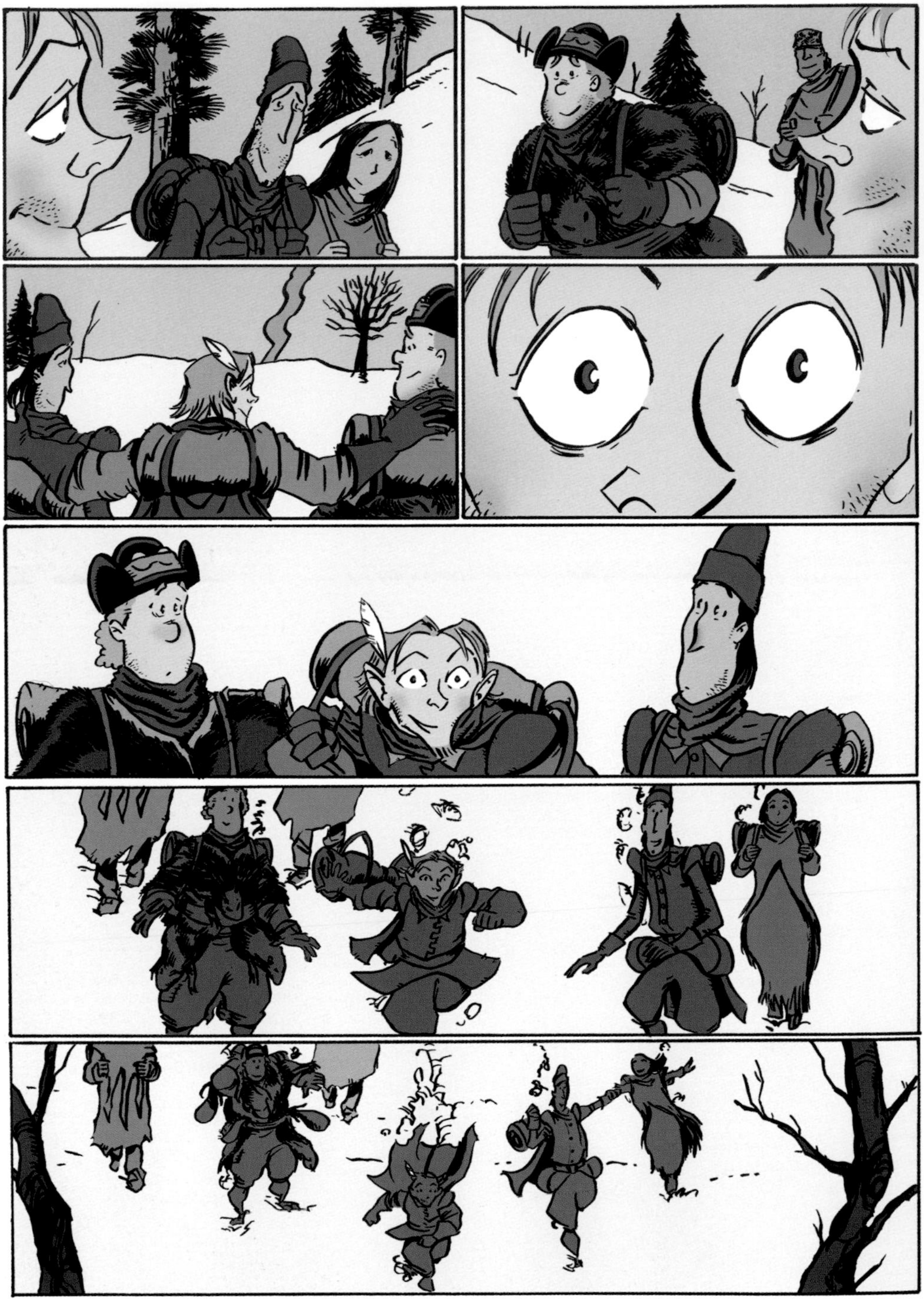

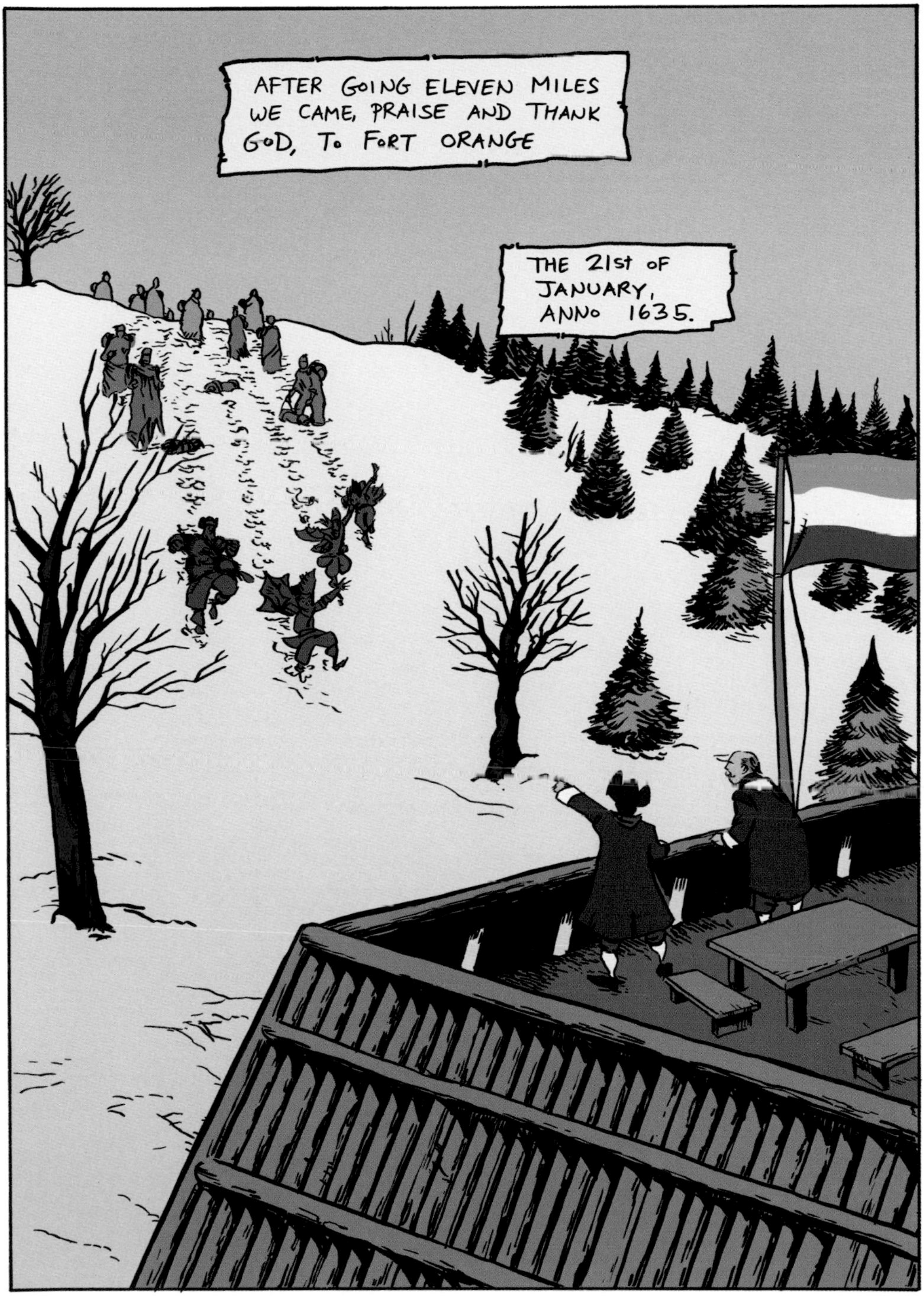
AFTER GOING ELEVEN MILES WE CAME, PRAISE AND THANK GOD, TO FORT ORANGE
THE 21st OF JANUARY, ANNO 1635.

Afterword

A few words of thanks are in order to all the people who made *Journey into Mohawk Country* possible. Firstly I'd like to give a loud, whooping shout out to *Mr. Charles T. Gehring* and *Mr. William A. Starna*, the gentlemen responsible for this translation of *Harmen's* journal. Anyone who has become intrigued by the lost world glimpsed through this graphic novel would be well-served by hunting down a copy of their text-only edition of the journal, *A Journey into Mohawk and Oneida Country, 1634-1635: The Journal of Harmen Meyndertsz van den Bogaert*. It is not as snappily titled as the book you're holding, and it's missing all the pretty pictures as well, but it does have an unbelievable amount of informative footnotes that help explain the mysteries of *Mohawk Country*. Of particular interest is the inclusion of a Mohawk/Dutch/English dictionary compiled by Harmen himself during his travels.

On the subject of informative footnotes, I am also indebted to *Mr. Gunther Michelson*. A native speaker, his translations of many of the *Mohawk* names and phrases recorded by *Harmen* during his travels can also be found in the above-mentioned volume. Many of my designs for the *Mohawks* drew inspiration from his translations of their names.

I should also thank *Mr. Russell Shorto* for introducing me to *Harmen* and company in his excellent book, *The Island at the Center of the World*. It is a fascinating history of *Dutch Manhattan* and hopefully will one day help restore that often-overlooked segment of history to its rightful prominence.

Credit should also be given to *Mr. Mark Siegel*, for letting
a guy who was best known, if at all, for picture books
about children dressed up as superheroes tell the epic story
of how *New York* almost wasn't. Through our discussions,
Journey into Mohawk Country was transformed from the fairly
dry and by-the-numbers adaptation of the journal I had
initially conceived of into the story you've just read.

Likewise, I couldn't have done it without the help of Ms.
Hilary Sycamore. Her wonderful colors helped bring the
pen and ink world of *Mohawk Country* to life. That, and
she was a wonderful sport, listening patiently as I droned
on and on, regurgitating useless factoids about *Mohawks*,
Dutchmen, and old timey *New Amsterdam.*

I'd like to thank *Arta* for being *Arta*.

And finally, I would like to acknowledge *Mr. Harmen
van den Bogaert*, my collaborator on this book. It is not
uncommon in comics for a writer and an illustrator never
to have met, but I doubt that many collaborators have been
separated by so wide a gulf as we. I doubt that *Harmen*
ever dreamed—even in his wildest imaginings—that his
journal would one day become the text of a graphic novel
(and in English, no less), but I hope that he would smile
at my depiction of him and his adventures. Thank you,
Harmen Meyndertsz van den Bogaert, not only for trekking
into the unknown under the harshest of conditions, with
no guarantee of survival, to ensure that the city I love
would one day exist, but thank you also for being the sort
of man who would want to buy a bear.

Glossary

CASTLE: A fortified village, typically with palisades

DUFFEL: An all-purpose *Dutch* cloth, popular in trades with Indians

ELL: A *Dutch* measurement equal to about 2 feet

FATHOM: A unit of measurement equal to six feet

FRENCH INDIANS: *The Huron,* a non-league *Iroquois* tribe allied with the *French.* The *Huron* tribe was a traditional enemy of the *Iroquois League* nations.

GUILDER: A *Dutch* monetary unit. A day's work was worth about one *Guilder.*

HAND: A unit of measurement approximately equal to approximately six inches

IRONWOOD: A common name for the *American Hornbeam Tree.*

MAHICANS: The *Mohawk's* neighbors; members of the *Algonquin* tribe and longtime enemies of the *Mohawk.*

MANHATAS: *Manhattan Island,* where the colony of *New Amsterdam* was located.

MAQUASEN: An early *Dutch* name for the *Mohawk* tribe, the easternmost of the *League of the Iroquois* tribes.

MINQUAS: A *Dutch* name for the *Susquehannock,* an *Iroquois*-speaking tribe whose territory neighbored that of the *Mohawk.*

MORGEN: A *Dutch* measurement equal to approximately 2 acres.

ONNEDAEGES: A *Dutch* name for the *Onondaga* tribe of the *Iroquois League.*

SAPPAEN: Corn mush stew

SATTEEU: Sateen, a type of cotton fabric

SEWANT: Also known as wampum. A string of beads made from seashells, often used as currency by *European* traders.

SINNEKENS: The *Dutch* commonly referred to all tribes west of the *Mohawk* as *Sinnekens*; when this term appears in *Van den Bogaert's* journal, it refers specifically to the *Oneida* tribe. The name is derived from the *Seneca,* the westernmost of the *Iroquois League* tribes.

SKIPPLE: A *Dutch* measurement, equivalent to a small basket